D0375012

THE
ISLAMIC
TSUNAMI

ISRAEL AND
AMERICA
IN THE AGE
OF OBAMA

DAVID RUBIN

Shiloh
ISRAEL*Press*

The Islamic Tsunami:
Israel and America in the Age of Obama
ISBN: 978-0-9829067-0-5

Published by Shiloh Israel Press

Contact The Author
David@ShilohIsraelChildren.org
1-877-742-2064 (toll-free)

Contact The Publisher
sipress@ShilohIsraelChildren.org

For Orders:
1-800-431-1579 (toll-free)

Book Layout and Emendation
Prestige Prepress
prestige.prepress@gmail.com

Cover Design and Layout
Christopher Tobias

Printed in The United States of America

This book is dedicated in loving memory to my father, Ruby Rubin. He lived a simple life as a dedicated father of three children, a caring husband, and a beloved teacher and camp director to thousands of children who benefited from his gentle guidance.

His young adult years were spent in New York City as a passionate liberal, but he gradually shifted as he recognized the hypocrisy of "political correctness," years before the term was even in use. He was a proud American patriot, often defending the principles of freedom and liberty that America stood for. At the same time, his passion for the miraculous rebirth of Israel and pride in his Jewish heritage was obvious to all who had the privilege of knowing him.

For all of those reasons, I have no doubt that he would have appreciated this book, as well as my work on behalf of the terror victim children in the biblical heartland of Israel.

May his memory be a blessing for all of our children, especially in Israel and in the United States of America.

We Strongly Endorse...

Dr. Pat Robertson
Chairman and CEO of the Christian Broadcasting Network (CBN)
Host of The 700 Club

The unholy alliance of Islamic ideologues and secular leftists is undoubtedly the greatest threat to Judeo-Christian civilization and the USA as we know it today. David Rubin is an American Israeli who lives on the front lines of the war on Islamic terrorism in the Biblical heartland of Israel. He has been a proud Israeli for many years and has been victimized by Islamic terrorists for that distinction, but he remains a proud American, as well. As he so poignantly illustrates, the Islamic challenge to Israel and America is varied in its methods and is certainly global, as is the plague of moral relativism in Western society, but the solution at this point in time needs to be much more directly focused, and depends on America reclaiming its formerly proud Biblical heritage, for that is what made America great. Last, but not least, we need to be courageous and proudly standing with those who are continuing the biblical mandate of Israel in our times and are bravely countering the aggressive Islamic challenge. David Rubin has written a powerful book about a crucial partnership for our times. Such a partnership against evil is good for Israel, good for America, and good for Judeo-Christian civilization.

David Horowitz
Founder and CEO of the David Horowitz Freedom Center
New York Times Bestselling Author

One aspect of the fundamental change that Barack Obama promised, which has now become disturbingly clear, is the weakening of America's support for our ally Israel and the strengthening of the aspirations of our enemies. David Rubin has written a powerful book that illustrates the strategic collusion between the aggressive Islamist forces and the secular Left. Written from the unique perspective of an Israeli and American patriot who lives with his family in Israel and has personally suffered the ravages of Islamic terrorism and hatred, *The Islamic Tsunami: Israel and America in the Age of Obama* is a unique and compelling read on the imminent and fateful challenges facing our great nation.

SE Cupp
Author of
"Losing Our Religion: The Liberal Media's Attack on Christianity"

The power of semantics has long been used by the Left, both in America and Israel, to deceptively pin labels on those who fail to toe the politically correct line. American-Israeli author David Rubin has written a powerful exposé of the dual approach adopted by the Islamic ideologues, in which he demonstrates how they exploit the cynical cooperation and support of their allies on the "liberal" Left, who bash conservative Americans and no-longer-politically-correct Israel. This strange alliance seems to have joined hands as they seek to transform American society, all in the cause of their contradictory versions of "liberty."

Rev. James M. Hutchens, Ph.D
Chaplain (Brigadier General) U.S. Army (ret.)
President & CEO, The JerUSAlem Connection, Int'l

Having his son, toddler Ruby, nearly killed by Jihadists, and being witness to such suffering from terrorism nearly every day due to his important work initiating and supporting projects for children in Israel, David Rubin is particularly sensitive to the needs of the terror victims. Likewise, as a lifetime student of history and a dual citizen of the USA and Israel, he has an unusual grasp of the constitutional guarantees of the U.S. founding documents, as well as the biblical covenants that decree modern Israel to the Jews. With a remarkable depth of knowledge of both the history of the conflict and its current ramifications, Rubin adroitly illustrates the danger of the spread of Islam to our liberty, as well as the harm that the Islam-pandering Obama administration is inflicting on both Israel and America. Reaping the insights of the Founding Fathers of our great republic, as well as biblical heroes like King David and Samuel the Prophet, he provides passionate and wise advice to a free people that has lost its way. David Rubin's powerful voice needs to be heard by every American and by every lover of liberty!

Barry Farber
Legendary Radio Talk Show Host

If you saw your children playing with fire in the kerosene distillery you'd raise hell and put a chunk under it. In addition to a galaxy of other worthy historic and political missions, that's exactly what David Rubin does between covers of *The Islamic Tsunami: Israel and America in the Age of Obama*. Rubin attacks and destroys those "kids" responsible for whatever rift is widening between the United States and Israel. He exposes the suicidal insanity of America and Israel doing anything but interlocking in their firmest embrace ever in the face of Islamic aggression; suicidal, not just for Israel and America, but for civilization itself. "Armchairs" are great, especially when they're snug within ivory towers belonging to think-tanks, but I prefer my geo-political scolding from the likes of Rubin who lives in Israel and was personally attacked by Islamic terrorists along with his three-year-old son who was shot in the head. This book belongs on that table close by, where alarm clocks go.

About The Author

David Rubin is a former mayor of Shiloh, Israel – in the region of Samaria, known to much of the world as the West Bank. He is the founder and president of Shiloh Israel Children's Fund – dedicated to easing the trauma of children who have been victims of terrorist attacks, as well as rebuilding the biblical heartland of Israel. The Fund was established after Rubin and his three-year-old son were wounded in a vicious terrorist attack while driving home from Jerusalem. He vowed to retaliate – not with hatred or anger, but with compassion – in order to affect positive change for Israel and its people.

Rubin's previous book, *God, Israel, and Shiloh: Returning to the Land,* recounts the struggles and the triumphs of Israel's complex history. He also illustrates the inspiring journey of the people of Israel returning to their biblical heartland, with all of the difficult challenges that they have faced.

A featured speaker throughout the United States and in Israel, David Rubin has appeared on national and international radio and television programs.

Prior to his current activities, Rubin learned crucial lessons during 25 years as an educator in the United States and Israel. He instructed students in college, elementary school, and all ages in-between; and thrived on the challenge of relating to children of varying ages and backgrounds. Rubin believes that the ability to adapt and relate to others and to address issues openly and honestly are essential skills – ideas that he also instilled in his students.

Born and raised in Brooklyn, NY, Rubin currently resides in Israel with his wife and children on a hilltop overlooking the site of Ancient Shiloh. This is the hallowed ground where the Tabernacle stood for 369 years in the time of Joshua, Hannah, and Samuel the Prophet.

Contents

Chapter One
    In God We Trust   13
Chapter Two
    Terror Is Not An Enemy   36
Chapter Three
    The Chosen People   60
Chapter Four
    The Real Face Of Islam   77
Chapter Five
    Eurabia And The Islamic Challenge   105
Chapter Six
    A Light In The Land Of Zion   128
Chapter Seven
    The Sleeping Giant   162
Chapter Eight
    Education In The Land Of The Free   178
Chapter Nine
    Those Who Bless Israel   199
Chapter Ten
    Facing The Challenge   224

Acknowledgments   245
Photographic Credits   245
Endnotes   246

THE
ISLAMIC
TSUNAMI

ISRAEL AND
AMERICA
IN THE AGE
OF OBAMA

Chapter One

In God We Trust

America is the greatest, freest and most decent society in existence. It is an oasis of goodness in a desert of cynicism and barbarism. This country, once an experiment unique in the world, is now the last best hope for the world.[1]

(Dinesh D'Souza)

I am a native American – a native American in the sense that I was born and raised and lived for many years as a young adult in the U.S. I now reside in Israel and have lived here for more than eighteen years. Today, most people know me as an Israeli – specifically as former mayor of the reestablished Shiloh, as a victim of terrorism in Israel, as an Israeli author, or as the founder and president of the Shiloh Israel Children's Fund. Nonetheless, despite almost two decades in Israel, I am often looked upon by my fellow Israelis as an American. Conversely, when visiting America, I am considered to be an Israeli, despite the fact that a majority of my life was spent in the U.S. The status of being between two worlds in a sense and a citizen of both countries is always fascinating, even though most of my days and nights are spent in the Holy Land.

As a second generation American, I am filled with gratitude to the nation that welcomed my Russian, Polish, and Romanian Jewish immigrant grandparents to its peaceful shores just 100 years ago. They came from poverty and suffered under the yoke of legalized and non-legalized discrimination against Jews. As with many new arrivals in their time, they were seeking a better life for their children in the land of opportunity; a land that they hoped wouldn't persecute them for being Jewish; and a land in which they could be rewarded for their hard work in whatever field they chose.

> *The Jews themselves, of whom a considerable number were already scattered throughout the colonies, were true to the teachings of their prophets. The Jewish faith is predominantly the faith of liberty.*[2]
>
> (President Calvin Coolidge, May 3, 1925)

Everyone becomes reflective at times, looks back nostalgically, remembers a different, seemingly simpler time in their lives, the lives of family members, or in the lives of their people or nations. The motivation that spurs the reflection often comes from surprising, unexpected places.

Apparently, the election of President Barack Hussein Obama was such a pivotal event for me, a revolutionary event for the United States and the world, but also causing both reflection and concern in my own life and in that of the country that is now my home, which is Israel. The years in Israel have certainly been painful at times, exciting at others, but never boring, and I have never regretted the move, not even once. In fact, with each passing day, I feel ever more privileged to be living here in this deeply historical land, where Israel was reestablished in 1948 as an independent, sovereign nation after nearly 2000 years of exile and dispersion, exactly as the biblical prophets such as Ezekiel predicted, many years earlier.

> *I will take you from the nations and gather you from all the lands, and I will bring you to your own soil.*
>
> (Ezekiel 36:24)

Even so, my passion for Israel doesn't negate my affection and appreciation for the land of my birth and the positive values that I acquired in the 33 years that I lived there. I didn't leave America as a way of escaping the country, but rather, as a way of embracing the history and the vision of another nation. I moved to Israel so that I could be living in the land of Abraham, Isaac, and Jacob, which is a spiritual elevation that the Founding Fathers of the United States would have appreciated. Those men were spiritually and biblically connected in ways that seem to have been forgotten by the average American. The concept of the Jewish people returning to Israel is a religious notion that has been known to biblically-literate people for thousands of years. The American colonial heroes were well-versed in its principles and lessons.

In fact, many of the early Puritan refugees settled in the New World to escape religious persecution. They too were inspired by the story of the ancient Israelites who fled their tyrant, Pharaoh, in Egypt, eventually reaching the Promised Land of Israel. The Puritans, along with many early settlers, saw themselves as instruments of Divine Providence, fleeing tyranny to build a commonwealth in a new land of hope and promise. They originally conceived the American holiday, Thanksgiving, as something akin to the Jewish holiday Yom Kippur, a day of fasting and deep introspection, to thank the Almighty for his blessings and to pray for His continued benevolence.[3] In true Jewish spirit, it evolved into a day of feasting, in this case on turkey and cranberry sauce, but the concept of giving thanks to the Creator was the central feature of the holiday.

In 2008, after his election to office, Barack Obama fundamentally attempted to change America's orientation in the world, thereby impacting Israel in very negative ways. After this, I began to understand my complex relationship with the United States. Americans who have moved to Israel are allowed to retain dual citizenship, but the reason for my strong feelings for the country of my birth is more complex than the legalities of citizenship. Those complexities are not readily visible to the average observer. I fully identify myself as an Israeli. I was married in Israel, my children were born in Israel, my message is fundamentally a message of Israel's mission, and my work is totally focused on building Israel's biblical heartland through the children of Israel. When I travel and speak to congregations and groups across the United States, and throughout the world, I am doing so as an Israeli, even though I may have insight into American realities that most Israeli natives don't possess.

Nonetheless, I will always identify myself as an American as well, a fact of which I am proud and have integrated into my worldview as an Israeli. We are a product of the many influencing factors that shape us throughout our lives. I firmly believe that President Obama and I would agree on this point from a sociological perspective. Obama's worldview includes his experiences from living in Hawaii and/or Kenya, Indonesia and the United States. Questions have been raised about Obama's religious upbringing in Indonesia. He later moved to the United States and became a long-time member of a particularly controversial church in Chicago. He now professes to be a Christian, even though he has referred to the Muslim call to prayer as *the prettiest sound on Earth*. Whatever the president's religious beliefs or geographic background may be, we are all products of where we come from and our, as is the case of Obama, complex backgrounds. I understand the positive and negative aspects of this, since I have a similarly elaborate (though different) background.

My early childhood in the United States began with a formal American education in Brooklyn, New York. As a young student in Public School 233, with its high, large windows and wood floors, I sat in classes of about 35-40 students. Every morning, we began our day staring at the flag that hung on the wall and pledged our allegiance to the nation. We also sang the *Star Spangled Banner*, with its proud words proclaiming the birth of the American nation. I stood at attention, placed my hand on my heart and recited the words:

> *I pledge allegiance to the flag of the United States of America and to the republic, for which it stands, one nation under God, indivisible, with liberty and justice for all.*

Perhaps as a young child, I wasn't cognizant of the fact that I was actually pledging allegiance, not to Betsy Ross's piece of decorative cloth that we call the American flag, but to an optimistic value system conceived by the founders of a unique union of states. The union was established mainly through pioneering efforts of the Dutch and the British settlers seeking religious freedom, but eventually was comprised of immigrants from around the world.

My four grandparents sailed from Eastern Europe to Ellis Island in the early part of the 20th century. Each group of immigrants brought their own culture, language, and traditions and were all seeking the same thing – freedom; whether economic, religious, or cultural.

> *Give me your tired, your poor, your huddled masses yearning to be free.*[4]
>
> (Emma Lazarus, *The New Colossus*, 1883)

Those words, written by the young American Jewish woman, Emma Lazarus, were engraved on a bronze plaque and mounted inside the Statue of Liberty. The statue itself was a gift from France and represents an enduring symbol of the liberty, the creativity, and the idealistic vision that the U.S. represents.

> *An Englishman is a person who does things because they have been done before. An American is a person who does things because they haven't been done before.*[5]
>
> (Mark Twain)

Creativity is not the first word that comes to mind when thinking of the Statue of Liberty. We think of freedom as the ability to create our own destiny, but freedom, within the proper framework, certainly encourages creativity.

The renowned American entrepreneurial spirit has had setbacks in recent years due to the economic downturn, while competition from several other countries continues to challenge the United States' leading entrepreneurial role. Nonetheless, the entrepreneurial spirit is a product of the free market capitalist system, which America has long championed. This does not include the bedlam, corruption and abuse of an economic and social system without constraints and without a soul. The unique combination of freedom with a moral system of biblically-based guidelines for life is the best recipe for creative juices to flow in a prolific, constructive direction.

This was aptly described in 1849 by Robert Winthrop, the United States Speaker of the House:

> *All societies of men must be governed in some way or other. The less they may have of stringent State Government, the more they must have of individual self-government. The less they rely on public law or physical force, the more they must rely on private moral restraint. Men, in a word, must necessarily be controlled either by a power within them, or a power without them; either by the word of God, or by the strong arm of man; either by the Bible or by the bayonet.*[6]

As we will discuss later, freedom is often defined as something unlimited, but in an ideal situation, it is anything but that! God gives us the freedom to make the right choices. Failure to do so can create chaos, unnecessary conflict, and suffering.

> *Men are qualified for civil liberty in exact proportion to their disposition to put moral chains upon their own appetites ... and the less of it there is within, the more there must be without.*[7]
> (British Statesman Edmund Burke, 1791)

Like many Americans, I attended numerous sporting events as a child. I stood for the National Anthem before the start of these games and cheered enthusiastically at the conclusion of its recitation. Without question, the fans were excited that the game was about to begin, but I have always believed that there was something else ... something *bigger* and much greater. I feel as if there is an element of instinct, that the crowd was cheering for their right not merely to enjoy the game but to celebrate the American vision of liberty and justice for all. These include the right to excel through hard work in any chosen field. It also encompasses freedom of speech, freedom of worship and freedom from excessive taxation. Perhaps the fans didn't consciously reflect on this as they were cheering at the anthem's conclusion, but the feeling of American pride was always there – as if it were an unspoken presence hovering over the stadium. What fascinated me about the United States of America was that, despite its remarkable cultural diversity, the nation was held together by a certain dignity and grace stemming from great accomplishments and its many freedoms – freedoms that most countries don't allow and their citizens can hardly fathom.

As a child growing up in the United States, when reprimanded by an adult, or asked to stop doing something, the standard response would so often be, "It's a free country!" The value of freedom is so ingrained in the American culture that it was seemingly embedded into the child's very DNA. At the same time, this liberty was never intended to be an unlimited, hedonistic, free-for-all, in which everyone disregards the common good and indulges in pleasures without considering the consequences. It was based on a moral system of values – a system which the Founding Fathers clearly reinforced – that stemmed from the number one all-time bestseller, the Bible.

> *I have examined all religions, as well as my narrow sphere, my straightened means, and my busy life would allow; and the result is that the Bible is the best Book in the world. It contains more philosophy than all the libraries I have seen.*[8]
>
> (John Adams, in a letter to
> Thomas Jefferson, December 25, 1813)

The Bible is the foundation on which the United States is established and from which many of its laws are based. Even some of the early leaders of this nation, such as Jefferson and Lincoln, who were known to possess some degree of intellectual skepticism about elements of the Christian dogma, came to the same conclusion that the biblical narratives should be employed as the guide for American life.

The Bible is the only history that claims to be God's Book – to comprise His law – His history. It contains an immense amount of evidence as to its authenticity.[9]

(Abraham Lincoln,
as related by Hon. L. E. Chittenden,
Register of the Treasury under Lincoln)

Lincoln continued:

But for it (the Bible), we could not know right from wrong... Now let us treat the Bible fairly. If we had a witness on the stand whose general story we knew was true, we would believe him when he asserted facts of which we have no other evidence. We ought to treat the Bible with equal fairness. I decided a long time ago that it was less difficult to believe that the Bible was what it claimed to be than to disbelieve it.[10]

(Abraham Lincoln)

So, too, was it understood that the Bible provided the embryonic American nation with a moral code, a way to control the negative inclinations of human nature and to channel human passion in the right direction. These were issues that were discussed openly, with the idealistic purpose of creating a model nation.

We have no government armed with power capable of contending with human passions unbridled by morality and religion. Avarice, ambition, revenge, or gallantry would break the strongest cords of our Constitution as a whale goes through a net. Our Constitution was made only for a moral and religious people. It is wholly inadequate to the government of any other.[11]

(John Adams, speech to the
U.S. military, October 11, 1798)

The second President of the United States was expressing the consensus philosophy of America's Founding Fathers. This philosophy provided the foundation on which they built the basic principles that were to be the pillars of the nation.

In Brooklyn, NY, I attended public schools and we were taught to always honor these principles and learned to revere the founders of the nation. George Washington, John Adams, Thomas Jefferson, and Abraham Lincoln were legendary figures who, as far as we were concerned, could do no wrong. I remember learning the famous story about George Washington and the cherry tree. I was often confused about whether the story was true or not, but it didn't really matter when I learned the moral behind it.

The Cherry Tree by M. L. Weems

When George was about six years old, he was made the wealthy owner of a hatchet, of which, like most little boys, he was immoderately fond, and was constantly going about chopping everything that came in his way.

One day, in the garden, where he often amused himself by hacking his mother's pea-sticks, he unluckily tried the edge of his hatchet on the body of a beautiful young English cherry tree, which he barked so terribly…

The next morning, the old gentleman, finding out what had befallen his tree, which, by the by, was a great favourite, came into the house; and with much warmth asked for the mischievous author, declaring at the same time, that he would not have taken five guineas for his tree. Nobody could tell him anything about it.

Presently George and his hatchet made their appearance. "George," said his father, "do you know who killed that beautiful little cherry tree yonder in the garden?"

This was a tough question; and George staggered under it for a moment; but quickly recovering himself; and looking at his father … he bravely cried out, "I can't tell a lie, Pa, you know I can't tell a lie. I did cut it with my hatchet."

"Run to my arms, you dearest boy," cried his father in transports.

"Run to my arms. Glad am I, George, that you killed my

tree; for you have paid me for it a thousandfold. Such an act of heroism in my son, is more worth than a thousand trees, though blossomed with silver, and their fruits of purest gold."[12]

Once again, the validity of the story is irrelevant. What did matter was the moral message that we should revere our elected leaders. That reverence should be derived not simply from their power and leadership roles, but from their admirable character traits and moral standing. This was the view of the Founding Fathers in my native country, not merely as politicians, but as men of moral character.

Aside from blatantly accepting the legendary status of the Founding Fathers as political and philosophical leaders, it is certainly worthwhile to question their insights regarding America's roots. More specifically, what motivated their deeply philosophical view that molded America? And, more importantly, what can we learn from their defining words that continue to shape the values of America?

An Almost Biblical Nation: *President Washington considered the United States to be a unique nation guided by the Almighty for a noble mission.*

Whereas it is the duty of all nations to acknowledge the providence of Almighty God, to obey His will, to be grateful for His benefits, and humbly to implore His protection and favor...[13]

(George Washington,
The Thanksgiving Proclamation,
October 3, 1789)

America's first President made it clear that this country would be unlike any other. Instead, this would be a nation that would be guided by Divine favor. The Founding Fathers united to create a God-centered nation that would provide an unparalleled level of respect for the rights of the individual. The Founding Fathers formed an extensive system of freedoms and repeatedly stressed these rights had been derived from the Creator.

> *God who gave us life gave us liberty. Can the liberties of a nation be secure when we have removed a conviction that these liberties are the gift of God?*[14]
>
> (Thomas Jefferson,
> Jefferson Memorial inscription)

In my first book, *God, Israel, and Shiloh: Returning to the Land,* I wrote about my speaking tours throughout the United States, during which I passed through cities or towns called Shiloh, the name obviously derived from the biblical Shiloh.

As the former mayor of Shiloh, Israel – the original Shiloh – often referred to as a "settlement" in the infamous "West Bank" of Israel, it was fascinating to me as I also came across inns, churches and schools with the namesake Shiloh.[15]

Despite my passion for the historic biblical town in Israel that has been my home for nearly two decades, it is important to note that the biblical names in the United States don't merely include the namesake Shiloh, but also include the many cities named Jerusalem, Jericho, Mount Zion, Bethlehem, Nazareth, and Bethel. This speaks volumes about the biblical and religious foundations of the United States as well as the specific type of religion that was intended. While religious liberty was granted to one and all, the population was overwhelmingly Christian. These people derived their guiding principles from what is often known as the Judeo-Christian heritage – the religious heritage that is based on the Bible, not on the Koran nor on any Buddhist or Hindu text. The public educational system, known then as the common school which was first established in Colonial America, commonly used

Focus On the Biblical Heartland: *With the exception of the far southern and northern parts of Israel, this map of Israel includes all areas of the country currently in Israel's possession, with a particular focus on the biblical heartland (often mistakenly called the West Bank).*

the Bible as its reading primer to teach young children how to read.[16] While it was clear that there would be no single established religion and that people would be free to worship God as they wished, in those days people were not obsessed with the need to separate church and state. No one complained about prayer or God in the classroom; it was expected that the Bible would be taught in schools, as it provided the basis of common principles that would bind the society together. It was also a given that children would learn to pray and be thankful for what they had. This ideology is the basis for the Thanksgiving holiday in America. This was also a biblical principle, and, perhaps unbeknownst to the average U.S. citizen, was deeply rooted in the oral traditions and lessons derived from the Torah of Israel, known to Christians as the Old Testament.

> *Who is rich? He who is happy with (i.e., thankful for) what*
> *he has.*
>
> (Mishna: Ethics of the Fathers 4:1)

Today, prayer and religious instruction in schools are indeed hot issues – both in the United States and in Israel. Much of the opposition to school prayer in the U.S. comes from the organized American Jewish community, which has objected based upon the grounds of church-state separation. I believe that their concern is understandable, but not on the basis of church-state separation – it is more likely an issue of establishment of religion. Are they objecting to the spiritual reflection or are they simply concerned about vocal Christian prayer, which Jews would feel uncomfortable with? American Jews often claim that school prayer would undoubtedly mean Christian prayer, and they may be right. The educational system would need to establish a way to protect the rights of the minority of children – those who don't pray in a Christian way. One way to include prayer without alienating non-Christian children would be to offer a moment of silent prayer or reflection. However, to not allow prayer at all is akin to establishing Atheism as the American standard, which would be a violation of the Constitution. It would also mean that Atheism would become the official religion in the common school.

As for the overall distinctions between Jews and Christians, I am in favor of confronting these differences sincerely and frankly, but not to dwell on them obsessively. There are some religious Jews who strongly object to the term *Judeo-Christian heritage*, claiming that any blurring of the distinct identity of God's *chosen people* is problematic. There is a distinct Jewish heritage that can be traced back to years before the birth of Jesus and the development of Christianity, so our identity is certainly not dependent on linkage with Christians. Those Jews' arguments have some merit, but difficult times often demand out-of-the-box thinking. These modern times demand ongoing Jewish-Christian dialogue and cooperation, with the primary goal of reaching agreement on the many things that we have in common. If Jews and Christians can't find a way to work together, death and destruction will be invited by those who seek to destroy us. I have personally taken on the challenge of living in Israel, and while I understand the Torah concept that Israel is *a nation that stands alone* (Numbers 23:9) both physically and spiritually, contemporary challenges demand that we identify ways to join together against the threats that the entire world faces. Many of the challenges and threats that Jews and Christians face are similar. We in Israel just happen to be on the front lines and are forced to bear the brunt of it on a daily basis.

As to the differences between Jews and Christians, Jews have always had an understanding of messiah that predates and postdates Jesus of Nazareth. It is a view that is quite different from the Christian concept, but there is no doubt that Christianity has its roots in Judaism. Therefore, when we speak of the biblical foundations of the United States, we must speak of the original Bible, the Torah, and of the nation of Israel, which brought that holiest of books into this world. America's Founding Fathers recognized the critical nature of that connection, which would ensure the success of their newly created nation and successive presidents recognized that historical connection.

> The patriots who laid the foundation of this Republic drew
> their faith from the Bible. May they give due credit to the people
> among whom the Holy Scriptures came into being. And as
> they ponder the assertion that "Hebraic mortar cemented the
> foundations of American democracy," they cannot escape the
> conclusion that if American democracy is to remain the greatest
> hope of humanity it must continue abundantly in the faith of
> the Bible.[17]
>
> (President Calvin Coolidge, May 3, 1925)

When examining the Jewish involvement in supporting the
American Revolution, one must acknowledge George Washington's
close relationship with Hayim Solomon, the Polish-born Jewish-
American financier and revolutionary activist based in Philadelphia.
Solomon reportedly loaned the newly-formed American government
over $600,000, a sum that was never repaid. In today's market that
would be equivalent to approximately $30 billion. According to the
research of Jacob Rader Marcus, the sum was closer to $800,000 or the
equivalent of $40 billion.[18] George Washington's appreciation for
Solomon's substantial behind-the-scenes role in the Revolution may
have been a factor in his

***Revolutionary Hero and American
Patriot:*** *Hayim Solomon, the humble Jewish
"financier of the American Revolution,"
epitomized one of the ideal personality traits
praised in the Jewish "Ethics of the Fathers"
book of wisdom – "Say a little, Do a lot."*

support for the people of Israel. On the other hand, Washington's statements reveal a philosophical-historical bond with the people of Israel that seems to go much deeper:

> *May the same wonder-working Deity, who long since delivered the Hebrews from their Egyptian oppressors, and planted them in the promised land, whose providential agency has lately been conspicuous in establishing these United States as an independent nation, continue to water them with the dews of Heaven, and to make the inhabitants of every denomination participate in the temporal and spiritual blessings of that people, whose God is Jehovah.*[19]
>
> (George Washington, speaking
> to the Hebrew Congregation of Savannah)

In other words, George Washington seemed to understand that there was a clear connection between the rise of the United States as a world power and its relationship with the not-yet-reestablished nation of Israel. The Founding Fathers, most of whom were Christians of deep faith, looked to biblical history for inspiration and guidance. They frequently noticed striking parallels between Israel's miraculous story and the making of the American nation. Thomas Jefferson, who would eventually become the third president, served on a committee to draft a seal for the newly-formed U.S. This seal would characterize the spirit of the nation. He proposed the following representation:

> *The Children of Israel in the wilderness, led by a cloud by day, and a pillar of fire by night.*[20]

Distinguished philosopher/inventor/statesman Benjamin Franklin served on that same committee. Using the imagery of Moses lifting up his wand (staff), and dividing the Red Sea, and Pharaoh in his chariot overwhelmed with the waters, he proposed this motto: *Rebellion to tyrants is obedience to God.*[21]

Franklin's analogy was actually very appropriate and matched ancient Israel's vision of leadership. Despite the fact that monarchy or dictatorship was the international norm in biblical times,

Learning from the Prophets: Benjamin Franklin, *certainly one of the philosophical leaders and visionaries in the American Revolution, often used biblical imagery and ideas to describe the new nation.*

Israel's form of monarchy was quite opposed to unrestricted political control. After the Exodus from slavery in Egypt, the Children of Israel (the Israelites) wandered in the desert for forty years, eventually entering the Land of Israel, which was then called the Land of Canaan. Israel's leadership and unity had been torn asunder by excessive individualism following a tumultuous several hundred-year-long period called the Judges. The people, in an unofficial spirit of rebellion and democracy, began to agitate for a king – a strong leader who would put an end to the painful division and instability that plagued Israel. However, this was to be no ordinary monarchy, but a monarchy with clear biblical guidelines that would obstruct Israel's eventual progression into dictatorship.

> In those days, there was no king in Israel; every man did what was right in his own eyes.
>
> (Judges 21:25)

Following Divine guidance, Samuel the Prophet cautioned the people against putting unlimited power in the hands of any one leader. He warned of the abuse of power and ruthless dictatorship that could result due to such lusting for strong leadership. But the people were not dissuaded – they persisted in their demand for a king.

> They said, "No! There shall be a king over us, and we will be like all the other nations; our king will judge us, and go forth

before us, and fight our wars!"

(1 Samuel 8:19-20)

The demand of the people was actually a plea for an end to the divisive Judges period. They hoped that a strong leader would bring unity and decisiveness through his leadership. The people's demand for a strong king was granted, but Samuel issued conditions that would bind the leader to a moral system of leadership, under which he would be unable to act solely according to his own whims and desires.

> *If you will fear the Lord and worship Him, and hearken to His voice and not rebel against the word of the Lord, then you and the king who reigns over you will be following the Lord your God. But if you do not hearken to the voice of the Lord, and you rebel against the word of the Lord, then the hand of the Lord will be against you, and against your fathers.*

(1 Samuel 12:13-15)

The biblical commentator known as the Radak teaches that the words *your fathers* in the above quote refers to the kings of Israel. In other words, Samuel was giving a clear warning that the king was expected to adhere to God's Torah. He would be held up to the same moral principles as the average citizen. For this reason, immediately upon taking office, the king was required to write his own Torah scroll and to keep it with him at all times. Thus, Samuel was showing the people who was really on the throne. Samuel made it apparent that the king was obligated to obey the guidelines given to him by the Almighty. Samuel the Prophet, 2,000 years before the Magna Carta, forged what was a cutting-edge, limited monarchy, complete with a king who was given power at the democratic demand of the people. However, this king and his citizens were subservient to the Real King. This system of checks and balances was immediately tested and proven efficient, when Saul – the first King of Israel – was rapidly deposed by Samuel the Prophet for not explicitly following the instructions given to him by God during the war against Amalek, the arch-enemy of Israel.

While not a prophet, Benjamin Franklin was a voice of morality and conscience in the American colonies. He spoke strongly against the unlimited rule of tyrants, but he also emphasized the need for leaders and citizens to follow the guidelines of Scripture as the way to constrain uncontrolled power. In lieu of prophecy as a means of enforcing human integrity, this philosophy was eventually developed into the comprehensive system of governmental self-enforcement, which included the brilliant concepts of Separation of Powers and Checks and Balances, which helped prevent abuse and corruption. However, it is important to remember that the focus on balance between strong leadership and spiritual guidance came from biblical lessons, as did the need for an enlightened, aware, and assertive citizenry.

> *A Bible and a newspaper in every house, a good school in every district – all studied and appreciated as they merit – are the principal support of virtue, morality, and civil liberty.*[22]
>
> (Benjamin Franklin, in a letter to the Ministry of France, March 1778)

The Bible as the most basic and central element of education was so widely accepted that it even permeated the halls of higher learning. A knowledge of Hebrew was necessary for early American scholars; many universities made it a prerequisite in their core curriculum. Hebrew was compulsory at Harvard until 1787. Harvard President Increase Mather (1685-1701) was an ardent Hebraist, as were his predecessors, Henry Dunster and Charles Chauncey. Mather's writings contain numerous quotations from the Talmud as well as from the works of Saadia Gaon, Rashi, Maimonides and other classic Jewish Bible commentators. To this day, Yale's insignia, which has been in use since 1736, has the Hebrew words *Urim V'Tumim*, meaning Light and Perfection, written on it. These words refer to the holy parchment on which God's Name is written. This parchment was positioned within the breastplate of the High Priest in the Temple in Jerusalem. Samuel

Johnson, first president of King's College (1754-1763), expressed the intellectual attitude of his age when he referred to Hebrew as *essential to a gentleman's education.*

So prevalent and popular was the study of the Hebrew language in the Ivy League schools of the late 16th and early 17th centuries that several students at Yale delivered their commencement addresses in Hebrew. Hebrew was one of three optional foreign languages in which a commencement speech could be given in the schools that taught the language. These schools included universities such as Yale, Harvard, Columbia, Dartmouth, Brown, Princeton, Johns Hopkins, and the University of Pennsylvania. The two other languages allowed were Latin and Greek.[23]

Beyond the educational sphere, the Jewish/biblical influence could also be seen in the legal system. The 15 Capital Laws of New England included the *Seven Noahide Laws* of the Torah, or what may be termed the *seven universal laws of morality*, the observance of which are incumbent upon all people. Six of these laws prohibit idolatry, blasphemy, murder, robbery, adultery, and eating flesh from a living animal, while the seventh requires the establishment of courts of justice. Such courts are obviously essential to any society based on the need for reason and persuasion rather than passion and intimidation.[24]

My general premise in this book is that the United States, for all of its current challenges, was created for such a time as this – an age of turmoil, terrorism, and various challenges to Western civilization. The foundations of the U.S.-Israel relationship seem to be self-evident, quite similar to the truths that President Abraham Lincoln spoke about in his Gettysburg Address. President Lincoln gathered his inspiration from the Preamble of the Declaration of Independence; but even before then, the Founding Fathers derived their basic principles from, you guessed it, the Bible of Israel. Those bonds between the American Constitution and the Bible were so great that it was considered to be an essential principle on which the nation was based. This included the concept of representative government. In the days of prophecy, there was

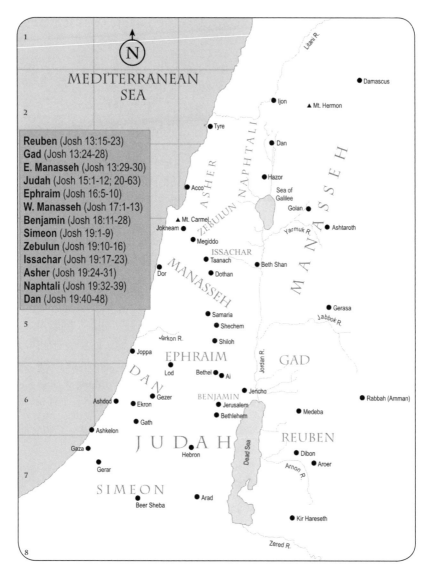

Reuben (Josh 13:15-23)
Gad (Josh 13:24-28)
E. Manasseh (Josh 13:29-30)
Judah (Josh 15:1-12; 20-63)
Ephraim (Josh 16:5-10)
W. Manasseh (Josh 17:1-13)
Benjamin (Josh 18:11-28)
Simeon (Josh 19:1-9)
Zebulun (Josh 19:10-16)
Issachar (Josh 19:17-23)
Asher (Josh 19:24-31)
Naphtali (Josh 19:32-39)
Dan (Josh 19:40-48)

Regional Representation: *The biblical system of land apportionment among the Israelite tribes was perhaps the first form of regional democracy that the world has known.*

the critical spiritual component of Divine supervision, but the notion of the people choosing leaders of character was similar to the American idea.

> *Select for yourselves men who are wise, understanding, and known to your tribes and I will appoint them as your leaders.*
>
> (Deuteronomy 1:13)

Rabbi Samson Raphael Hirsch comments:

> *Each tribe (shevet in Hebrew) is to choose out of its own midst men whose character can only be known by their lives (hence whose character) is known only to those who have associated with them.*

This is the biblical source of residential requirements for Representatives and Senators in the United States.[25]

> *In the spirit and essence of our Constitution, the influence of the Hebrew Commonwealth was paramount in that it was not only the highest authority for the principle, "that rebellion to tyrants is obedience to God," but also because it was in itself a Divine precedent for a pure democracy, as distinguished from monarchy, aristocracy or any other form of government.*[26]
>
> (President Woodrow Wilson, May 7, 1911)

> *And proclaim freedom throughout the land for all its inhabitants (thereof).*
>
> (Leviticus 25:10 – Inscribed
on the Liberty Bell in Philadelphia, PA)

In our times, the values that the Liberty Bell represents are under dual attack. The first prong of this assault comes from secularists and extreme leftists. Both of these groups say that they support liberty, but, in reality, are trying to undermine America's biblical foundations, simply because of the Judeo-Christian nature of these foundations. The second prong of this assault comes from those who oppose the entire concept of liberty. They have been known to exploit the very liberties that they disdain in order to undermine the system and the foundations on which it was built.

As you can see from this basic outline, the problem that has been placed on our shoulders is a multi-faceted one. The United States and Israel share historic bonds, but the many values that the two nations have in common will mean nothing if we lack the courage and firmness of heart to stand up for what we believe.

Terrorism in recent years has been combined with more subtle attempts to change the very character of the United States into a caricature that would have shocked the nation's founders. In recent years, Israel has faced similar challenges; the two nations are deeply intertwined since they are both primary targets.

Will the U.S. and Israel accept the challenge? This is only possible if we understand that the current struggle is not about disputed territories, multicultural freedom, or economic justice. It is a religious war, or more accurately, an anti-religious war, against Judaism, Christianity, and the magnificent Western civilization.

Chapter Two
Terror Is Not An Enemy

The face of terror is not the true faith of Islam. That's not what Islam is all about. Islam is peace. These terrorists (who carried out the September 11 attacks) don't represent peace. They represent evil and war.[1]

(President George W. Bush, speech at the Islamic Center of Washington, September 17, 2001)

We (Muslims) have ruled the world before, and by Allah, the day will come when we will rule the entire world again. The day will come when we will rule America. The day will come when we will rule Britain and the entire world – except for the Jews. The Jews will not enjoy a life of tranquility under our rule, because they are treacherous by nature, as they have been throughout history.... Listen to the Prophet Muhammad, who tells you about the evil end that awaits Jews.[2]

(Sheikh Ibrahim Mudeiris, Sermon on official Palestinian Authority TV, May 13, 2005)

While the topics discussed throughout these chapters have always concerned me, the horrific terror in Mumbai, India during November 2008 compelled me to seriously consider writing this book. The death toll reached nearly 200 along with the more than 300 wounded.

This extensive terrorist operation included a series of well-coordinated, wide-ranging attacks on at least ten distinct targets in Mumbai – India's financial capital.

Although India is a vibrant and populous democracy, it is a poor country that is often considered to be a part of the Third World. India has increasingly become a target of terrorism, especially from hostile terror groups based in Pakistan – its Islamic neighbor.

The targets of the November 2008 terrorist attacks included a murderous rampage at the two largest hotels in Mumbai, in which people of many nationalities were killed or wounded. This was the largest single attack on a major democracy since 9-11 and was a poignant reminder that the U.S. and Israel are not isolated targets. The long arm of terrorism extends to the destruction of any nation that embraces value systems different than their own; and in particular, a nation that will not negotiate with terrorists. Political scientists have spent millions of dollars and expended thousands of hours to research terrorism, which is a much more complex issue than academicians can decipher. It strikes at the heart of mankind's quest for liberty and human dignity. Those who have experienced its wrath are forever changed. This is not a theoretical conflict that will be resolved in ivory towers or in research institutes, for it is an issue that will only be resolved when it is determined that terrorism is a symptom, not an enemy. To understand terrorism, one must truly comprehend that behind terrorist acts, a dangerous ideology is seething with the intent of destroying human dignity and creating havoc. This ideology seeks to exterminate any civilization that opposes its version of what is holy and right – based upon its own sources of authority.

The nature of Islamic terrorism is aptly described by German historian Koenraad Elst and American historian Will Durant who recall the history of Islamic terror attacks in India.

> *The Muslim conquests, down to the 16th century, were for the Hindus a pure struggle of life and death. Entire cities were burnt down and the populations massacred, with hundreds of thousands killed in every campaign, and similar numbers deported as slaves. Every new invader made (often literally) his hills of Hindus skulls. Thus, the conquest of Afghanistan in*

the year 1000 was followed by the annihilation of the Hindu population; the region is still called the Hindu Kush, i.e. Hindu slaughter. The Bahmani sultans (1347-1480) in central India made it a rule to kill 100,000 captives in a single day, and many more on other occasions. The conquest of the Vijayanagar Empire in 1564 left the capital plus large areas of Karnataka depopulated. And so on.

As a contribution to research on the quantity of the Islamic crimes against humanity, we may mention that the Indian (subcontinent) population decreased by 80 million between 1000 (conquest of Afghanistan) and 1525 (end of Delhi Sultanate)...[3]

(Koenraad Elst, German historian, *Negation in India*)

The Islamic conquest of India is probably the bloodiest story in history. It is a discouraging tale, for its evident moral is that civilization is a precious good, whose delicate complex of order and freedom, culture and peace, can at any moment be overthrown by barbarians invading from without or multiplying from within.[4]

(Will Durant, U.S. historian)

Voices from around the globe have discussed the challenge of terrorism in contrast to conventional warfare. Targeting innocents (including the capture of hostages) is a fairly recent phenomenon which requires a new approach to combat enemies. For example, we see the inhumane military techniques that are being employed by the terrorist organizations Hamas and Hezbollah, who have based their armies inside of functioning hospitals and schools, where we could expect enormous civilian casualties if they are attacked. This is also a very successful propaganda strategy because it forces the Israeli army to attack these locations in an effort to fight the terrorist enemy. When such an attack occurs, the perception throughout the world is not that the enemy is endangering their civilians by using their hospitals and schools as human shields, rather, that the Israeli army is targeting these locations an effort to injure civilians. Israeli military officers have notified civilians well in advance of impending attacks so they may leave the site even though this often endangers the lives of Israeli soldiers. Yet, little media attention has been dedicated to exposing the reality that terror groups cynically exploit the lives of innocents to win the propaganda war, as well as to prevent Israel from responding to the Hamas rocket fire coming from those very schools and hospitals. Even though war tactics are changing, this does not mean that terrorism itself is a new phenomenon.

The United States has combated terrorists since the days of Presidents George Washington, John Adams and Thomas Jefferson. Although these men were battling the Barbary Pirates and not today's terrorists, the psychology is the same now as it was two hundred years ago. Contrary to popular wisdom, the bitter lessons learned by those early American leaders still hold true. If the lessons continue to go unheeded, our children will be doomed to suffer the consequences of our stubbornness, fear, and ignorance; and must fight the same battles facing the world today.

Those who cannot learn from history are doomed to repeat it.[5]

(George Santayana,
Spanish-American philosopher, 1905)

Terrorism is not a new topic to me and is certainly not one that I have merely read about in books. Anyone who dwells within the biblical heartland of Israel has experienced terrorism to varying degrees. Often known as the West Bank – or by the historical names of Samaria or Judea – these pioneering Jewish communities are under perpetual attack and the terrorism is constant in our day-to-day lives. Some communities have suffered from terrorist infiltrations while others have endured roadside bombings or terrorist ambushes. During the most intense periods, there were commuters that were living in my township (Shiloh) who wore bulletproof vests and helmets while driving to work each morning. Since many individuals only travel by bus, the intercity buses became armored after enduring intense waves of terrorism. After numerous reports of both parents being murdered in an attack, parents began travelling in separate cars, in fear of orphaning their children.

This is to say nothing of the psychological damage inflicted upon children who carried the weight of an uncertain future each and every day. This daily terror is magnified within Samaria, the biblical heartland of Israel; located in the area north of Jerusalem. The same daily uncertainty occurred in Judea, the area south of Jerusalem. These regions – where most of the biblical and historical sites are located – account for the most intense and disproportionate incidents of terrorism which has inflicted an enormous amount of damage to adults and children.

In merely one city of Shiloh, the neighborhood I call home, there have been seemingly endless accounts of death.

Take for instance the Eldar family. Their 16-year-old son Yonatan was a serious student and a kind-hearted boy who was a popular counselor in his youth group (the Israeli equivalent of Boy Scouts). I still recall the Sabbath before Yonatan and his classmates were killed. Yonatan stood in the synagogue and eloquently read a passage from the Torah, never knowing that this would become his last time. He was murdered near the entrance of his high school library, along with seven other boys, who were shot dead by a terrorist and left laying in an ugly pool of blood on the library floor.

In the house next door to the Eldar family lives the Yerushalmi family. Their 17-year-old son Shmuel was slaughtered while doing something as ordinary as waiting for his bus. The friendly young student was on his way home from Jerusalem, where he had taken an exam and taken the time to visit with his grandmother. As he stood at the crowded bus stop, a suicide bomber detonated an explosive that killed Shmuel alongside other innocent Israelis.

The very next house belongs to the Kessler family. Their energetic 19-year-old granddaughter, Gila Sarah, was robbed of her adulthood at the hands of the very same terrorist who had killed Shmuel.

Only three houses down from the Kesslers is the home of the Sitone family. Their tall, active, 17-year-old son Avi was at his high school when terrorist infiltrators with assault rifles attacked the boys on the basketball court. They shot to kill and continued their rampage by hunting down those who had fled into dormitories. Avi did not survive.

Yonatan Eldar

The Shoham family lives around the corner from Avi's family. Their five-month-old baby Yehudah was murdered after a large rock was thrown at his parents' car. They were driving home from a visit with the infant's grandparents. The rock crushed the baby's head and he died several days later.

Shmuel Yerushalmi

There are many others in my town of Shiloh who have suffered from terrorism – including me and my three-year-old son Reuven (known to all as Ruby). Ruby was a friendly, happy little boy who was very attached to me. I was his role model and he would imitate me in his adorable three-year-old style. For example, when I would put on my *talit* (Jewish prayer shawl), swaying back and forth with the rhythm of prayer and with prayerbook in hand, he would imitate me by putting a green head kerchief around his shoulders, doing the same with a children's picture book in his little hands. His sincerity, and love of life was contagious and enveloped all who came into contact with him.

Gila Kessler

Avi Sitone

Ruby's life was filled with the innocence of childhood until that night in December 2001

Yehuda Shoham

when everything changed. It was a cold, dark night, the last day of Chanukah, and we were returning home after spending an afternoon together in Jerusalem. We were riding on the dark, country road known as the Road of the Patriarchs, because that is the historic north-south mountain-ridge road that the biblical Patriarchs – Abraham, Isaac, and Jacob – used to travel on (In our times, it's been given a modern name – Route 60). As I was listening to a news report on the radio about a terror attack that had just occurred several miles away from there, the radio suddenly went dead, as a massive hail of bullets struck my car! I saw four orange sparks whizzing past my eyes and I felt a bullet ram into my leg and blood started pouring out, almost like an open fire hydrant on an inner-city street.

I had been shot in the left leg and my little boy was shot in his head and neck. I will never forget the feeling of panic after the bullets hit their targets – me and my son. The blood was furiously pouring out of my leg, but I hadn't yet realized that Ruby had also been wounded. He was still sitting quietly behind me in his baby seat. When I turned to him, I was shocked to see that his mouth was wide open, his eyes were wide open, but he couldn't move. He looked like he was trying to cry or scream, but there was only a deafening silence. I didn't see any blood on him, so I assumed he was just in shock and other than that, he was okay. Meanwhile, my attention was refocused on the bullets that were still flying and I couldn't get the car to start. I had already turned the ignition several times, but the car stubbornly refused to start. I don't know if I was even breathing during the next five or six failed attempts. Finally, after what seemed an eternity, but was probably only a few seconds, the car finally sprung to life as if there hadn't even been a problem. I thank God for the moment. I thanked Him then and still thank Him now.

I drove the car nearly 120 mph to the next community and prayed someone would be able to call for an ambulance. I was continuously hitting the button on my CB radio, trying to reach the security forces in the area, but they weren't responding. I tried

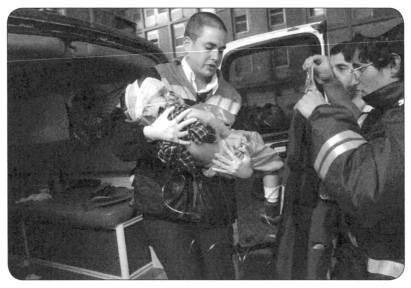

Targeting Innocent Babies: *Three-year-old Ruby Rubin being carried from the ambulance into the hospital. The Muslim terrorists exploited the new freedom given to them by the Israeli government under world pressure, to launch hundreds of terrorist attacks against innocent Israeli civilians, including babies and young children.*

to focus on the road and not think of the pain, the blood pouring from my left leg, or that it was pounding so violently.

We reached the community several minutes later and I started screaming for help. A gas station attendant ran to the car shouting that he was also a paramedic. I don't know what I would have done without him. He ripped off my shirt and wrapped it tightly around my leg to try to stop the blood flow. After the wound had been attended to, he handed me his cell phone and told me to call my wife. I remember looking down at my trembling hand the same time that he did. Without even a word, he took the phone and dialed the number for me.

When my wife Lisa answered the phone, I told her that I had been shot, but that Ruby was okay. She was actually relieved that I called, because the security services had contacted her, telling her that I had been trying to reach them, that something had happened, but that they couldn't get through to me. She had feared that I was dead.

After what felt like hours, the ambulance arrived and that was when my entire life changed.

The EMT examined Ruby, for what we all assumed was merely a formality. Instead, he discovered that Ruby had been severely wounded. A bullet from what was later determined to be a Kalashnikov assault rifle, otherwise known as an AK-47, had pierced his skull at the point where it meets with the neck. This in turn caused a skull fracture and internal bleeding in the cerebellum (which controls motor and cognition functions). In a flurry of activity, Ruby's head was wrapped with bandages, an oxygen mask was placed on his face and he was lifted onto a stretcher. At the same time, I was hoisted onto a stretcher and we were whisked away to a hospital in Jerusalem. This seemingly easy task became complex due to Israeli ambulances often being fired upon in the area. During a tense 40-minute ride that seemed to take hours, I was in tears. I so wanted to comfort my three-year-old, to provide the fatherly support that he so needed, but I was helpless. Finally, we reached a hospital on the far side of Jerusalem.

Shortly after arriving, I was told by the hospital's public relations director that I was the hospital's 1,000th victim of terrorism. They had begun counting only a year and a half prior. I wasn't quite sure how to respond to that dubious honor and wondered if I would be presented with an award – one I certainly would not cherish. I can laugh about it now, but I certainly wasn't laughing then. The director explained that he was telling me this because the media was amassing outside the emergency room to interview the 1,000th terror victim. He promised that he would do his best to keep them away and protect our privacy. As I pondered this, I did not think of the television cameras outside. Instead, images of the 999 other victims were flashing in my head. There was nothing private about this. Everyone had been suffering from ongoing terror attacks and the resultant anxiety each and every day. And now, I knew exactly how many victims had been in this exact hospital in only 18 months. So, I told him that the media should come in. There was nothing private about this anyway and that I would tell my story to them. The violence had to stop. I've been telling my story ever since. There have now been thousands of additional terror victims in Israel but I still continue to tell our horrifying, but miraculous story. I am enormously thankful that the car inexplicably started while bullets were flying by. That engine turning over enabled us to reach the ambulance. I'm also fortunate that the bullet hit only my left leg, even though the terrorists were shooting from the right side of the road. Because of this, I was able to drive my automatic car after the attack.

Last but not least, I was later told by the surgeon that the bullet which entered the head and traveled through the neck of my three-year-old boy missed his brain stem by one millimeter. One precious millimeter. Our miraculous survival pierced through my ever-present New York skepticism and I am grateful to the Almighty to this day.

After several weeks of hospitalization, numerous operations, and extensive post-trauma psychological play therapy for my son, we eventually had a full recovery. Since then, I've had the privilege of responding to terrorism by doing the opposite of what the terrorists and their masters intended. They wanted to kill and terrorize Jewish communities in the biblical heartland of Israel. Instead, we are strengthening future generations in Israel through an organization I established after the attack. It is the Shiloh Israel Children's Fund; and it supports a wide variety of child-centered psychological therapy and educational programs in the communities within Israel's heartland that have been traumatized by the terrorism.

As an individual who had been terrorized, it would have been understandable – if not acceptable – for me to vow taking revenge against those who had attacked us. It also would have been reasonable to many if I sunk a deep depression after my son and I were wounded. But, I do not believe that this is the Jewish way to contend with adversity.

Once a Symbol of American Pride: The Twin Towers, before the terrorist attacks on September 11, 2001.

The medieval Jewish text – The Zohar – says that in order to get into the heavenly yeshiva (the equivalent of a Bible College), one needs to turn darkness into light and bitterness into sweetness. I have focused my energies on this during the years since the attack. Entire communities have been traumatized by the terrorism in Israel and the domino effect of PTSD (Post-Traumatic Stress Disorder) is particularly destabilizing in the lives of children, for whom the sense of security and self-confidence is always crucial.

After experiencing the effects of terrorism in Israel daily, I am not surprised when I hear about attacks in other parts of the world. I know that the architects of terrorism have goals that stretch far beyond Israel. As in Israel, terror victims are often neglected during the news analysis of the day; but the pain of the victims – especially the children, even if those who weren't physically wounded themselves – is very real. Children feel the residual effects from a friend, neighbor, or teacher being killed or wounded. They are often suffering from serious emotional wounds which very few notice. Attention is given to those who are physically wounded, and because of that, the psychological trauma of these victims is usually neglected and left untreated.

In Israel, the ongoing terrorism, frequent wars and resulting traumas are part of a difficult reality that we live with every day. During 2001 and 2002, when it was the most intense with attacks occurring daily, Israelis were understandably obsessed with terrorism. The conversations on the street were almost always about the latest attack or the most recent miracle survivor. When a Jerusalem bus driver would tune his radio to the news station, everyone on the crowded bus would sit or stand in tense silence as the next attack was reported. Everyone listened to the morbid details of how many were killed and wounded. The people of Israel have always been determined not to let terrorists disrupt their lives, but the continuous stress eventually takes its toll. This always seemed to be a challenge that only Israelis faced, that is, until the attacks of September 11, 2001 sent shockwaves around the world when my second home, New York City, was gripped in terror while 3,000 innocent American lives were lost.

The 9-11 attacks occurred only a few months before my son and I were wounded in Israel. Until that fateful day, the words "terrorism" and "Israel" were synonymous, even exclusive, in the eyes of the American public. When the Twin Towers and the Pentagon were attacked, everything changed. For a brief amount of time, Americans understood the pain that no one should ever have to endure – the pain that Israelis comprehend on an unmatched scale. Until that day, it was almost impossible for Americans to understand the Israeli's reality, which had become a morbid routine that consisted of watching gruesome video footage on TV, hearing the numbers of those killed and wounded, and in many cases, identifying the names with real people who have touched your lives.

Immediately after the attack in New York, my brother phoned from Manhattan to tell us that he was okay. It was almost surreal for me and my wife after the years of concerned phone calls from my brother and other family members in the U.S. who would ask if we were okay after each terrorist attack in Israel. Terrorism had suddenly gone global, and in a big way. The thousands who were murdered and wounded were multiplied by those who were left psychologically scarred for life. Throughout the daily treatment of children in our therapeutic programs, coupled with the relevant research, I have learned that the trauma never truly goes away. The goal is to learn to recognize it, contend with it, and put it in its proper place. If that is done successfully, the young victim becomes stronger and has actually grown because of the experience.

Children aren't like adults. An adult can sit in a therapist's office and verbally relive his or her trauma, as painful as it may be. Children are different. Children need intermediaries, such as animals, music, movement or art to help the trauma emerge. That is the first step on the road to recovery and how youngsters learn to integrate the understanding of that trauma into their young lives. The Shiloh Israel Children's Fund has programs that are structured with this knowledge in mind; and thankfully, we've had a lot of success.

However, adults also need to learn from their traumas, not just for each individual victim, for their friends and their neighbors, but for the society as a whole. While many Israelis, through no choice of our own, have become somewhat knowledgeable about treating victims, can we also say that we have learned the necessary lessons in our society that will combat the growth of terrorism? The same question is certainly applicable for the United States as well. Can we honestly say that Americans have learned anything of significance from the trauma relating to the attacks on 9-11? Have strategic conclusions and long-term goals been enacted to protect America in the future and to defeat its enemies? These are complex questions to answer.

When I heard about the 2008 Mumbai massacre in India, it struck a chord in me about the true global nature of terrorism. In particular, the glaring fact that political leaders in the East and West are missing the magnitude and the true meaning of terrorism. The massacre in India was horrific and the pain of the victims is still very real. Yet, the reactions from around the world were somewhat predictable and disappointing given that seven years had passed since the events on 9-11. In those seven years, leaders from around the world had not unambiguously identified the enemy. And, even more frightening, they had not taken serious and consistent action against it. After this attack, the usual calls were heard to wipe out "the ugly head of terror."

On November 29, 2008 – while standing on the White House South Lawn – George W. Bush gave one of his last public statements while serving as U.S. President. He began by stating what must have appeared obvious to all who had observed the events of previous days. Bush referred to the "brutal and violent" nature of the killers and declared that terror will not have the final word.[6] After several Indian leaders accused their Muslim neighbor, Pakistan, of involvement in the attack, Husain Huqqani – Pakistan's ambassador to the U.S.– said that his country was confronting the menace of terrorism with great vigor.[7] In further reaction to the attacks in India, The Associated Press (AP) reported that incoming President-elect Barack Obama intended to stand with India against terrorism … and his promise that this attack would not shake the will of a global coalition to defeat terrorism.[8] Even Reuven Rivlin, Speaker of the Israeli Knesset (the parliament) who is one of the rare politicians who calls a spade a spade, fell into the trap of identifying terrorism as an enemy. He said:

> *Terrorism is trying to paralyze and silence democracies fighting against it.*[9]

(Reuven Rivlin, Speaker of the
Israeli Knesset, February 23, 2010)

There has been a multitude of bold statements by world leaders vowing to fight against terrorism, yet there are questions which remain unanswered such as:

- Who is Terrorism?
- Does Terrorism have a head and a long arm that speaks only to silence its people?
- Is there a nation or a person called Terrorism?
- Is there an organization called Terrorism?

What is fascinating to me about all of these seemingly brazen assertions by world leaders is that (aside from the brief and passing accusation of Pakistani involvement), none of these concerned leaders pointed to any specific perpetrator for the attacks in India. In recent years, world leaders have not dared to call terrorism by a name that identifies specific enemies or ideologies. They only refer to an act – a symptom if you will – of a sick ideology. How then, is an average citizen supposed to make sense of these horrific attacks? There is nothing that is more confusing than this lack of moral clarity from the leaders in the free world that spans the boundaries of nations and religion.

European countries such as France, Austria, Holland, and the United Kingdom have had internal problems which make it difficult to voice a clear message, despite their obvious interest in solving the problem. The large and growing Muslim minorities and the ever-present concern for political correctness have emasculated the once-strong nations that now comprise the European Union. Absent from this list are the United States and Israel – the "Great Satan" and the "Little Satan." They are left to weather the storms facing the Western world and to confront the enormous challenge of "World Terrorism," that is, once the leaders agree exactly what the challenge is and how to address that challenge. This allows the leaders of world terrorism to spew venomous criticisms against their two main "enemies." Iranian President Mahmoud Ahmadinejad said during a joint news conference held on February 25, 2010 with Syrian President Bashar al-Assad:

(The Americans) want to dominate the region, but they feel Iran and Syria are preventing that. We tell them that instead of interfering in the region's affairs, to pack their things and leave. If the Zionist regime wants to repeat its past mistakes, this will constitute its demise and annihilation.

Ahmadinejad declared that Iran, Syria, Iraq and Lebanon will stand against Israel. In response, Assad publicly stated his strong support for Iran. He contended that America's stance on Iran is a new situation of colonialism in the region.[10]

The people of Syria and Iran should be so fortunate as to have a little old-fashioned American "colonialism." Would that be so terrible? They would suffer from the so-called "oppressive" nature of the freedoms of religion and speech, the respect for individual rights, and the ability to work to the best of their abilities in a field that aligns with their interests. They would be forced to endure "life, liberty, and pursuit of happiness." In all seriousness, American colonists were idealists who established a wholesome and positive way to live their lives, even with limited means. Did they make mistakes? Of course they did. In any experimental undertaking, mistakes are made and lessons are learned. The ability for Americans to learn from, and correct, their mistakes has been nothing short of remarkable. This has resulted in countries around the world reaping the wealth and benefits of the American way of life. This is certainly not appreciated in countries such as Iraq and in places like Gaza. The inability to value American greatness stems from a cultural and ideological problem that may not be surmountable (discussed in more detail in subsequent chapters). The tiny nation of Israel has worked to spread its know-how around the world to those in need – the earthquake rescue in Haiti being one notable example. On the other hand, the truly oppressive regimes of Ahmadinejad and Assad bring undue suffering to their people and nuclear threats to the world. Nonetheless, their hatred and verbal genocide is fierce and knows no bounds.

To adequately respond to such haters of freedom, both America and Israel will have to develop the courage to identify their true enemies. Is it just Ahmadinejad and Assad? If so, what happens when their reign ends? What and who is the terrorist we must defeat? Until there is an answer to those questions, we won't have the fortitude to move forward by even the tiniest of steps.

On September 17, 2001, President George W. Bush identified Islam as a peaceful religion. Then, on September 20, 2001 – now nine days after the September 11 attacks on the Twin Towers and the Pentagon – the President spoke to the U.S. Congress and to the American people. This address nearly grasped the moral clarity that is needed to confront the Islamic threat.

> *(Terrorists) want to drive Israel out of the Middle East. They want to drive Christians and Jews out of vast regions of Asia and Africa. These terrorists kill not merely to end lives, but to disrupt and end a way of life. With every atrocity, they hope that America grows fearful, retreating from the world.... They stand against us, because we stand in their way.... And we will pursue nations that provide aid or safe haven to terrorism. Every nation, in every region, now has a decision to make. Either you are with us, or you are with the terrorists.*[11]
> (George W. Bush, September 20, 2001)

The relative clarity in his message was impressive, but didn't stand the test of time. The moral clarity soon evolved into an inconsistent policy of pandering to staunchly Islamic states such as Pakistan and Saudi Arabia and terror organizations such as Fatah – President Mahmoud Abbas's ruling component in the Palestinian Authority. The pressure that was sworn to defeat terrorists quickly became pressure that was misdirected to Israel. The United States wanted Israel to surrender vital strategic and historic territories, as a down payment for the cooperation of Saudi Arabia and other Islamic countries in the war on terrorism. When Barack Hussein Obama became President, Iran's nuclear threat and massive support for major terrorist organizations around the world became less of an issue for the United States. In its stead was a sudden urgency to reason with Iran as a means of placating the Muslim world.

The American ambassador to Syria then returned to the Middle Eastern country, in essence reversing President George W. Bush's decision to remove him as a way of officially protesting Syrian support for terrorism. This about-face signaled an American reconciliation with Assad's terror-supporting state – which provides extensive support to Hezbollah in its attempts to dominate Lebanon and to destroy Israel. Compounding the decision, the travel advisory that had been issued to warn about the dangers of travel in this terror-supporting country was lifted.[12] The U.S. no longer viewed Syria's support of terrorism as an obstacle to peace. The Israeli "occupation" of the West Bank (Samaria and Judea) had emerged as the "real issue" in the eyes of America. In addition, the United States decreed that the only way it would be able to confront terrorists was if Jewish construction in Samaria and Judea came to a halt. It seemed as though simple construction, even something as trivial as an addition to a house, suddenly presented a much greater strategic threat to Western civilization than an Iranian nuclear bomb.

The moral clarity of President Bush's September 20, 2001 speech was totally discarded, first by Bush himself during the disappointing second half of his administration, and then by Obama, as despotic leaders such as Venezuela's Chavez, Iran's Ahmadinejad, and Syria's Assad became people with whom the U.S. needed to understand and reason. Allies who were in need of defense and assurances – such as South Korea, Japan, Czechoslovakia, Poland, Taiwan, and Israel – were either ignored or castigated.

Since the inauguration of President Obama there has been a resurgence of the plague of "moral relativism" – the belief that truth is relative and that there is no such thing as good or evil. I distinctly remember when I was a teenager growing up in New York, at the fringes of the nihilistic values of the 1960s. The expression "everything's relative" was regarded as a basic truism in life. Today, in the age of Obama, it seems to be making a comeback. I would be standing with the half of America who is cheering this on, but too much has happened since the rose-colored 60s and my early teenage years. The peace, love and unbridled hedonism of the 60s became the norm in many parts of America, and was revealed to be merely an illusion. This ideology has led to sky-high divorce rates, an increase in children born out of wedlock and has been tearing at the very fabric of the nuclear family.

Many years ago, I was teaching a fifth-grade class in an inner-city school in Brooklyn, New York. Only nine of those twenty-seven children had fathers that they saw on a regular basis. Moral relativism and lack of commitments seemed to go hand-in-hand. I learned that there is value in being faithful in marriage and in relationships; and that a person's word is gold, or, rather, it should be. I also realized that there is a distinct difference between good and evil as shown with the Holocaust. Last but not least, I've learned, as my father used to try to teach me during my rebellious years when I never wanted to listen, that there is a God above us who guides this world according to a greater plan. There are those who consider themselves above all of this "primitive thinking," as I once did. They think that this amazing world fell into place by happenstance.

The emphasis on relative truth applies to the political arena as well. Since the dawn of the "Age of Obama," the expression "War on Islamic Terrorism" was quietly done away with, the belief that all ideas need to have moral equivalence, and all cultures and religions are equal. The American concept of life, liberty, and the pursuit of happiness is no longer the most significant ideal for which to strive.

Consequently, America's international public relations have been shattered. They have returned to the days of President Jimmy Carter, when the United States was placed on the defensive and frequently apologetic. The 1960s and 1970s culture of moral relativism – while its motives and intentions may have been truly idealistic at some point – got hijacked by the anti-Americans and the anti-Zionists of the Left. They have formed a strange alliance with the Islamic fascists and call self-defense a "war crime" and freedom is now referred to as "imperialism." There is a public message being delivered via this old-new approach of moral relativism, which states that the U.S. hasn't shown enough respect and understanding for the other great cultures and religions in the world, such as Islam. The latest unspoken mantra is that the United States is at fault for terrorism. This belief is fueled by America's lack of appreciation and respect for other cultures and due to the inability of Americans to accept other points of view, especially as they relate to Communist or Islamic dictators. Thus, it is no longer moral relativism and moral equivalence that we are speaking about, but more appropriately, an attempted upheaval of American values.

> *...I know it is possible to reconcile Islam with modernity and respect for human rights and a rejection of violence.*[13]
> (President Barack Obama, May 21, 2009)

This upheaval of values has become the new policy when dealing with the Islamic world. The newspeak of Islamic-friendly terminology is justified by the distorted system: "I'm okay, you're okay" – otherwise known as tolerance – is and has seemingly become the slogan of many Westerners.

Yet, according to the modern Islamic ideology and public policy, one cannot set foot into Muslim countries like Saudi Arabia or Qatar reciting public words of praise for Judaism, Christianity, or any religion other than Islam. In fact, public tolerance toward other religions is illegal. Where then is the justification for moral relativism? Tolerance has to go both ways. There are churches and mosques in Israel; and there are places for nearly every form of worship within U.S. Why then is such tolerance unknown in the Persian Gulf or even in what is dubbed the "U.S. ally" of Egypt? In fact, Egypt is known for the signing of a (very cold) peace agreement with Israel and for which they received the promise of unconditional aid from the United States.

Egypt is a primarily Islamic nation, although there is a significant 15 percent minority of Coptic Christians. This group experiences persecution on a daily basis that includes killing, destruction of their property, deportation from their homes, and the forced Islamization of their minor daughters.[14] In countries like Egypt, in which Presidential dictator Hosni Mubarak rules with an iron fist, such persecution wouldn't be possible without government consent or, at the very least, indifference. There is no end to the tyranny in sight since Mubarak is reportedly grooming his son to carry on the tyranny.

In the Islamic world, moral relativism isn't even recognized. Tolerance certainly does not exist either, and peaceful Christians and Jews are at a distinct disadvantage if they accept the values engulfing countries such as Egypt as equal to our own. The hand that we eagerly extend to them may be cut off, perhaps literally.

When I was a child living in Brooklyn, NY, I can vividly recall the neighborhood kids having vicious fights in the Public School 233 schoolyard. If there was an attempted truce, which was very rare indeed, it would start from the less aggressive of two children asking for a compromise in an attempt to resolve the disagreement peacefully. Even more uncommon was for the stronger of the two boys to agree. In most cases, the aggressor, who was often sitting on top of the weaker boy, would reject the offer and punch the kid even harder. In such a scenario, what did the weaker of the two boys accomplish by begging for a peaceful resolution? The stronger boy often sensed the physical and psychological weakness of his counterpart and saw little, if any, incentive to end the fight. The lessons learned on that playground extend to adult conflicts as well. If the Islamists see any signs of respect and tolerance, they are interpreted to be signs of weakness. This results in Islamists trying to "up the ante" and continue to push – whether violently or peacefully – for their belief system to supplant the Judeo-Christian norm in the free world. Terrorism is merely one of the many abhorrent tools that are present in a far-reaching global strategy.

In February 2010, President Obama appointed Rashad Hussain – who had been one of his top White House legal advisors – to the position of special envoy to the Muslim world. Specifically, Hussain was assigned to focus on the 57-nation organization that comprises the Organization of the Islamic Conference (OIC) – which is based in Qatar – a wealthy Persian Gulf State. The OIC is an organization that openly and proudly supports global implementation of *Sharia* (Islamic law). On the surface, Hussain certainly seemed like the right man for the job. He is a

Yale-educated Muslim lawyer and appeared to be an exceptional choice as the person to represent the American way of life to the Islamic world. Hussain seemed more than capable of presenting an enlightened and modern face of Islam to Islamic countries, even though they are the primary funders of and apologists for terrorism – that is, until an exhaustive examination of his views uncovered the disappointing truth.

Merely one year before being appointed to the position, Hussain and his colleague and fellow Muslim, Al-Husein N. Madhany, penned the following Brookings Institute paper on counterterrorism:

> First, rather than characterizing counterterrorism efforts as "freedom and democracy versus terrorist ideology," policymakers should instead frame the battle of ideas as a conflict between terrorist elements in the Muslim world and Islam.
>
> Second, policymakers should reject the use of language that provides a religious legitimization of terrorism such as "Islamic terrorism" and "Islamic extremist." They should replace such terminology with more specific and descriptive terms such as "al-Qaeda terrorism."[15]

Hussain typifies what is the American Muslim mask – which proclaims that Islam is not the problem. To the contrary, this belief holds that the problem is only from specific terror organizations. Rashad was reportedly instrumental in helping to craft President Obama's Cairo speech, in which he called for a new relationship with the Muslim world that would be based upon mutual respect and appreciation.

Is it truly that simple? Hardly. The question that no one seems to be asking is: If Islam is not the problem, what is? On what ideological system is this violence and hatred based? What can terrorists in Chechnya, Yemen, Holland, Lebanon, the UK, the U.S., Israel, and India possibly have in common, aside from the ideology or religion of Islam that they all adhere to?

If Islam is not the enemy, then what is it that motivates

Muslim terrorists in such geographically and culturally diverse countries to attack – and to gladly die – for the cause of Islamic domination? Is it possible that we are being confronted with an ideology that is in itself evil? How can a Yale-educated Muslim who dons a suit and tie and speaks out against terrorism be the same man who calls for a new and cooperative relationship with those who support terrorist acts?

During the 1960s and 1970s, traditional values in the United States and Europe became untrendy and were often ridiculed. So much so, that the expression "good and evil" was met with guffaws, outright laughter, harsh ridicule and even criticism due to supposed closed-mindedness and primitiveness of the speaker. A political leader in America who dares to use that expression, particularly a Republican leader, is stereotyped as ignorant, superficial, or simply of having low intelligence. One such leader was Ronald Reagan. His understanding of human nature and psychological warfare to bring down the Soviet Empire was nothing short of brilliant. In a speech that the media – who ranged from hostile to skeptical – called his "Evil Empire Speech," President Reagan described the need to stand up to evil, and not to be fooled by its sugar coating and propaganda. He said:

> *It was C.S. Lewis who, in his unforgettable Screwtape Letters wrote: "The greatest evil is not done now in those sordid 'dens of crime' that Dickens loved to paint. It is not even done in concentration camps and labor camps. In those we see its final result. But it is conceived and ordered (moved, seconded, carried and minuted) in clear, carpeted, warmed, and well-lighted offices, by quiet men with white collars and cut fingernails and smooth-shaven cheeks who do not need to raise their voice."*
>
> *Well, because these "quiet men" do not "raise their voices" because they sometimes speak in soothing tones of brotherhood and peace; because, like other dictators before them, they're always making "their final territorial demand," some would have us accept them at their word and accommodate ourselves*

to their aggressive impulses. But if history teaches anything, it teaches that simple-minded appeasement or wishful thinking about our adversaries is folly. It means the betrayal of our past, the squandering of our freedom.[16]

(Ronald Reagan, March 8, 1983)

In Israel, the media often responds to a terror attack by discussing how the attack occurred, in extensive detail, the degree of wounds the victims suffered, and the name of the killer. The problem is that the terrorist who fires bullets or sets off bombs is typically not the one who planned the attack, escape, and cover-up, when no one will claim responsibility for the attack.

When my son and I were wounded, there were no claims of responsibility. The actual terrorists who shot us weren't caught until years later. For me, that didn't matter because the men who should be held truly responsible are the ones who sit in the back rooms, who, as Reagan said, were "in clear, carpeted, warmed, and well-lighted offices ... men with white collars and cut fingernails and smooth-shaven cheeks who do not need to raise their voices." These men are often the so-called reasonable politicians and academicians who the media loves to praise.

PA President Mahmoud Abbas and his ally Muhammad Dahlan are examples of the men who are cleanly-shaven (or have neatly trimmed mustaches) and wear top-of-the-line suits. They sit in comfortable offices, generally speak in soft tones – at least when they are speaking English. These men are two of today's worst terrorist criminals and yet they are praised as moderates.

This is not reality. Evil has to be identified, whether the perpetrators are in terrorist uniforms with *keffiyeh* (Arabic-style kerchief) masks on their faces or in Brooks Brothers suits. Until leaders have the courage to establish consistent moral clarity toward evil, we will not be able to overcome the grasp of the enemy.

Terror is not the enemy. The evil ideology behind that terror is the true enemy. Only when nations face the ideology and its followers, will we finally begin moving forward to thwart the enemy and its goals.

Chapter Three
√The Chosen People

They said, "Come, let us cut them off from nationhood, so the name Israel will not be remembered any longer."
(Psalms 83:5)

Terrorism and Israel are two words that are frequently used in the same sentence, usually by the media reporting the latest terrorist attack aimed at Jewish targets. The juxtaposition of words is often used by Israel's enemies who are attempting to slander Israel. This is done by accusing Israel of what is cynically referred to as "war crimes" or "state terrorism." In the case of Israel, this refers to the nation's response to ongoing and merciless Islamic terrorism, usually by the terrorist organizations known as Hamas, Fatah, Islamic *Jihad*, or Hezbollah. Is it merely a coincidence that Israel is, without a doubt, the most disproportionate victim of terrorism? Why is that so? Why is the geographically tiny Jewish State, with its land mass not much larger than the state of Delaware, the most popular target for the terrorists' wrath? How can the deep-seated hatred that permeates nearly every discussion about Israel in the United Nations be explained?

Millions of dollars have been spent by the organized American Jewish community to fund extensive studies examining the causes of anti-Semitism, otherwise known as the hatred of Jews. The cumulative national trauma of almost 2,000 years of exile from the Land of Israel led to seemingly endless persecution. This culminated with the Holocaust, which resulted in the senseless murder of six million Jews by the Nazis. In fact, the Holocaust has become so central in the traumatic Jewish history that it is often the primary element in the American Jewish identity because there are so many American Jews who lack a rudimentary Jewish religious or historical education of any positive nature.

Based on my experiences of growing up as an American Jew with a public school education, I think it is accurate to say that the majority of American Jews cannot name five positive events in Jewish history before the Holocaust. Part of the reason is due to the lack of a Jewish education, but it is also related to the horrific magnitude of the Holocaust, and therefore, it has become the primary event studied while learning secular Jewish studies in universities. Unless an individual receives an education in a private Jewish school that is focused on teaching the full Jewish history and religion, there is little else that is learned. I have no intention of adding yet another extensive analysis to those texts that already exist about anti-Semitism, yet it is paramount in understanding the tense relationships that exist between Judaism, Christianity, and Islam. The background surrounding the anti-Jewish hatred and its sad history is a defining factor in how Jews evolved into the people they are today. However, anyone who defines Judaism only through the prism of persecution, pogroms, and the Holocaust cannot truly claim to understand the importance of Israel. It is essential to study the roots of Judaism, starting with Abraham, the Founding Father of Judaism, also known in Israel's history book, the Bible, as Abraham the Hebrew.

In fact, for thousands of years, Hebrew has been known as the language of Israel and therefore, Israelis have often been called Hebrews – particularly during biblical times. During the Exile from the Land of Israel, Hebrew was mainly used as a written language in books and in correspondence by rabbis and other Jewish scholars. In modern times, Hebrew is used in its written form and has been revitalized in Israel as a spoken language. The Zionist scholar Eliezer Ben-Yehuda, is credited as initiating this process – which began in the early 1900s. He embarked on the ambitious project of reviving a spoken language that was nearly extinct, and was then followed by other scholars who continued his pioneering spirit. Today, Hebrew is once again a living, thriving language that is not merely used in synagogues and study halls, but also can be heard on the street and at almost every dinner table in Israel.

Unlike English, most of the words used in Hebrew have a literal meaning and are based on roots within the word; this even includes the name of the language itself. Hebrew is an English translation of the word *Ivri* – which literally means "on the other side." This denotes a form of separateness; a distinction between oneself and others and the willingness to stand firm for what is right – even when everyone else is against you. When Abraham, the first Jew, lived nearly 4,000 years ago, the world was filled with idolatry. This is defined as the "worship of any cult image, idea, or object, as opposed to the worship of a monotheistic God."[1] Abraham stood against idolatry and championed the truth of God who created us in His image and who is the sovereign that guides human existence. Needless to say, this was not a popular view in Abraham's day, though the ideology quickly began to spread.

Abraham's son was named Isaac, and Isaac had a son Jacob, who often went by the name Israel. They were direct descendants and became patriarchs of the embryonic nation of Israel. They believed that there was one God, who stood against all idol worshippers of that time. Abraham's great grandson, Joseph, continued this belief, but added an interesting worldly twist, as Joseph overcame adversity and anti-Semitism and achieved prominence as governor of Egypt. In this role, he developed a positive working relationship with the King of Egypt – more commonly known as the Pharaoh, or simply Pharaoh. Joseph's step-sibling rivalries had forced him out of Israel and he became the first example of a successful Jew in the Gentile world. It was a theme that was to be repeated many times in history, but it is notable to the history of Jews that Joseph was the first recorded case of the prototypical hard-working Jew who achieved a prominent position of distinction and influence in the Gentile world, despite adversity and obstacles in his path.

Joseph was eventually reunited with Jacob – his father – and his many siblings. They had arrived in Egypt at a time when the Land of Israel – then known as Canaan – was undergoing severe famine.

Joseph, along with his nuclear and extended family, remained in Egypt and they were treated with honor and respect by Pharaoh, who had come to greatly appreciate Joseph's important contribution to the rebuilding of Egypt.[2]

After Joseph's death however, Egypt underwent significant change. Joseph's descendants adopted many Egyptian customs and abandoned their own. Their assimilation into Egyptian society even resulted in their abandonment of the central commandment of circumcision, known as the physical sign of the covenant between Israel and the Almighty.[3] The desire for Jews to fit into their new Egyptian society by abandoning many of their own customs and norms to adopt the new Egyptian ones was to be repeated in many nations throughout the course of ancient and modern history. These results seemed positive at the time, but ultimately led to conflict and persecution against the Jewish community.

> *And a new king arose over Egypt who did not know Joseph.*
>
> (Exodus 1:8)

Upon his death, the adulation and honor that Joseph had earned in Egypt was quickly forgotten. The anti-Semitic saga of organized hatred against the Children of Israel (also known as the Israelites) began at this time and continued on to the next generation of Hebrews in Egypt, the direct descendents of Joseph.

> *Behold, the people, the Children of Israel, are more numerous and stronger than we. Come, let us deal wisely with this, lest they multiply and if a war will take place, they will join our enemies*

and wage war against us and go up from the land.

(Exodus 1:9-10)

This marked the beginning of the bitter enslavement of the Children of Israel. Despite the harshness and cruelty of this slavery, the Hebrews continued to grow in number. This resulted in Pharaoh serving an edict to the primary Hebrew midwives – Shifrah and Puah – that they must kill all male Hebrew newborns that they helped to deliver.

But the Egyptian ruler had foolishly underestimated the courage and fortitude of the Hebrew women, the pillars of strength that has always held the Jewish family together. Risking their own lives by defying Pharaoh, Shifrah and Puah boldly ignored his demand.

But the midwives feared God and they did not do what the king of Egypt had told them to do, and they kept the male babies alive.

(Exodus 1:17)

Pharaoh had not only underestimated the midwives, but apparently didn't recognize the conviction that the women of Israel possessed. He was unaware that these women would not surrender to his edict against Hebrew families in Egypt. There is a story told from that difficult period in Israel's history that illustrates the simple wisdom of a young girl. The main characters in this story are the Hebrew woman Yocheved, her husband Amram, and their five-year-old daughter, Miriam. When Amram, the leader in the Israelite community, heard about Pharaoh's edict to kill all male babies, he called for all men and women in Israel to cease having marital relations. In the age before birth control, this meant either divorce or separation. Amram promptly separated from Yocheved, knowing that there was little logic in bringing a child into the world and then having to kill him. Because he led the community, many followed his example and also divorced. His young daughter Miriam became very critical of her father's lack of faith, asserting that his decree was even harsher than that of the Pharaoh since her father seemingly punished both males and females. In other words, since all the Israelite men had withdrawn from their wives, neither sons nor daughters would come into the world. Furthermore, while Pharaoh was robbing the male Israelites of their lives, Amram was taking away the chance for them to experience the wonders of the world-to-come. In her young perceptive eyes, it was unacceptable that her father, who was considered to be such an esteemed and learned member of the Hebrew community, would surrender to the blatant anti-Semitism of Pharaoh. Amram became convinced by his daughter's prophetic faith in God, and that He would stand against Pharaoh's evil decree. Therefore, if the community truly believed that the Almighty would stand behind the justice of their cause, they would be successful in rebelling against the tyrant and would be victorious in the end.[4]

This account extends to everyday life; when we are confronted by tyranny and seemingly hopeless situations, God may have a bigger plan. As a result of Miriam's prophetic faith, assertiveness and vision, her brother Moses was born. He grew to lead the children of Israel from slavery in Egypt into the desert, where they received the Torah on Mount Sinai and forever changed the world.

> *And who is like your people Israel, one unique nation in the Land?*
>
> (1 Chronicles 17:21)

> *I am the Lord your God; who has taken you out of the Land of Egypt, out of slavery. You shall have no other gods besides Me...*
>
> (Exodus 20:2-3)

This was probably the greatest single event in Jewish history, if not the world. An entire people assembled at the base of Mount Sinai as Moses stood on its peak in the Almighty's presence. The mountain was in flames and shook while the sound of the *Shofar* – the ram's horn – blew loudly. The King of kings gave His people a mission to become a kingdom of ministers and a holy nation (Exodus 19:6). Thus was born the concept of the *chosen people*, which is perhaps the most misunderstood concept in world history. This was not intended to be just another religion or another country, like France or New Zealand. Instead, this was the birth of a religious nation with a unique mission to be God's witnesses in this world; to proclaim His glory; and to bring His Torah – His Bible – to the world as a blueprint for life.

Israel was given an awesome mission. This chosen nation was not to have superior people with special privileges; rather it was to be a nation whose people had special responsibilities and obligations as described by the commandments in the Bible.

As a child, I did not come from a very religious background and only started to follow all of the commandments later in life. I can honestly say that obeying all of the commandments that a Jew is expected to adhere to is a daunting task. Nonetheless, what may seem a burden to some is something that I view as a privilege. Our sages teach us that mankind was created in God's image to spread righteousness in this world. It is because of the corruption and violence that had reigned over justice and kindness that the mission was limited to a particular group of people. Even though we are all created in God's image and are all expected to keep the basic laws of civilization, God's specific purpose for Israel was to have us abide by a spiritual leadership role with the intention of spreading His message to the world through example. This was to be done through positive and non-coercive means, as "a light unto the nations."[5]

Despite that mission to be God's witnesses in this world, the intention was to never spread His Word by force, coercion, violence or submission. In fact, when a Gentile approaches a rabbi to ask him if he can convert to Judaism, the rabbi is supposed to try to dissuade him by telling him that it is difficult to be a Jew. The Gentile is then supposed to be sent away so that he can ponder this knowledge. If he returns to the rabbi a second time, the rabbi is supposed to dissuade him again. It is only on the third visit that a Gentile can be accepted as a student that will begin the extensive process of learning Torah and of how to fulfill its precepts. The premise behind this process is that a Gentile must be able to handle the challenge of being a Jew. This also means that they must be prepared to stand up to discrimination and persecution, which is no simple task.

Jews are obligated to inform the potential convert of these obstacles before they make their decision. In order to begin the conversion process, one's sincerity must be confirmed beyond reasonable doubt. In short, it is not expected nor desired for all Gentiles to disrupt their lives to become Jews; it is only that they must live the lives of righteous and peaceful people – but not necessarily doing that while being a Jew.

Throughout history, this non-coercive approach has contrasted with the practices of many Christian – usually Catholic – communities. Christians often forced Jews to convert to Christianity. For example, in Spain in the year 1492, Jews were ordered to convert to Christianity or be expelled from the country, while others went into spiritual hiding – meaning that they maintained Jewish traditions in secret and publicly pretended to be Christian converts. They were known as the "Marranos," which was a derogatory term that meant pigs or swine. In Hebrew, their descendants are called by a more neutral term, *B'nei Anusim*, which translates to "the descendants of those who were forced" (against their will).[6]

In the centuries that followed, there were additional European countries in which the forced conversion approach was adapted. Subsequently, this evolved into pogroms – organized violent mob attacks against Jews – which were often totally unrelated to conversion issues and were instead, a more general hatred against the Jews in general. Examples of the most vicious forms of anti-Semitism – meaning anti-Jewish hatred – originated in the Russian Empire and other parts of Eastern Europe. The spread of the Russian Empire in the 18th century had certain unintended effects; specifically the increase in its Jewish population. As a result of the annexation of a substantial portion of Poland in 1772, Russia inherited 200,000 Jews. The partitions of 1793 and 1795 increased the number of Polish-Lithuanian provinces to the empire – and the Jewish population grew to 900,000. These annexations and/or partitions presented the Russians with a dilemma. Their historic prejudices prevented them from allowing the Jews to integrate with the Russian population, so specific ordinances were enacted, limiting Jewish residence, work, and movement to certain provinces and districts, which became known as the Pale of Settlement.[7]

Even those Jews who lived outside of the Pale of Settlement had restrictions placed on their work options, making it nearly impossible for them to find work in most of the Russian Empire. These measures became increasingly intense in the 19th century. During the late 1800s, organized massacres took place throughout the Russian Empire. These organized physical attacks on Jews included the plundering of property and businesses; and many Jews were beaten or killed. When the Russian authorities began to acquiesce and allowed the brutality to reach a fevered pitch, the mass expulsion of the Jews from Moscow in 1891-1892 came as little surprise.[8]

Without question, the Nazi Holocaust was the ultimate anti-Semitic act. Occurring before and during World War II, Jews were forced to live severely restricted lives in enclosed ghettos and were eventually shipped to death camps, which resulted in at least six million murdered.

Much of the Christian world has altered its intolerance toward Jews that stemmed from different theological opinions since the cruel history of prejudice in Europe was brought to light and understood in recent years. The official Catholic Church was more gradual to make changes and their intentions have been questionable in both their endurance and their sincerity. On the other hand, much of the evangelical Protestant community seems to have abandoned its coerciveness, although there is still a long way to go toward the ultimate goals of total tolerance and unconditional love.

Many Christians still proselytize among Jews asserting that the people of Israel must have an intermediary for their relationship with God in order to achieve salvation. The Jews, on the other hand, affirm that they have had a direct relationship with the Almighty God ever since the great events on Mount Sinai. Some Christians find this hard to accept, but I think a bit of humility on their part is in order. As a Christian friend once commented to me, "We believe in spreading the Gospel, but it would be arrogant for me to try to convince you to accept our view of Jesus. Our path to God is through y'*all*. You are the root and we are just a branch. We think we're an important branch, but the branch can't survive without the root."

In short, Jews take their relationship with God very seriously. When Christians proselytize among Jews, however well intentioned, there is the potential of destroying a fragile but crucial and growing alliance of Jews and Christians on behalf of Israel and for the sake of liberty around the world.

One recent morning I was visited by a journalist from Germany who was seeking information about communities in the biblical heartland of Israel. He was interested in discussing Shiloh due to its deep religious-historical significance. He wanted to know how it was possible for me to cooperate with Evangelical Christians, knowing that they believe that an Armageddon is coming and that all of the Jews will have to become Christians or they will perish. My answer was simple and to the point. Christians are not monolithic and they have the right to have their own beliefs about what will occur in the future. We Jews also have our own scenarios of how we think events will play out over time. None of us are prophets, although we believe that we have some insights from original Hebrew texts. My answer is that I have little doubt that God will make everything clear to us in due time.

God will be King over all the land; on that day the Lord will be One and His Name will be One.

(Zechariah 14:9)

Meanwhile, there is too much for us to accomplish until the day when God resolves all of our theological disagreements. Everything is leading in the direction of unity and clarification. Even terrorists are inadvertently playing a role in this, as the concepts of good and evil become increasingly clear in our eyes. Eventually, we will all want to do the right thing:

Many peoples will go and say, "Come and let us go up to the mountain of the Lord, to the house of the God of Jacob (Israel); and He will teach us of His ways and we will walk in His paths; for from Zion will go forth the Torah and the word of the Lord from Jerusalem. He will judge among the nations and will settle the arguments of many peoples..."

(Isaiah 2:3-4)

The growing tolerance, as well as strong and often passionate support in parts of the Christian world for Israel and its people is a sign that this trend should be welcomed. We should work together on all of the biblically-based goals that we have in common, because radical Muslims whose world-view is derived from the Koran are seeking the destruction of both of our houses.

Jews are a determined group of people who strive to overcome all obstacles. It is in our nature after encountering so much adversity. We choose to view this adversity with optimism – asserting that the core of the Bible is true. How else could we explain our existence, survival, and return to nationhood after everything that we have endured?

Anyone who doesn't believe in miracles is not a realist.[9]

(David Ben Gurion,
first Prime Minister of the State of Israel)

In essence, the Jewish people chuckle at all forms of anti-Semitism. Think all you want and you will not be able to find one form of brutality or strategy that has not been used in warfare against the Jewish people.

I cannot be defeated says Judaism. All that you attempt to do to me today has been attempted 3,200 years prior in Egypt. Then tried the Babylonians and Persians… afterwards, tried the Romans and then others and others.

There is no question that the Jews will outlive us all. This is an eternal people… They cannot be defeated, understand this! Every war with them is a vain waste of time and manpower. Conversely, it is wise to sign a mutual covenant with them. How trustworthy and profitable they are as allies! Look at their patriotism, their commercial benefit, and their ambition and success in science, the arts, and politics! Be their friends and they will pay you back in friendship one hundred fold. This is an exalted and chosen people![10]

Jon DeBileda, French author

The survival of the Jewish people through centuries of exile, expulsion, subjugation, and persecution is the best proof of God's existence. The Bible is not merely a nice collection of stories, but is a very real series of historical facts and prophecies that are taking place even today through the people of Israel. Whether the events that have taken place in the annals of Jewish history are positive or negative, they are often of a scope and magnitude that seems to defy common logic. The history of the Jewish people, both in and out of the Land of Israel, operates on a plane that is separate from world history. It befits a chosen nation that has been selected for these challenges like no other nation in history.

Yes, we can marvel at the survival of the Jewish people throughout history, but how do we theologically explain all of the persecution and suffering? If we are God's *chosen people*, doesn't that include some unconditional Divine protection? The Bible has clear answers to this perplexing question that were foretold thousands of years ago. Simply explained, the responsibilities that we were given as a people have consequences when they aren't carried out.

And if you continually hearken to my commandments that I command you today, to love the Lord your God, and to serve Him, with all your heart and all your soul, then I will provide rain for your land in its proper time, the early and late rains, that you may gather in your grain, your wine and your oil. I will provide grass in your field for your cattle and you will eat and be satisfied. Beware, lest your heart be seduced and you turn astray and serve gods of others and bow to them. Then the wrath of the Lord will blaze against you. He will restrain the heavens so there will be no rain and the ground will not yield its produce. And you will swiftly be banished from the goodly land which the Lord gives you.

(Deuteronomy 11:13-17)

The Jewish people have always correlated their state of existence to their relationship with the Creator. They believe that there are spiritual ramifications for their actions, similar to a system of rewards and punishments. Along with this line of thinking, it is believed that God is actively involved in their lives. There are also extreme situations in which God temporarily removes Himself from active involvement in human affairs to leave people to their own devices. When this happens, all havoc can, and sometimes does break loose, not only for the nation of Israel, but for the world in its entirety. Unfortunately, the human race does not have a stellar history when left to handle circumstances on its own. In Hebrew, this theological concept of temporary abandonment is known as *Hester Panim,* or "The Hiding of the Face."

Hester Panim is related to Israel's waywardness and may be regarded as an ultimate punishment... It is terrifying because it signifies rejection. A child can stoically bear a father's reprimand, but to be totally ignored and treated as persona non grata in one's own home is a frightening experience.[11]

Rabbi Dr. Joseph B. Soloveitchik

When the Jewish people have suffered at various times in history, it is relatively simple to see the theological comparison to reward and punishment. On the other hand, extreme events like the Holocaust fall into the category of *Hester Panim* – the world going haywire – when the Almighty had removed Himself from active involvement. The theological explanation for this concept is one where the punishment does not seem to fit the crime.

> *Then My anger will flare up against them on that day and I will abandon them and hide My face from them, and many evils and distress shall befall them...*
> (Deuteronomy 31:17)

We know that God's Covenant with Israel is unbreakable. Jews have experienced many miracles because of that Covenant and will no doubt see many more in the future, but that doesn't mean that the Covenant will be not tested and that Israel will not continue to have painful ups and downs along the way.

> *You only have I known of all the families of the Earth, and therefore, I will hold you accountable for your iniquities.*
> (Amos 3:2)

I am reminded of a story that is personal to me – a bit mundane perhaps, but very real nonetheless. It has occurred to countless parents and their children throughout history. My wife and I had to reprimand our son for misbehaving on a school trip. His retort was the all-too-common, "But the other kids did it too!" We responded by saying, "Perhaps this is true, but you are our son and it is our duty to hold you accountable for your actions." This is how we view Israel's relationship with God. God is not implying that He does not care about how His other children reacted in that situation. It is that, in our view, He has special expectations of us. It can be called a higher standard or having additional responsibility, but no matter semantics, if we do not live up to the Almighty's expectations, we can't be removed from blame because "the other kids did it too."

> *This people I have formed for Myself, that they might declare My praise.*
> (Isaiah 43:21)

We are living in magnificent times, when much of the Christian world is waking up to the fact that God's Covenant with Israel is eternal. Unfortunately, there are some who are still asleep to this realization and believe that God has forsaken His people. For Christians with this mindset, I recommend that they read what God said to the patriarchs and matriarchs of Israel:

> *I will establish my covenant as an everlasting covenant between Me and you and your descendants after you for the generations to come ... and I will give to you and your descendants the Land of your sojourns, all the Land of Canaan, for an everlasting possession, and I will be their God.*
>
> (Genesis 17:7-8)

Is God indecisive and apt to change His mind about such a central part of world history and the Divine plan? Israel and the Almighty were bound together by an eternal covenant that was never to be broken. This covenant obligates both partners, but the redemptive process is not an exclusive one. This includes the active participation of righteous non-Jews, who believe that God's written words in the Torah, and the writings of his prophets, are true and eternal. They have a vital role in fulfilling today's prophecies.

There is a dynamic process taking place in history before our eyes. The frightening terrorist threats that occur at airports, in cities around the globe, the upheavals in the global economy, and the increasingly frequent clashes in the Middle East are all indicative of an historic process that makes sense and has solutions.

In a March 2010 discussion between Israeli Knesset Member Tzipi Livni and U.S. Senate Foreign Relations Committee Chairman Sen. John Kerry (D-MA), Livni lamented that "the diplomatic conflict between Israel and the Palestinians is about to turn into a religious one that will be impossible to solve."[12]

Livni may well be troubled by diplomatic conflict, but the reality is that the religious war that is raging is far greater than the

"Israeli-Palestinian diplomatic conflict." In fact, this war is beyond the scope of terrorism, instead Islamic ideology is the true source of the conflict. There are those who will say it is unfair to place the blame on one religion; that the religion is a peaceful one that is burdened by radical extremists. I truly wish that it was that easy. I am not ascribing blame to every Muslim. Instead, I am referring to a particular ideology. In order to properly understand a specific religious ideology, it is essential to look at the roots of that belief. I have explored the roots of Judaism and detailed how Christianity is an offshoot of Judaism that is based upon a philosophical message that was espoused by the Jew who is known throughout the world as Jesus. Jesus' approach was not accepted by mainstream Judaism, yet he never intended to reject Judaism:

> *I did not come to abolish the Law of Moses or the writings of the prophets...*
>
> (Matthew 5:17)

General acceptance of Torah Law was unquestioned by the first followers of Jesus, who were all Jews. Attitudes only started to change with some of the steps taken by the Apostle Paul, who, seeking to attract Gentiles, began to emphasize the element of faith in Jesus, at the expense of the commandments. However, the most serious shifts, creating Christianity as a separate religion and rejecting Israel's God-given mission, were only carried out generations later. However, Jesus of Nazareth never rejected the basics of Judaism – he prayed only to the God of Israel, not to himself.

As a personal aside, there was an event that reminded me of this distortion of history when I was traveling in America. I was scheduled to speak in a church in New Mexico. I was looking forward to the event partly because I had come to know that there were many supporters there for my work with Israeli children. This was scheduled to be my last stop before I returned to Israel. A few weeks prior to departing for my trip to U.S., I received an unexpected email from my host – a Sunday School pastor in the church. He apologetically informed me that he needed to disinvite me from speaking to his congregation. He had discovered that his church had a policy that non-Christians were not allowed to speak at the church. Furthermore, it was not permissible to have a collection take place for non-Christian organizations. I responded that aside from my disappointment at the inconvenience and extra cost to the Shiloh Israel Children's Fund due to the sudden change in plans, I felt that it was tragically ironic that this policy would have precluded Jesus, a Jew, from speaking in that church! To me, this illustrated just how far the organized church has digressed from the roots of its faith.

I don't personally know the individuals who established that particular policy, but I am certain that Jesus had more in common with my religious practices than he did with the decision-makers in that church. The recent movement in much of the Christian world to reconnect with their Hebraic roots and express support for Israel reflects a very sad reality. While much of the Christian world is still skeptical of these movements, as are many wary Jews, who fear that this is a veiled attempt to proselytize among Jews. I must respectfully disagree. I believe that the trend should be seen as a mostly sincere expression that stems from a genuine movement to reconnect with the original roots of the Bible – not only for Christianity – but for the U.S. in its entirety.

On the other hand, Islam falls into a unique category, even though many people are unaware of what Islam is truly preaching. They see terrorism as a threat and sense that there is a connection with something called *radical Islam* – but do not understand the roots of the religion. So, what are the roots of Islam? How do they explain the phenomenon that is called Islamic terrorism? Only when we understand these questions can we examine the ramifications being felt today and hope to understand what may be in store for us tomorrow.

Chapter Four
The Real Face Of Islam

America and Islam are not exclusive and need not be in competition. Instead, they overlap, and share common principles – principles of justice and progress; tolerance and the dignity of all human beings.[1]

(President Barack Hussein Obama, June 4, 2009)

We (Muslims) will conquer the world, so that there is no God but Allah, and Muhammad is the Prophet of Allah will be triumphant over the domes of Moscow, Washington, and Paris... We will annihilate America.[2]

(Iraqi Ayatollah Ahmad Husseini al-Baghdadi)

On November 5, 2009, Major Nidal Malik Hassan, a psychologist serving in the United States Army, went on a rampage at a U.S. military base in Fort Hood, Texas. With two handguns, he murdered 13 of his fellow soldiers and wounded 28 others. The American media kicked into high gear, analyzing the case and conducting interviews with anyone who ever knew this crazy individual. His cousin, interviewed on FOX News on the day of the attack, claimed that Hassan was *a good American* who was born and grew up in the U.S., but was afraid to go to war in Afghanistan or Iraq. In fact, some *experts* were interviewed, claiming that Hassan suffered from Post-Traumatic Stress Disorder (PTSD), the same affliction that thousands of children in Israel who are victims of terrorism suffer from. Many children who lost parents in the 9-11 attacks undoubtedly still suffer from this trauma, as well as other family members, friends, and neighbors of the victims. So too, the Fort Hood families suffer similar trauma to this day. As a person who is very involved in helping children who are victims of terrorist attacks, the mere suggestion that Hassan was suffering from PTSD greatly disturbs me, especially given what we later discovered about his background and convictions.

The most reasonable and convincing argument, perhaps, was that Hassan was a conscientious objector. America has known many cases of conscientious objectors or draft evaders who, due to fear, principle, or psychological instability, have asked not to be sent to war. In a time when young Americans were being drafted – being required to serve in the U.S. armed forces against their will – this objection was understandable, if not controversial. However, that is not the situation in the United States today, when unlike Israel and many other countries, the U.S. employs an army comprised completely of volunteers; those who enlist have no misconceptions about what they are signing up for. Forty years ago, this was not the case.

During the Vietnam War, the streets of America were filled with massive protests by those opposed to the war – the debates were intense and, at times, even violent. Draft evasion was not insignificant, and soldiers who went AWOL (Absence Without Official Leave) were heroes to some, traitors to others, and the country was nearly torn apart by the painful division. In Israel, too, where military service has always been mandatory for most citizens, there are occasional cases of conscientious objection for various psychological, political, or religious reasons. However, a soldier who is already serving is expected to fight valiantly against the country's enemies. The point here is that conscientious objection exists throughout Western society and has its own proponents and opponents, all of whom maintain that their opinion is correct. The question is: In an existential war against evil, can we afford such division and ambivalence? Doesn't this dissension merely help the enemy who, cynically exploiting that division within a democracy, seeks to destroy our morale?

Mankind must put an end to war, or war will put an end to mankind. War will exist until that distant day when the conscientious objector enjoys the same reputation and prestige that the warrior does today.[3]

(President John F. Kennedy,
Speech to UN General Assembly)

For many years, lobbyists against wars have been known as *anti-war protesters*, or alternatively, *peace activists*. When heard in the media, most people accept them at face value, but in reality, these terms are extremely loaded; they imply that those who do not disapprove of war are in favor of war and are, therefore, against peace. The fact is that, as a matter of principle, most people are actually against war and support peace, but a mature person understands that – just as a good teacher will not let an unruly, violent child prevent all the others in the class from enjoying a positive learning environment – there are times when nations need to stand up to evil, and sometimes war is the only solution that works.

President Kennedy often spoke poetically about the ideal of world peace and bringing an end to war, but when push came to shove, he initiated America's involvement in the Vietnam War. Yes, the same controversial war for which Kennedy's successor, President Lyndon B. Johnson was demonized by the American people – Vietnam was actually Kennedy's war. To his credit, despite his conviction that war should be avoided whenever possible, Kennedy understood that there was a struggle between good and evil and that the spread of Communism – a totalitarian system of government which had developed into tyranny – needed to be stopped before it took over the world. Kennedy also understood, as did the wise King Solomon of Israel a few thousand years earlier, that when confronted with evil, war is often the only workable option on the table.

A time to love and a time to hate. A time for war and a time for peace.

(Ecclesiastes 3:8)

Other bold leaders throughout history have understood that there are times when evil needs to be confronted before it overtakes everything in its path, like a tsunami mushrooming out of control. In almost every century, there have been challenges that could not be avoided, even when it seemed less painful to look the other way. A true leader recognizes that ultimately, there will be a day of reckoning, that the day will come when major risks will need to be taken to confront evil head-on and stop it in its tracks. If we elect leaders who do not recognize this, we are destined to pay a price that is far greater than that of any war. In order for good to overcome evil, one must have moral clarity, determination, and the willingness to sacrifice. These are the necessary prerequisites for success.

> *I have nothing to offer but blood, toil, tears and sweat. We have before us an ordeal of the most grievous kind. We have before us many, many long months of struggle and of suffering. You ask, what is our policy? I will say: It is to wage war, by sea, land and air, with all our might and with all the strength that God can give us; to wage war against a monstrous tyranny, never surpassed in the dark lamentable catalogue of human crime. That is our policy. You ask, what is our aim? I can answer in one word: victory; victory at all costs, victory in spite of all terror, victory, however long and hard the road may be; for without victory there is no survival.[4]*

(Winston Churchill)

> *No nation can appease the Nazis. No man can tame a tiger into a kitten by stroking it.[5]*

(Franklin D. Roosevelt,
Fireside Chat, December 29, 1940)

The above statements, made by clear-thinking leaders, grasped the simple idea that evil must be confronted in whatever form it takes. Communism was praised by its supporters as a social, economic and political ideology that would liberate the workers from oppression. Nazism was also a self-proclaimed socially and economically-liberating ideology, but just as Churchill and FDR recognized, evil needed to be confronted with tools other than sweet talk, diplomacy, and understanding for our enemies' concerns. This is also true today. We are faced with an enemy no less destructive but potentially more dangerous than Communism and Nazism ever were. The form of Islam that comes under the guise of American or European Islam masquerades as a religion consisting of peaceful immigrants or children of immigrants who simply yearn to be free. This is personified by the high-achieving, educated American Major Nidal Malik Hassan. However, we need only to explore the basics of Islam to reveal the most deceitful misrepresentation of a religion that mankind has ever known. Islam has never been the religion of peace that it too often claims to be. Of course, that doesn't mean that there are no peaceful Muslims, but the Islamic ideology in itself is exceedingly troublesome.

The argument that Nidal Hassan was fearful of going to war is a specious one at best. The truth is quite the opposite. Hassan's issue was that his loyalty and devotion was to the wrong armed forces and to the wrong cause. He was committed to the precepts of Islam, which would not allow him to wage war against a Muslim nation or Muslim terrorist groups. Islam, in fact, commanded him to make *jihad*, or war against the infidels, the non-Muslims. Furthermore, Hassan was no isolated nut-case. Yes, what he did was crazy, but it was consistent with his world view, a radical ideology deeply rooted in and financed by mainstream Islam as practiced in *moderate* countries such as Saudi Arabia. According to widespread reports, this was a man whose professional business card said on it *SOA (SWT)*, which means Soldier of Allah – literally translated: Glorious and exalted is Allah.[6] It has also been frequently reported that Hassan had ongoing correspondence and consultation with an American-Muslim *imam* (religious leader/scholar). According to his website, this imam, named Anwar al-Awlaki, previously served in Denver, San Diego and Falls Church, Virginia. Al-Awlaki has also benefited from the

American educational system, having achieved a degree in civil engineering from Colorado State University and a master's degree in educational leadership from San Diego State University.

After the attack at Fort Hood, al-Awlaki, who reportedly had been giving ongoing advice to Hassan, wrote the following commentary on his blog:

> *Nidal Hassan is a hero. He is a man of conscience who could not bear living the contradiction of being a Muslim and serving in an army that is fighting against his own people. Any decent Muslim cannot live, understanding properly his duties towards his Creator and his fellow Muslims, and yet serve as a U.S. soldier. The U.S. is leading the war against terrorism which in reality is a war against Islam. Its army is directly invading two Muslim countries and indirectly occupying the rest through its stooges.[7]*

Al-Awlaki's father, Nasser al-Awlaki, was also a beneficiary of Western higher education, receiving a master's degree in agricultural economics from New Mexico State University in 1971 and a doctorate at the University of Nebraska. The family returned to Yemen in 1978, where Nasser served as Agriculture Minister and as President of Sanaa University. Certainly, one cannot claim that this family was drawn to terrorism due to poverty, or that American higher education, as it stands today, is the antidote to extremism.

Speaking on CNN, the elder al-Awlaki pleaded his son's case, proclaiming:

> *He has been wrongly accused, it's unbelievable. He lived his life in America, he's an all-American boy. My son would love to go back to America, he used to have a good life in America. Now he's hiding in the mountains, he doesn't even have safe water to drink.[8]*

Such is the plight of the *all-American boy* who seems to have been an important source of inspiration for another *all-American boy*, Major Nidal Hassan. The frightening reality appears to be that Hassan, who shouted the Islamic war cry *allahu Akhbar* (Allah is greater) before shooting his victims, was himself a Muslim terrorist in American army uniform. Hassan was driven by the violent ideology that is mainstream Islam – often referred to as one of the three great monotheistic religions, with Judaism and Christianity. But is it really?

How did this *great religion* begin? Contrary to what some Muslim revisionist historians may tell you, Islam is less than 1,400 years old. The founder of the religion was a man named Muhammad, who was born in the year 570 Common Era (CE) into the Quraysh tribe – the ruling tribe in Mecca – in the Arabian Peninsula, what is now called Saudi Arabia.[9] Muhammad is believed to have been a direct descendant of Ishmael, the wayward son of the biblical figure Abraham and his maidservant Hagar. Abraham is, of course, well known as the founder of Monotheism and Judaism. Ishmael was the controversial progenitor of the (now almost exclusively Muslim) Arab nation.[10]

> *And he (Ishmael) will be a wild man; his hand will be against everyone and (therefore) everyone's hand will be against him...*
>
> (Genesis 16:12)

The word *Islam* means *submission*, ostensibly submission to the will of Allah – what they call God – but a more careful examination of the history of this religion is needed to fully understand the meaning of this word. Through a study of the life of Muhammad – Islam's founder – we can more accurately understand why the term *submission* is appropriate, both in Islam's emphasis on the founder's philosophy on social relations and how he actually relates to people of other religions.

Muhammad was born into a very difficult family situation; psychologists would surely concur that his tragic and topsy-turvy upbringing undoubtedly affected his ability to relate to others throughout his life. Muhammad's father, Abd Allah, passed away six months before Muhammad was born and his mother, Amina, died when he was just six years old. After her death, he was left in the care of his grandfather, Abd al-Muttalib, who died two years later. From then on, Muhammad was raised by his uncle Abu Talib, a textile merchant who often traveled with his nephew on cross-country camel caravans. It was on these travels that young Muhammad learned about different cultures and religions. As he was illiterate, this wealth of knowledge was acquired solely by listening to stories and oral traditions about Judaism, Christianity, Zoroastrianism, and the various Arabian pagan religions that were prevalent at the time. He eventually would adopt bits and pieces of all of these while creating his new religion, even appealing to certain key beliefs – such as briefly advocating the Jewish practice of facing Jerusalem in prayer – as a way to lure people in. When his claims of prophecy were rejected by the Jews and other groups, he officially established that all prayer should be directed toward Mecca. After his painful rejection by Jews, Christians, and pagan Arabs in Mecca, Muhammad fled to Medina, where he officially established the religion of Islam in the year 622. Unlike their leader, some of his followers were literate, and began to write down his sayings and stories. These narratives eventually evolved into the writings of the Koran, divided into 114 Sura (chapters), as well as the Hadith, the written version of the Islamic oral tradition, the instructions of how to lead a proper life, according to the teachings of Muhammad.[11]

Muhammad's life is known to Muslims as *the Sunna*, which means *the usual practice* or *the example*. In Muslim terminology, *the Sunna* refers to the life and ways of Muhammad as the prime example of how to act. In other words, Muslims have always looked to the life of Muhammad for guidance about how to relate to other people and other nations. For this information, Muslims reference the Koran, which is considered the *word of God*, or the Hadith, which recorded the sayings of Muhammad and his followers. The Hadith is considered the *tradition of the prophet*, and consists mainly of what Muslims consider to be the valuable lessons about how to live life, according to *the prophet* Muhammad.[12] This is the key to understanding the Islamic mentality, because some dissenting Muslims have referred to Islamic terrorism and other abhorrent acts as an aberration. They say that terrorist acts are a perversion of Islam, just as many Christians say that the rampant killing during the Crusades was a perversion of Christianity. Former Iranian Muslim Ali Sina vehemently disagrees:

> *In the West, people ask whether Islam can undergo a reformation like the one that Christianity underwent. That's a poor parallel. In Christianity, it wasn't the religion that needed to be reformed, but the church; what Jesus preached was good. In Islam, it's not the community that is bad, but the religion.... Islam is full of hatred, and the hatred is in Muhammad himself.*[13]

Let's go to the Islamic sources, where we will learn some real lessons from the life of Muhammad, starting with his attitude towards women and social relationships. According to the list in the Hadith, as compiled by Muslim scholar Ali Dashti, the founder of Islam had at least 31 wives. Although polygamy was (and still is) permitted in Islam, the Koran (Sura 4:3) officially limited men to four wives. Nonetheless, Muslims are allowed by the Koran to have an unlimited number of concubines and can have sex with *women their right hands possess* (Sura 23:5-6, Sura 33:50, Sura 7:29-30). Even Muhammad seemed to have taken advantage of this abuse of women, which has become the model behavior for observant Muslims to emulate.

> *Men are the protectors and maintainers of women, because Allah has given the one more (strength) than the other, and because they support them from their means. Therefore the righteous women are devoutly obedient, and guard in (the husband's) absence what Allah would have them guard. As to those women on whose part you fear disloyalty and ill-conduct, admonish them (first), (next), refuse to share their beds (and last) beat them (lightly); but if they return to obedience, seek*

not against them means (of annoyance): for Allah is Most High,
Great (above you all).

(Sura 4:34)

It is clear to any objective non-Muslim that Muhammad considered women to be playthings, which would satiate his own hedonism and enjoy his position of power. Shockingly, his abusive behavior is described in some detail and praised in Muslim sources. The amazing thing is that the idea of repentance is completely absent from any discussion of Muhammad's abuse of power. This is a sharp contrast to the punishments meted out for any misguided behavior of leaders in the Bible, as well as the emphasis on their need to repent – to admit their mistakes and to correct them in the future. The verses in the Koran justify and even give a so-called *divine* stamp of approval for Muhammad's much more frequent abuses:

> *Aisha remarked, "It seems to me that your Lord hastens to*
> *satisfy your desire."*
>
> (Hadith Sahih Muslim: 2:8:3453-3454)

Muslims believe that Muhammad was a direct descendent of the father of the Arab nation, Ishmael, the wayward son of Abraham and Sarah's Egyptian maid, Hagar. We read in the Bible that Abraham's wife, Sarah, had been unable to bear children, and that she gave Abraham the go-ahead to have a child with Hagar. However, as Ishmael reached adulthood, his problematic behavior had to be dealt with.

> *And Sarah saw the son of Hagar the Egyptian woman*
> *playing. So she said to Abraham, "Drive out this slave woman*
> *with her son, for the son of that slave woman shall not inherit*
> *with my son, with Isaac!"*
>
> (Genesis 21:9-10)

The Jewish source of wisdom, the Midrash, teaches a lesson about Ishmael and Islam from the original Hebrew by the great Torah sage, Rabbi Akiva, who, in his uniquely concise style, hits the nail on the head:

> *Rabbi Akiva expounded ... "Playing" (in this context) can only mean sexual sin ... This teaches that Sarah would see Ishmael breach garden fences, hunting down men's wives and raping them.*
>
> (Genesis Rabah 53:11)

> *Ten measures of sexual sin descended to the world – Arabia took nine.*
>
> (Talmud, Kiddushin 49b)

There are commentaries in the Talmud that define the word *playing* as murder. In this context, however, it is not meant that way, but nonetheless, just as Muslims follow the ways of Muhammad, Muhammad had a well-known role model of his own. The extent to which Muhammad was influenced by his progenitor Ishmael is open for debate, but it is impossible to ignore the likelihood that he was, indeed, influenced by Ishmael in some way. Although many centuries have passed since the days when Muhammad *played*, there is no doubt that his free-wheeling, no-limits lifestyle is imitated and legitimized by those who revere his memory, as well as his behavior. For example, in Shiite Muslim society, there is a phenomenon called *pleasure marriages*, which is basically a form of legalized and religiously sanctioned prostitution. The following report describes its resurgence in the new, democratic Iraq:

> *In the days when it could land him in jail, Rahim al-Zaidi would whisper details of his muta'a only to his closest confidants and the occasional cousin. Never his wife.*
>
> *Al-Zaidi hopes to soon finalize his third muta'a, or "pleasure marriage," with a green-eyed neighbor. This time, he talks about it openly and with obvious relish. Even so, he says, he probably still won't tell his wife.*
>
> *The 1,400-year-old practice of muta'a – ecstasy in Arabic – is as old as Islam itself. It was permitted by the prophet Muhammad*

as a way to ensure a respectable means of income for widowed women.

Pleasure marriages were outlawed under Saddam Hussein but have begun to flourish again. The contracts, lasting anywhere from one hour to 10 years, generally stipulate that the man will pay the woman in exchange for sexual intimacy. Now some Iraqi clerics and women's rights activists are complaining that the contracts have become less a mechanism for taking care of widows than an outlet for male sexual desires.

Most Shiite scholars today consider it halal, or religiously legal. Grand Ayatollah Ali al-Sistani, the highest religious authority in Shiite Islam, sets conditions and obligations for muta'a on his Web site. ("A woman with whom temporary marriage is contracted is not entitled to share the conjugal bed of her husband and does not inherit from him...")

"We have reports about one-hour pleasure marriages that are flourishing among students," says Sheik Ali al-Mashhadani, a Sunni imam at the Ibn Taimiya mosque in Baghdad. "I'm advising parents to watch their sons very carefully, particularly those who are in the colleges and universities."[14]

Such practices in the *new* democratic Iraq call into question the wisdom of the democracy for Iraq movement. This theory asserts that if Islamic countries are given the right to democratically elect their own leaders, they will become good practitioners and valued proponents of the European/American model of democracy. This model displays a tradition of freedom of speech, freedom of religion, peaceful tolerance, and rights for women. At best, this is wishful thinking. Any societal change that leaves the prominence of Islamic religious culture intact is bound to fail. This is evidenced by the situation that arose when the Palestinian Authority's violently anti-Israel and anti-American Hamas terrorist group in Gaza captured an electoral victory. Prior to that election, Israel had withdrawn from the region, and, as a result, the American and European Union-sponsored elections brought the Hamas to power. There has been an ongoing dispute between the Hamas and Fatah terrorist groups – the two main components in the Palestinian Authority. These groups unwillingly share power in their quasi-government, which is comprised of Gaza, Judea and Samaria. This power struggle often results in violent conflict. Nonetheless, Hamas has seized full control in Gaza, the result of this being a continuing process of societal change, leading to a complete theocratic dictatorship and a gradual implementation of *Sharia* – Islamic Law – in Gaza. The Muslims of *Fatah*-ruled Samaria and Judea (the West Bank) are, on average, a bit more cosmopolitan and less extreme in religious observance, and they aren't yet under *Sharia* rule. However, certain indicators suggest that, despite a current lust for materialistic pursuits in the Palestinian autonomous cities (which is a result of massive Western and Israeli governmental financial assistance), societal and demographic trends favor the radical Islamic activists and the glorification of *jihad*. Likewise, the democratic elections in Iraq, far from bringing an enlightened form of westernized Islam, have encouraged the will of the people. That will, apparently, is fiercely Islamic, which means the implementation of *Sharia* law is fast approaching. Demands for full-fledged *Sharia* in Iraq are increasing, and it is only a matter of time before it is fully implemented.

In Islamic countries, democracy will eventually lead to *Sharia*, which is the opposite of the Western concept of *liberty and justice for all*. One thing should be clear and should override our Western multicultural tolerance: *Sharia* doesn't mean high morality and spiritual dignity for all citizens. Whatever justification Muhammad gave for the practice of *pleasure marriage*, it doesn't sound any different than one-night stands, long-term sexual affairs, cheating, or prostitution, which is prevalent in secular Western society. The difference is that in the United States, there is still the pretense that such unethical behavior is unacceptable. In the Islamic society, however, that type of behavior has *the prophet's* stamp of approval and is generally accepted by Islamic legal code. This perversion of their so-called *moral example* can be traced back to

Muhammad himself and the religion that he created 1400 years ago. As long as we continue to legitimize, and show tolerance or respect for such an ideology, positive change will not come to Iraq or Gaza. The imams who give sanction to that kind of reckless, abusive behavior in Iraq are simply following their teacher – how can they be blamed? More importantly, how can democracy modify this behavior? The problem lies within the value system, not within the system of government.

The founder of Islam drew no red lines when it came to the sexual and consequential emotional abuse of young children. The stories from the life of Muhammad reveal his penchant for raping young girls with uncontrollable lust and abuse of power. He then justified and gave his indiscretions a legal framework, saying that it was the will of Allah:

> *The Prophet engaged me when I was a girl of six (years). We went to Medina and stayed at the home of Bani-al-Harith bin Khazraj. Then I got ill and my hair fell out. Later on my hair grew (again) and my mother, Um Ruman, came to me while I was playing in a swing with some of my girl friends. She called me, and I went to her, not knowing what she wanted to do to me. She caught me by the hand and made me stand at the door of the house. I was breathless then, and when my breathing became all right, she took some water and rubbed my face and head with it. Then she took me into the house. There in the house I saw some Ansari women who said, "Best wishes and Allah's blessing and a good luck." Then she entrusted me to them and they prepared me (for the marriage). Unexpectedly Allah's Apostle came to me in the forenoon and my mother handed me over to him, and at that time I was a girl of nine years of age.*
> (Hadith Sahih Bukhari 5:58:234 Narrated Aisha)

> *…the Prophet married her when she was six years old and he consummated his marriage when she was nine years old, and then she remained with him for nine years (i.e., till his death)*
> (Hadith Sahih Bukhari 7:62:64 Narrated Aisha)

Aisha said, "The Apostle of Allah married me when I was seven years old. (The narrator Sulaiman said: 'Or six years.') He had intercourse with me when I was nine years old."
(Hadith Sunan Abu Dawud, Volume 2:2116)

According to the above quotes from the Hadith, it's not difficult to conclude that Muhammad was a child molester and a serial rapist who subjugated women and young girls, and abused his position to a shocking extent. In the United States, these are the crimes of statutory rape and, at the very least, sexual harassment. However, in the rose-colored world of political correctness, harsh criticism of Islam is considered to be *Islamophobia*, which is really just a way to prevent people from honestly examining the issues. The politically-correct mob tells us that we need to try to understand such behavior through the prism of respect for Islamic mores and cultural differences. In modern newspeak, one might say that Muhammad was a charismatic leader, but a flawed individual who perhaps *stretched* the boundaries of what was acceptable. If we adhere to the strange premise that truth is subjective and/or relative, then we need to be respectful of the *cultural uniqueness* in the Muslim world that enabled such morally warped behavior, but only if we *unfairly* judge him according to westernized social norms.

On the other hand, however, if we have the courage to examine such behavior objectively, we perceive a mentally sick and abusive individual who used his spiritual, physical, and political position of authority to take advantage of young girls. In essence, his position of importance served his megalomania and hedonistic lifestyle at the expense of those who were unable to object. If a Jewish or Christian spiritual leader today behaved in such a manner – and we have certainly seen such unfortunate examples – he would not only be lambasted through the media, condemned, and removed from his pulpit or position, but he would probably be arrested for statutory rape and/or sexual harassment. And he would deserve it.

I think that those who believe in liberty, dignity and respect, would agree that Muhammad's behavior – as described in the Islamic religious texts – was abhorrent and criminal. Nonetheless, these are among the behavioral examples that mainstream Muslims look to for guidance. The reality of this is frightening. In this case, the *submission* that Islam refers to appears not to be to God or even to Allah – the legendary Moon God that Muhammad created as an Islamic replacement of the God of Israel – but a submission to Muhammad's very own decadent whims and desires.

This is not just an ancient and sad fictional fairy tale. According to Islamic religious text, these are actual accounts of Muhammad's life. His model of behavior is being followed in many parts of the world today, even in the same country with an Islamic

king who President Obama bowed down to in 2009. Let's read one more recent example, this time from Saudi Arabia:

Saudi women's rights advocates are outraged after a 12-year-old girl was sold by her father into marriage with an 80-year-old man.

A Saudi father, whose name has not been released, sold his 12-year-old daughter to his 80-year-old

Questionable Presidential Etiquette: *President Obama bowing down to Saudi Arabian King Abdullah bin Abdul Aziz Al Saud at Buckingham Palace in London. It's perhaps interesting to note that he didn't bow to his host, Queen Elizabeth of England.*

cousin for the equivalent of $22,600... The girl, already in the custody of the elderly man, was reported to have shouted, "I don't want him, save me!" when contacted by phone by a journalist from the Al Riyadh, a local newspaper in the Saudi capital. He has previously married three other young girls... The girl's mother, who had objected strongly to the marriage, took the case to local media after her lawyer's efforts to get it legally annulled failed... Saudi Arabia's religious leadership defends child marriages, often citing the marriage by Muhammad ... the founder of Islam, to Aisha bint Abu Bakr when ... she was six or seven years old ... moving in with Muhammad and consummating the marriage when she was nine.[15]

Such child abuse, while not necessarily legal in more modern Islamic societies, is often tolerated, perhaps because similar abuses were carried out by the founder of Islam himself. In Afghanistan, there is a widespread practice known as *bacha bazi*, or *boy play*, in which young boys are taken from their families and forced to dance or be sex slaves for powerful men.

A spring there, called Salsabîl. And round about them will (serve) boys of everlasting youth.

(Sura 76:18-19)

The number of boys involved is unknown – the practice has been going on for centuries in countries where they are overshadowed by conflict and war. It is widely known that in many cases, military officials and high-ranking commanders and their friends partake in the abuse of these boys. However, it is a rarity to hear these practices spoken about. Is this because of the ongoing state of war, or because of the quiet Islamic tolerance of such practices that is based on the abusive behavior exhibited by Muhammad himself?[16]

Even modern Muslim Indonesia – a country with 220,000 citizens, 87% of whom are Muslims – falls prey to Muhammad's example.

In a *Los Angeles Times* article, written by Robin Wright,

a 16-year-old Indonesian student was interviewed about how modern Muslim young women balance ambition and career with Islamic rules. She arrived in full Islamic dress from head to toe, and responded to a question about her role model with this answer:

> *My role model?.... Muhammad the prophet, may peace be upon him. I want to spend my life as his messenger.*[17]

When this girl is ready to pursue her ambitions as a modern career woman, will she be tripped up by her blind obedience to Islamic ideology? What will happen as she tries to assert her ambitions as a young woman looking to fully achieve her potential? Muhammad as her role model is certainly an obstacle, as the spread of Islam inevitably restricts the rights of women. This pattern is seen in leading Islamic nations such as Saudi Arabia and Iran, in the tradition of Muhammad. Human rights restrictions apply to women of all ages. In Saudi Arabia, where women are not allowed to drive or to vote, a 75-year-old woman was sentenced to 40 lashes and four months in prison for mingling with two young men, one of whom was her late husband's nephew. The Saudi newspaper Al-Watan reported that the two men were responding to her request to bring over several loaves of bread.[18]

The uncontrollable abuse of authority and suppression of freedoms in the name of Islam – as bad as it is when it concerns child abuse and abuse of women – is ever more shocking when we examine the next central precept in Islam, that of *jihad*, or holy war. This obligation to carry out *jihad* is forced upon every Muslim, and the Islamic texts are replete with verses exhorting the faithful to make violent, holy war against the non-believers. This is especially directed at Jews and Christians, who once rejected Muhammad's false claims of prophecy.

> *Allah's Apostle said, "I have been ordered to fight with the people till they say, 'None has the right to be worshipped but Allah'..."*
>
> (Hadith 4:196 Narrated Abu Huraira)

> *The Jews call Uzayr a son of Allah and the Christians call Christ the son of Allah. That is a saying from their mouths; (in this) they but imitate what the Unbelievers of old used to say. Allah's curse be on them: how they are deluded away from the Truth!*
>
> (Sura 9:30)

Obviously, someone with a knowledge of Judaism and/or Jewish history would understand that Ezra (listed as Uzayr in the above quote) – the Scribe from the Second Temple period in Jerusalem – was a great leader, but was never considered to be the son of anyone but his earthly mother and father. This, of course, reveals Muhammad's ignorance about one of the primary targets of his antagonism. Aside from his apparent lack of knowledge of basic Judaism, we see Muhammad's central philosophy of *jihad*, which is to violently destroy those who disagree with him. This doctrine has been passed on and carried out as an ideal through the generations, and sharply sets Islam apart from God's word in the Torah, which makes it clear that respect for all and the dignity of each individual is a central premise in Judaism. The Koran's punishment of mandatory death and beheading to those who disagree with its precepts certainly isn't consistent with the words of the Jewish sages:

> *Hillel says, be like the disciples of Aaron: Love peace and pursue peace. Love all living things and bring them closer to Torah.*
>
> (Mishna: Ethics of the Fathers 1:12)

> *Ben Zoma said: Who is wise? He who learns from all people, as it is written (Psalm 119:99) I have gained understanding from all of my teachers.*
>
> (Mishna: Ethics of the Fathers 4:1)

Christianity emerged from Judaism, but eventually evolved into its own religion, and throughout this progression continued to teach many fundamental teachings derived from Judaism. This is in stark contrast with Islam, and concurs with the Judaic message of peace and tolerance:

> *Treat others the same way you want them to treat you.*
> (Luke 6:27-36)

That quote from the New Testament is actually a variation derived from the wisdom of Torah, as enunciated over two thousand years ago by Hillel, the great rabbinic sage in the Land of Israel. A pagan once came to Hillel saying:

> *I wish to convert, on the condition that you teach me the entire Torah "while I stand on one foot" (A Hebrew expression meaning quickly). Hillel accepted him as a convert and then told him, "What is hateful to you, do not do to others, this is the entire Torah, everything else is commentary. Go and learn."*
> (Talmud, Shabbat 31a)

It is no secret that Jews and Christians disagree about a number of theological issues, and there is a long and painful history of Christian persecution of Jews and of forced conversions and expulsions. However, most Christians today explain those atrocities and criminal acts against the Jewish people as a perversion of the teachings of Christianity – more specifically the teachings of peace and tolerance. Jesus never taught violence and forced conversion against Jews, not only because he didn't believe in it, but because he was a Jew, not a Christian. In fact, at that time there was no such thing as the Christian faith. Many of Jesus' other teachings, while not necessarily accepted by mainstream Judaism, were nonetheless spread peacefully. Although there were many in Jerusalem who strongly disagreed with much of what he preached, he was never accused of spreading his message in a violent way.

Christianity gradually developed as a separate religion many years after Jesus was killed by the Roman rulers, and the concept of Replacement Theology soon emerged. This theory states that God chose Israel as His *chosen people*, but then rejected them, and that the Church had somehow become the new Israel. Hatred for the Jews, which spanned centuries, were a result of this arrogant and blind reading of history, which certainly could not have been derived from the Five Books of Moses or the Writings of the Prophets. However, while Replacement Theology is still taught in many Christian denominations, it has also been refuted in many others. One basic truth in our times about Judaism and Christianity is that despite all our theological differences and our painful past of pogroms and persecution of Jews and the mass murder of Jews in Europe, most Christians now preach peace and tolerance in addressing divisive issues. It is definitely difficult for many Jews to forgive and forget the pain of the past, but I, for one, believe that mutual tolerance and respect is the best way to move on and move forward. We don't need to agree on every issue, but Jews have always believed that sincere repentance needs to be received and welcomed.

> *The Holy One says to Israel: "Return to me, and I shall return to you."*
>
> (Malachi 3:7)

That approach is consistent with the mutual tolerance and respect demanded by the famous prophetic vision of what is sure to come in the Messianic era:

> *From Zion will go forth the Torah and the word of the Lord from Jerusalem. He will judge among the nations, and will settle the arguments of many peoples. They shall beat their swords into plowshares and their spears into pruning hooks; nations will not lift sword against nation and they will no longer study warfare.*
>
> (Isaiah 2:3-4)

In other words, God will clarify the issues of disagreement for those who are sincerely seeking His guidance, but until then, the way to resolve difficult theological issues is by agreeing on what we have in common and working passionately to accomplish those mutual goals. As a pastor friend of mine once wrote to me after we had a friendly disagreement about theology, *Let's leave the messiah issue for Him.*

On the other hand, the Islamic way of dealing with differences of opinion, as written in the Koran, is quite the opposite from the mutual tolerance described above. The Koran's way of expressing differing opinions, expressed through Islamic brutality through the ages and in our times, is evidenced through numerous murders and death threats on the lives of those who disagree. The Koran and other Islamic sources, as well as words spoken in many mosques around the world, encourage the average Muslim to view non-Muslims as an enemy and even to kill them. Can this truly be regarded as a religion of peace?

> *O you who believe! Take not the Jews and the Christians as Auliya (friends, protectors, helpers), they are but Auliya of each other. And if any amongst you takes them (as Auliya), then surely he is one of them. Verily, Allah guides not those people who are the Zalimun (polytheists and wrong-doers and unjust).*
>
> (Sura 5:51)

> *Then, when the sacred months have passed, slay the mushikrun (non-believers) wherever ye find them, and take them (captive), and besiege them, and prepare for them each ambush. But if they repent and establish worship and pay the poor-due, then leave their way free. Lo! Allah is Forgiving, Merciful.*
>
> (Sura 9:5)

> *Allah's Apostle said, "You (i.e. Muslims) will fight with the Jews till some of them will hide behind stones. The stones will (betray them) saying, 'O Abdullah' (i.e. slave of Allah)! There is a Jew hiding behind me; so kill him."*
>
> (Hadith Sahih Bukhari 4:52:176
> Narrated Abdullah bin Umar)

These are not mere quotes or fables. These verses are based on the life and teachings of Muhammad, the founder, self-anointed prophet, and the original ideologue of Islam.

Let's look at a few examples. In the year 627, Muhammad

and his warriors laid siege to Medina and organized the takeover of a Jewish tribe – known as the *Banu Qurayzah*. Once they gained control, Muhammad ordered the construction of trenches around the city. Ibn Ishaq, Islam's earliest biographer of Muhammad, describes what happened next:

> Then they (Banu Qurayzah) surrendered ... then he sent for them and struck off their heads in those trenches as they were brought out to them in batches ... There were 600 or 700 in all, although some put the figure as high as 800 or 900 ... This went on until the Apostle made an end of them.[19]

One of the least-acknowledged and most horrific genocides in history was the genocide of Armenians by the Ottoman Turks, who brutally and systematically murdered at least 1.5 million Armenians from 1915-1918. After years of conflict and abuse of the educated, Westernized Christian Armenians by the illiterate Muslims of the Ottoman Empire, the *Young Turk* regime decided to exploit those omnipresent tensions. The Turks, who sided with the Central Powers (Germany and Austria-Hungary) as World War I broke out in 1914, dominated and disarmed the entire Armenian population, including 40,000 who were serving in the Turkish Army. The Armenians were then put in slave labor battalions, under the pretext that they were naturally sympathetic toward Christian Russia. The decision to annihilate the entire Armenian population came directly from the ruling triumvirate of the Young Turks. The actual extermination orders were transmitted in coded telegrams to all provincial governors throughout Turkey. Armed roundups of Armenians began on April 24, 1915, as 300 Armenian political leaders, educators, writers, clergy, and dignitaries in Constantinople (present-day Istanbul) were taken from their homes, briefly jailed or tortured, then hanged or shot. Subsequently, the mass arrests of Armenian men, women, and children, were followed by mass killings. Many children were taken from their families and coerced into denouncing Christianity and becoming Muslims, including a large number of girls and young women who were kidnapped, raped, and then forced into involuntary servitude. Following this, a million Armenians were forced to march hundreds of miles in the nude under the scorching Middle Eastern sun, until they dropped dead from exhaustion, if they weren't shot first – these were called *death marches*. An estimated 75% of the Armenians on these marches perished. Those who survived were herded into the desert without a drop of water.[20]

To this day, this Armenian genocide has been denied by much of the Turkish and the Muslim world, but the evidence is too great to refute. What is even more horrifying than the genocide itself is that the Turks and Muslims insist that such a well-documented series of events never happened.

> *I am confident that the whole history of the human race contains no such horrible episode as this. The great massacres and persecutions of the past seem almost insignificant when compared with the sufferings of the Armenian race in 1915.*[21]
>
> (Henry Morgenthau, Sr.,
> U.S. Ambassador to the Ottoman Empire)

In early 2002, the world was shocked by the savagery of the videotaped beheading of American journalist Daniel Pearl, a reporter with The Wall Street Journal who was murdered by Muslim terrorists in Pakistan. This was just one of many brutal terrorist-related crimes that al-Qaeda mastermind Khalid Sheikh Mohammed confessed to during a hearing at Guantanamo Bay more than five years after the murder. Standing before the American military tribunal, he proudly proclaimed:

> *I decapitated with my blessed right hand the head of the American Jew, Daniel Pearl, in the city of Karachi, Pakistan. For those who would like to confirm, there are pictures of me on the Internet holding his head.*[22]

Certainly a modern and liberalized citizen of the free world would be shocked by such acts and by the sick minds that proudly mastermind and subsequently brag about these attacks. The Koranic quotes that inspire such terrorism are not widely known, and the average person doesn't want to connect them to the present events because the ramifications of such an admission wouldn't be comfortable for the liberal, *truth is relative* mindset. It's much more comfortable to believe that such barbarism, which masquerades as religion, isn't relevant to the Muslim faith observed by many respectable, westernized Muslims. As one radio talk show host once commented to me, *Surely you are speaking about Radical Islam, not Islam itself!* To this I responded, *Go to the sources and tell me if I am wrong.* If Islam is the peaceful religion that its English-speaking spokesmen claim it is, why do the original quotes from those spokesmen or, more importantly, from the Koran and related sources, repeatedly reveal a violent, intolerant nature?

> *I studied the Koran a great deal ... I came away from that study with the conviction that by and large, there have been few religions in the world as deadly to men as that of Muhammad.*[23]
>
> (Alexis De Tocqville, French Thinker/Historian)

Even the seemingly moderate Islamic countries, which are supported by billions of dollars of American aid, such as Egypt, reveal views that are diametrically opposed to the views of most Americans. We see this in a ruling from one of the foremost religious authorities in Egypt. As reported on Al-Moheet Arab News Network:

> *Sheikh Ahmed Ali Othman, supervisor of the Da'awa (Islamic Indoctrination) of the Egyptian Waqf (Islamic Holy places), has issued a religious ruling (fatwa) that pigs in our time have their origins in Jews who angered Allah, such that he turned them into monkeys, pigs, and satan-worshippers, and it is obligatory to kill and slaughter them (the pigs).*
>
> *Othman based his ruling on this respected Koranic verse:*
>
> *Say (to the People of the Book – Jews and Christians), Come*

and I shall make known to you who receives the worst retribution of all from Allah: those whom Allah has cursed and upon whom He has poured His wrath, whom He has made into monkeys and pigs, and who have served abominations. Their place is worst of all, and their deviation is the greatest of all...

(Sura 5:60)

Sheikh Othman noted that this verse concerning the nation of the prophet Moses descended (from Allah to the Koran), and the books of commentary confirm this. There are two opinions among the Ulama (Islamic scholars) in this regard: The first is that the Jews, whom Allah transformed and turned into pigs, remained in that state until they died, without producing descendants. The other opinion is that the Jews who turned into pigs multiplied and produced descendants, and their line continues to this day, Sheik Othman also cited Hadiths (traditions attributed to Muhammad) as support...

Sheikh Othman said that whoever eats pig, it's as if he ate meat of an impure person, and stressed that this religious ruling is backed by the Islamic sages of Al Azhar (Sunni Islamic University) but they are afraid to say this publicly – so the sages won't be accused of anti-Semitism. Sheikh Ali Abu al-Hassan, head of the Fatwa Committee at Al-Azhar, said that the first view is accurate, because when Allah punishes a group of people he punishes only them. When Allah grew angry with the nation of Moses, He turned them into pigs and monkeys as an extraordinary punishment... but they died out without leaving descendants.[24]

In other words, the reason why Muslims are forbidden to eat pork is because, according to the Koran, pigs are descended from Jews! The pig itself is not problematic – it's the Jews that are. These *words of wisdom* from the supreme religious leaders of Islam are rotten fruit from the trees that Muhammad himself planted. His example lives on and is followed around the world. As former President Harry Truman's brilliant expression states, *The buck stops*

here, meaning that a moral leader must take full responsibility, not only for his own actions and behavior, but also that of his subordinates and followers. Why was the life of Islam's founder filled with angry words, repression of women, brutal teachings and vicious acts? What does it say about his so-called "religion of peace?"

The ramifications for the future are frightening, as the spread of the teachings of Muhammad and Islam continues. How this will play out during our lifetimes remains to be seen, but the signs are not encouraging. The reality that nearly all acts of terrorism are committed by

Taking Responsibility: *President Harry Truman was known for his expression, "The buck stops here," demonstrating the importance of taking personal responsibility for one's actions.*

Muslims is troubling, but the fact that Islamic terrorism is rapidly being transported to America in the guise of immigration from Islamic countries is even more frightening. On the surface, Muslim immigrants often resemble hard-working Europeans, Asians, or other immigrants that came before, and there are undoubtedly Muslim immigrants who only want to work hard, succeed and support their families, but there is one catch: their brethren won't allow it.

I'll give an example of what I mean by this by telling you a story about an Arab I know here in Israel, who I will call by a fictional name – Ahmed – in order to protect his privacy and safety. Ahmed once worked in Shiloh and in other Jewish communities in Samaria. About 12 years ago, without warning, he suddenly stopped coming to work. When I ran into him several months later, he had black and blue marks and bandages all over his body. I asked him what had happened. Ahmed told me that he had been taken into custody by the Palestinian Authority and was in jail for a number of weeks. During his time in jail, he was repeatedly beaten and tortured and he was warned to *never work for the Jews ever again*.

I never saw Ahmed again after that day. While he may still be alive, he has apparently chosen to live by avoiding what most Muslims call *the Zionist Enemy*. While Muslims in America are not as able to capture and torture their innocent brethren as in the Palestinian-ruled territories, the threat of violence is ever-present because of those who base their existence on a violent, intolerant guidebook. Their religious ideology makes it difficult for them to become truly loyal American advocates of liberty and the Judeo-Christian civilization that the Founding Fathers so honored. Even if they are *lapsed* Muslims in terms of their religious observance, the strictures of Islam eventually get in the way. Only Muslims who renounce Islam can escape these constraints. The modern story of American-born Nidal Malik Hassan and his Fort Hood victims reveal painful realities that non-Muslims prefer not to confront. The Westernization of Muslims in America will be a nearly impossible and uphill battle, a fact that is due to the poisonous roots of Islam and the hatred it preaches. No matter what, the shocking facts about this violent religion remain the same; all signs indicate that the ongoing encounter with Islam does not bode well for the future of Western civilization.

Chapter Five
Eurabia And The Islamic Challenge

Now when you meet those who disbelieve, smite their necks until when you have slain them greatly, then make fast the bonds; then, thereafter let them off either freely or by ransom, until the war lay down its burdens.

(Sura 47:4)

But my foes abound with life, and those who hate me without cause grow great. Those who repay evil for good harass me for my pursuit of good.

(Psalms 38:20-21)

The United States was established on idealism, and its people are well-known for their goodness, their giving nature and their openness. For all of those reasons, it is both shocking and understandable to even consider the possibility that the Land of the Free may soon fall prey to the Islamic beast which seeks to destroy it. Perhaps a vision of the U.S. twenty years from now can be predicted due to the frightening trends that the European continent has witnessed in the year 2010. The conversation and debate in Europe is not one of denial as in most parts of the U.S., but is one of awareness and caution. In Europe, it is more of a question of when, how, and what can or should be done about it.

In August 2009, the Telegraph (U.K.) reported in the latest census, the name Muhammad, in its various spellings, was the most popular name for baby boys in London and other British cities. Murtaza Shibli of the Muslim Council of Britain said he was not surprised to find that Muhammad had become the most popular boys' name in parts of the country.

> *People choose it because of their love of the prophet Muhammad, and they believe the name will bring happiness and abundance. Also because of its meaning – the praised one … There is a belief that if you do name your children Muhammad they will follow the good example of the prophet.*[1]
>
> (Murtaza Shibli, Muslim Council of Britain)

This is clearly a reflection of ominous population trends in Europe, where non-Western immigrants from Muslim countries and their Muslim children are vastly outpacing the indigenous Christian birthrates. Christian population totals aren't even reaching the levels necessary to maintain their own current numbers. Other data from the July to September 2008 Labour Force Survey showed that the Muslim population is growing ten times faster than the rest of the British population.[2] In Brussels, the capital city of Belgium, the top seven baby boys' names, as reported in a related article in the same series, were Muhammad, Adam, Rayan, Ayoub Mehdi, Amine, and Hamza. This state of affairs is a demographic time bomb and is prevalent throughout Europe, as Europe's Muslim population has more than doubled in the past 30 years and is expected to double again by 2015.[3] Even putting aside for a moment the ongoing threat of Islamic terrorism, the European continent is self-destructing before our very eyes. The historic populations of Western Europe, having become post-Christian populations, seem to have lost their desire to have children and the basic survival instincts that maintain any society or culture seem to be fading quickly. All of this is occurring while an aggressive Islamic population of immigrants and second-generation Europeans is on the rise. Demographic studies from a variety of reputable news sources in recent years have reported the following Muslim demographics in several major European cities:

- Marseilles, France – 25%
- Malmo, Sweden – 25%
- Amsterdam, Netherlands – 24%
- Brussels, Belgium – 17-20%
- Copenhagen, Denmark – 12.6%[4]

Given the rapidly rising Muslim birthrates, as compared to the majority Christian populations, it's not hard to project what the next twenty-five years will be like, as Europe gradually becomes Eurabia. It has been reported that Muslim leaders are well aware of this trend, and are actively promoting it to fruition.[5] The following is but a sample of what is being planned for Europe in the near future. The same is being planned for America further down the road.

We have 50 million Muslims in Europe. There are signs that Allah will grant Islam victory in Europe – without swords, without guns, without conquest – will turn it into a Muslim continent within a few decades.[6]
(Libyan dictator Muammar Gaddafi)

The conflict in the West is a fateful war between unbelief and Islam, between the army of Muhammad, the army of belief, and the people of the cross.[7]
(Osama bin Laden, al-Qaeda leader – December 27, 2004)

Our aim is to put down roots in the European continent, and to act quietly and in accordance with the laws, so that one day we may see all of Europe Muslim![8]
(Nijmuddin Erbakan, former Turkish Prime Minister)

The day will come when we will rule America. The day will come when we will rule Britain and the entire world...[9]
(Sheik Ibrahim Mudeiris, Friday sermon on official Palestinian Authority TV)

Should we be concerned? A growing Muslim minority

– which will perhaps soon become the majority in nuclear-armed Europe, the core of the NATO alliance – is certainly a threat to Western civilization, as it stands in stark contrast with its Islamic culture of violence, intolerance, and its doctrinal goal of world domination. Should we be concerned? An Islamic takeover of the European nuclear power should ring alarm bells in the ears of those who haven't lost the ability to hear or to see through their political correctness. This weakness is causing Europe to lose its basic sense of self-preservation.

They have eyes, but they cannot see, they have ears but they cannot hear.

(Psalms115:5-6)

Oh Muslims everywhere, I call on you to fight and become martyrs in the war against the Zionists (Jews) and the Crusaders (Christians) … It is a jihad for God's sake and will last until

Fighting for the Founder: *Muslim women demonstrating in front of the Justice Palace in Brussels, Belgium after a cartoonist drew a picture of Muhammad, the founder of Islam, in a Danish newspaper.*

(our) religion prevails ... from Spain to Iraq.[10]
(al-Qaeda Deputy Leader Ayman al-Zawahiri)

Then what would happen? What would happen if the radical Islamic vision of world hegemony came to pass in Europe, whether through terrorist violence or through peaceful demography? The alliance in Europe would, overnight, become nuclear-armed enemies of the United States and other remaining elements of the free world. Those are the global ramifications of an Islamic takeover of Europe. NATO would cease to exist or, at the least, be submerged into the Islamic alliance of nations. The United States and Israel would stand alone – as the sons of Muhammad captured the once-proud European continent.

If this takeover were to come to pass, the societal oppression that could be expected would shock the passive, liberal Europeans who currently seem to be ignoring what is about to happen. If we study the Islamic doctrine of *dhimmitude*, we can see the precedents of what Islamic sovereignty would entail. *Dhimmitude* specifically defines the status of Jews and Christians – referred to in the Koran as *People of the Book* – under Islamic rule, while the status of others was even worse. The concept arose in the year 629 CE, when Muhammad and his military forces conquered the Jewish oasis of Khaybar – 95 miles from Medina in the northwestern part of the Arabian Peninsula – in what is now Saudi Arabia. In the course of battle, the Muslims carried out a substantial massacre, in which 75% of the Jews were either killed or wounded. Those who survived were forced to accept a pact (*Dhimma*) that officially established their inferior status under Muslim rule.[11]

The rules that were established in the case of the Jews of Khaybar evolved over the centuries into a doctrine which distinctly resembles the *Jim Crow Laws*. These laws, established in the American South after the Civil War, severely limited the freedoms of African-Americans. Today, this could more accurately be described as a harsh form of sanctioned religious apartheid. Unlike the Jim Crow laws, which have long since been considered

American history, the laws of *Dhimmitude* have not lost their luster in the Islamic world. Therefore, it is vital that the citizens of Western countries pay close attention to its doctrine.

In the 13th century, those who agreed to pay *jizya* (servitude tax) were to be treated as *Dhimmi* only if they submitted to the following 20 disabilities. If they chose not to submit, their status would have been far worse:

- They are not to build any new places of worship.
- They are not to repair any old places of worship which have been destroyed by the Muslims.
- They are not to prevent Muslim travelers from staying in their places of worship.
- They are to entertain for three days any Muslim who wants to stay in their homes, and for a longer period if the Muslim falls ill.
- They are not to harbor any hostility towards the Islamic state, or give any aid and comfort to hostile elements.
- They are not to prevent any one of them from getting converted to Islam.
- They have to show respect towards every Muslim.
- They have to allow Muslims to participate in their private meetings.
- They are not to dress like Muslims.
- They are not to name themselves with Muslim names.
- They are not to ride on horses with saddle and bridle.
- They are not to possess arms.
- They are not to wear signet rings or seals on their fingers.
- They are not to sell or drink liquor openly.
- They are to wear a distinctive dress which shows their inferior status, and which separates them from the Muslims.
- They are not to propagate their customs and usages amongst the Muslims.

- They are not to build their houses in the neighborhood of Muslims.
- They are not to bring their dead near the graveyards of the Muslims.
- They are not to observe their religious practices publicly, or mourn their dead loudly.
- They are not to buy Muslim slaves.[12]

The Islamists have established an unofficial, yet bizarre, alliance with leftists of all nationalities to cover up the laws of *Dhimmitude* – they have succeeded to an extent that would have made George Orwell cringe. Muslim bigotry and newspeak has become legitimized by the European and American Left to such a degree that former U.S. President Jimmy Carter could write a scandalous book blasting embattled Israel as an apartheid state, without paying attention to the uncomfortable fact of the 100-year Islamic war seeking the annihilation of the State of Israel in the name of Allah, and while also shamefully ignoring the centuries-old religious apartheid, and slavery in the Muslim world, an oppression that has afflicted Christians as well as Jews.[13] This unusual alliance of secular leftists and Islamic activists can be seen in the modern Swedish city of Malmo, which typifies the strange political alliance of Muslim anti-Semites with some of their leftist counterparts, for whom Israel ceased to be *politically correct* a long time ago. Read this analysis by political commentator Caroline Glick:

Malmo is one of the most dangerous places for Jews in Europe. The city's small Jewish population is fleeing. The situation in Malmo was graphically demonstrated last March when Israel's tennis stars Amir Haddad and Andy Ram faced off against Swedish rivals at a Davis Cup tie in Malmo and Swedish authorities closed their game to the public. Malmo's Muslim residents and their post-Christian partners on the Left threatened to attack them. Malmo's authorities didn't think it was their responsibility to protect their Israeli guests, so Haddad and Ram were forced to play in an empty stadium.

Interviewed in a local paper this week about the rise of anti-Semitic attacks in his city, (Mayor Ilmar) Reepalu blamed Israel. In his view, the violence against Jews in Malmo by the far Left and Muslims, "spilled over from Gaza." (He was apparently referring to Israel's long-delayed retaliatory war against the Hamas terrorists in Gaza, a defensive struggle for which it was lambasted in the European media.)

By his lights the Jewish national liberation movement is just as bad as the Jewish annihilation movement. As he put it, "We accept neither Zionism nor anti-Semitism. They are extremes that place themselves above other groups they think are less important."[14]

When I read this description of Malmo, I found it especially disturbing, since I actually have very fond memories of Malmo. I remember visiting the formerly peaceful Swedish port city almost thirty years ago. As one who was used to the fast and often rough pace of New York, I was impressed by the gentle, well-mannered people who stood patiently at traffic lights and waited to cross the street. I had quite a few friends and acquaintances in Malmo and throughout Sweden at the time, so I had a number of people to visit there. I must admit that, as a New Yorker and card-carrying member of the melting pot, it did feel a bit strange that there wasn't much physical variety among the mostly blond-haired and blue-eyed Swedes. Nonetheless, I liked the Swedish people's mellow and easy-going nature, as well as the total feeling of safety, which I didn't have in New York City. It was certainly a different Sweden than what it seems to have become.

I recently had a conversation with a native and current New Yorker named Tom, who is married to a Swedish woman, Agneta. Tom described the year and a half that he had lived in Sweden over twenty-five years ago:

It was a socialistic society and it wasn't easy to find work at

The Call to Muslim Prayer/Action From The Minarets: *The mosques and their minarets now tower over the city of Malmo and many other European cities, symbolizing the changing demographics in nuclear Europe.*

first, but I took nothing from the society, except for a Swedish language course, which was subsidized. I worked really hard at learning the language and even dressed like the Swedes. I was almost obsessed with fitting in to Swedish society at the time, but things have changed since then. When we visit Malmo these days, it feels different. The Muslim immigrants don't seem to make any effort to fit into the society.

Tom's wife, Agneta, is a native Swede who has lived with Tom and their son in New York City for many years, but she regularly goes back to Sweden to visit family and friends. Agneta added:

It's not safe in Malmo like it used to be. People are afraid to go walking in the park. It also is a different feeling when going out in Malmo. The public buses are often 60% Muslim passengers and half of the women are wearing burkas. In a way it's nice that there is ethnic variety now, but it's not as safe as it used to be. One day, not so long ago, when we were sitting outside at a café on the walking street, a police car zoomed up with sirens blaring, screeched to a halt at the café, and the police officers ran out to chase after some criminals, waving their guns in the air. Now, I don't know if all of this is because of the demographic changes in Malmo, but the atmosphere is not what it once was.[15]

I think it's probably accurate to say that many of the Muslims in Malmo aren't thinking about a Muslim takeover of Europe – they are likely just living their day-to-day lives, without much thought for the bigger picture – but, rest assured that the Islamic religious and political leaders are. People either have short memories or they did not pay attention in history class, but we have definitely been in this movie before, and it doesn't end happily.

In 1930s Europe, a megalomaniac by the name of Adolf Hitler, with clear goals derived from a clear ideology, exploited Christian and Western tolerance and democratic freedoms to become the Chancellor of Germany. He then proceeded to gradually do away with the liberties that he exploited in his rise to power.[16]

Did German civilians think day and night about the grand takeover of Europe and the subsequent mass murder of its Jews and other undesirables? Probably not, but most did nothing to stop it.

That same tolerance and democracy is being exploited once again, as the passive Christian populations of Europe, with a barely existing and continually-falling birthrate, gradually self-destruct. The lapsed Christians of Europe have become disconnected from their rich cultural and historical values, a fact which has resulted in a lack of faith in the future that has been manifested in the plummeting birthrates among indigenous Europeans. The growing pro-Israel, pro-family evangelical Christianity that has energized many American communities is minimal in Europe – leaving a spiritual/cultural vacuum in a post-Christian Europe. Secularism as an ideology is a self-destructive force that is leading to the rapid extinction of the European nuclear family, and Islam is racing full steam ahead to fill the void. It is rapidly taking over the European continent, with its large families and religious passion, spreading Muhammad's message, whether demographically, violently or both. Many Muslim clerics are now calling for the imposition of *Sharia*, or Islamic Law, in European countries and the cries are getting louder as their population grows. They usually claim that they just want *Sharia* to serve the needs of the Muslim populations. The long-term goal, however, is the imposition of *Sharia* on everyone. They have many well-polished tools of propaganda, with which they hope to accomplish this. Well aware as they are of the West's aversion to the various forms of discrimination, the Islamic *thought police* have invented a new psychological ailment, which they call *Islamophobia*. The idea is to keep the West on the defensive, i.e., if you are against Islam, then something must be wrong with you. The idea is that if you are against Islam, you surely must suffer from a terrible neurosis that you are trying to pass along to others – you need to do some serious self-introspection or seek treatment, instead of doing the unthinkable: seriously examining the content of the malignant Islamic dogma and the fatal actions that result from it.

In June 2008, the Organization of the Islamic Conference (OIC) announced its plan for fighting Islamophobia. Here's what Ekmeleddin İhsanoğlu, their Secretary-General, had to say:

> *We are encouraged to see however, that an awareness of the dangers of Islamophobia is gradually setting in the West. The condemnation by many Western leaders and governments of Islamophobic acts such as the Fitna (Dutch movie which is critical of Islam) are positive confidence building measures that lead us to believe that all is not lost and that the gap can be closed*

in time. But mere condemnation or distancing from the acts of the perpetrators of Islamophobia will not resolve the issue as long as they remain free to carry on with their campaign of incitement and provocation on the plea of freedom of expression.[17]

Dr. İhsanoğlu unveiled a ten-point program, which he proposed in order to meet the OIC's ambitious goals. The OIC is an activist Islamic organization. On the surface they are peaceful, but they promote *Sharia* by keeping Christian Europe on the defensive, thereby limiting the willpower of the average European to resist this assault on liberty and to identify it as such. Not many Europeans understand the implications of this aggression, but they are submitting to its dictates.

In 2007, the European Ministers of Education underlined the importance of measures to improve understanding between cultural and/or religious communities through school education. In 2008, the Council of Europe published a white paper on Intercultural Dialogue entitled *Living Together As Equals in Dignity*.[18]

Islamophobia was repeatedly singled out as a form of *discrimination and racism* that needed to be ruthlessly stamped out through indoctrination as well as legal means across the entire European continent – a policy which is being implemented at an accelerating pace. The White Paper lists many institutions to cooperate with, most of them Islamic organizations or organizations geared towards appeasing Muslims. For instance, the Anna Lindh Euro-Mediterranean Foundation for the Dialogue between Cultures, which is one of the EU's most important instruments for Eurabian cooperation.[19] The network of Islamic banks funding the promotion of *Sharia* in Europe is quite extensive. This peaceful, gradual takeover is being eagerly promoted and supported by such *Europe-friendly* nations as Saudi Arabia, Dubai, Kuwait, and Qatar. Lest one think this is a new process being led by the relatively *new* Wahabi stream of Islam, which is dominant in Saudi Arabia, let's see what the great British leader Winston Churchill had to say about this movement – years before the Kingdom of Saudi Arabia was even established:

> *The Wahabis profess a life of exceeding austerity, and what they practise themselves they rigorously enforce on others. They hold it as an article of duty, as well as of faith, to kill all who do not share their opinions and to make slaves of their wives and children. Women have been put to death in Wahabi villages for simply appearing in the streets. It is a penal offence to wear a silk garment. Men have been killed for smoking a cigarette, and as for the crime of alcohol, the most energetic supporter of the temperance cause in this country falls far behind them. Austere, intolerant, well-armed, and bloodthirsty, in their own regions the Wahabis are a distinct factor which must be taken into account, and they have been, and still are, very dangerous to the holy cities of Mecca and Medina, and to the whole institution of the pilgrimage, in which our Indian fellow-subjects are so deeply concerned.*[20]

(Winston Churchill, June 14, 1921)

The Wahabi promotion of *Sharia* isn't new, but as their oil-wealth has grown, their techniques have become much more sophisticated. They are joined by their Shiite rivals in Iran and elsewhere in the aggressive promotion of *Sharia*. The internal rivalries throughout the Islamic world can be violent and fierce, but their ultimate goals are the same: world domination for Islam. Determining which Islamic nation will be the one to dominate should be irrelevant to us, since, in any event, we would be the ones to suffer from its rule. Nonetheless, the essence of what a *Sharia* system imposed on the free world would entail remains a mystery to most of its potential victims. An imposition of *Sharia* would most likely include the following changes and deviations from current systems of law in the West:

- There would be no religious freedom. Islam would be the only religion permitted and *infidels* would be subject to severe punishment, including death.

- Muslim leaders would command offensive, aggressive and unjust *jihads*.
- Unmarried fornicators would be whipped and adulterers stoned to death.
- Husbands would be allowed to hit their wives, even if the husband merely fears aggressiveness from his wife.
- Homosexuals would be executed.
- Critics of Muhammad, the Koran and even *Sharia* would be put to death.
- Highway robbers would be crucified or mutilated.
- An injured plaintiff would be allowed to exact legal revenge, *physical eye for physical eye.*
- As punishment, a thief's hand would be cut off, regardless of whether the thief was male or female.
- Drinkers and gamblers would be whipped.[21]

Is this the system of law that Europeans and Americans want to live under? Like it or not, an aggressive process is underway to make this become a reality throughout Europe. As the Muslims grow demographically, the demands will become stronger. We notice the terrorists and we rightly fear the bombings and shootings, but the real threat is far more discreet and ostensibly peaceful. The threat of a democratic, demographic takeover is the real genie at the door and it is waiting for the right moment to enter.

It was reported by correspondent Arthur Moore that near the site of recent attempted car bomb attacks in London, nationally syndicated talk radio host Rusty Humphries, together with WorldNetDaily (WND) Jerusalem bureau chief Aaron Klein, visited the London Central Mosque, where they recorded Muslim leader Abu Saif at a gathering of 3,000 Muslims.

The purpose for this gathering wasn't peaceful prayer and meditation; rather, it was a call for the overthrow of the British government, as part of their world vision which included an eventual Muslim takeover of the White House. Abu Saif, among others, kept his voice at a fever pitch through declarations such as:

"Brothers and sisters make no mistake. Make no mistake. The British government, the queen, the MPs in this country, they are enemies to you, enemies to Allah and enemies to the Muslims."

Abu Saif spoke with disdain of former Prime Minister Tony Blair's appointment as a special envoy to the Middle East, issuing an apparent threat.

"Inshallah (meaning Allah willing, he told the crowd, Blair) will go to the Middle East as an envoy, and he'll come back in a box. Inshallah. What box that is, we leave up to you."

Humphries estimated nearly 3,000 Muslims were gathered in front of the mosque in north London on June 22, after Friday prayers, to protest Queen Elizabeth's knighting of Indian author Salman Rushdie, the target of a death-sentence fatwa for insulting Islam's prophet Muhammad in his 1988 book, The Satanic Verses.

"One day my dear Muslims (shouted Anjem Choudary,) Islam will govern Britain!"

Choudary was a co-founder of Al-Muhajiroun, the now-banned group tied to suspects in the July 7, 2005, London transport bombings and a cheerleader of the 9-11 attacks.

"Democracy, hypocrisy (Choudary chanted as the crowd echoed him) Tony Blair, terrorist! Tony Blair, murderer! Queen Elizabeth, go to hell!"

For Humphries, the response of the Muslims at Islam's largest house of worship in the U.K. was telling: Not one said, "You're not speaking for me" or "not in my name." They stood there and watched and applauded.

Like the U.K., Humphries said, the U.S. has three major vulnerabilities to patient, fundamentalist Muslims who believe their *purpose for living in the West is to help fulfill Islamic prophecies: The loss of border control, the inability to say no and lack of assimilation.*

"I feel like I'm Rusty Revere. I'm out there yelling the Muslims are coming, the Muslims are coming, he said. But we don't want to hear it. We don't want to hurt people's feelings."

The Muslim leader Abu Saif said he does not believe in democracy and insists there is no such thing as freedom of religion:

> *"...because freedom is an absolute term. Are we to say that Muslims can fully practice religion in America? ... Say, for instance, I was a Muslim in America. Could I call for the destruction of the American government and establishment of an Islamic state in America? No. So where is the freedom of religion? There is none."*

Humphries asked: "Do you call for that?"

> *"Of course, he replied, we want Islam to be a source of governance for all of mankind. And we also believe that one day America will be ruled by Islam."*

Islamic leaders in the U.S. largely have been careful to not assert publicly the Muslim belief that Islam ultimately will gain worldwide supremacy.

"There's nothing we can do to be friends?" Humphries asked. Abu Saif replied:

> *"There is something you can do to be friends. You can become Muslim."*[22]

Dr. Ahmad Abu Matar, one of the rare outspoken Muslim reformists, wrote on his elaph.com website about the Islamic exploitation of democratic freedom to accomplish its non-democratic aims. Writing specifically about England, he mentions:

> *...the Islamic Liberation Party, which announces from London its political platform – to establish the Islamic caliphate over all corners of the earth – and declares that the party will suggest to*

the Queen of England that she convert to Islam, and thus will
not have to pay the Islamic poll tax on non-Muslims (jizya).

As another example, he cited the activities of Abu Hamza al-Masri, the imam of Finsbury Park Mosque in London, who called for *jihad* and suicide bombings in *Palestine*, Iraq, and Afghanistan. The third example he gave is the thousands of mosques and Islamic charitable organizations in Europe and America that publicly collect contributions, and in addition, receive annual budgets from European countries.[23]

While some recent polls seem to indicate that the Muslim populations of Europe aren't necessarily becoming more politically radical, they aren't becoming peace-loving Christians or Jews either, and their Islamic religious fervor doesn't seem to be diminishing, as evidenced by the substantial increase in the number of mosques throughout Europe. Unfortunately, in Islam it's very difficult to separate passion for religious observance from the passion for *jihad*, or holy war, so the demographic threat is also a political, social, and military threat to Western civilization. The trends are not encouraging and seem to defy the common wisdom concerning cultural assimilation in Western countries.

Policy Exchange, a British Study Group, found that more than 70% of Muslims over 55 years of age felt that they had as much in common with non-Muslims as with Muslims. When the 16-24 year old group was asked, the number dropped to 62%, which seems to be the opposite of what we would expect, the common wisdom being that the second and third generation European Muslims would identify stronger with the culture that they have supposedly grown up with.[24] Consequently, the threat to Europe is ominous, because a devout Muslim must, by commitment to his faith, be a soldier for Allah. This means that they are against everyone else in the spirit of Muhammad, whether or not he is outwardly violent and intolerant. That is the real danger and for that reason, I must say that until we see Muslims converting to other religions en masse, the threat to the world as we know it will only become greater as the demographic threat increases.

The lack of Islamic tolerance for free speech, as well as the hatred for Jews, was apparent at Oxford University on February 9, 2010, when Israeli Deputy Foreign Minister Danny Ayalon was heckled repeatedly by hostile Muslim protestors throughout his speech. In the course of the heckling, one of the protestors stood up and shouted the Islamic war-cry, well-known to us in Israel, *Itbah Al Yahud (Slaughter the Jews!)*.[25]

Just one week after a talk by historian and Ben-Gurion University Professor Benny Morris was cancelled at Cambridge University due to Muslim accusations of Islamophobia, an event which featured Azzam Tamimi, founder of the Institute of Islamic Thought and avowed supporter of Islamic terrorism and suicide bombings, was allowed to commence. In a nationally televised BBC interview in November 2004, Tamimi had declared that, given the opportunity, he would happily carry out a suicide bombing against Israel.[26]

Such is the situation on many university campuses in Europe, a situation in which Israel isn't even given the opportunity to defend its very existence against Islamic onslaught. Due to the present relevance of this issue, it may seem to us that it is only since 9-11 and the growing Islamic infiltration into Europe that these trends and focus are coming to the fore. However, it is also vital that we learn from the past. Through European history we can predict the future; the Islamic threat was perceived long ago by certain world leaders and visionaries who knew the scent of danger and sounded the warning for all to hear, long before it was on anyone's mind:

> *How dreadful are the curses which Mohammedanism lays on its votaries! Besides the fanatical frenzy, which is as dangerous in a man as hydrophobia in a dog, there is this fearful fatalistic apathy.... Far from being moribund, Mohammedanism is a militant and proselytizing faith. It has already spread throughout Central Africa, raising fearless warriors at every step; and were*

*it not that Christianity is sheltered in the strong arms of science,
the science against which it had vainly struggled, the civilisation
of modern Europe might fall, as fell the civilisation of ancient
Rome.*[27]

(Winston Churchill, 1899)

After reading Churchill's words, I can't help but wonder
what he would have thought when looking at his beloved Europe.
Perhaps in his time the Islamic propaganda machine wasn't
as well-oiled, but we are in a different era in which they have
learned to play the game, and better than most. *The strong arm of
science* doesn't seem to be helping much anymore, as universities
seem defenseless. Europe's vaunted higher education has been
infiltrated and confronted with a force of rampant Islamic
population growth and intensely passionate hatred. All the
PhD's in France, England, Spain, and Holland can't help to find
the solution for this in their laboratories or research institutes,
short of confronting the dual plagues of Islamic intimidation
and political correctness.

The almost religious belief that exposure to science and
higher education will overcome an evil ideology reminds me of
the story of Rashid. I met Rashid, a young Moroccan, while I was
traveling through Europe and Morocco as a college student on
summer break in 1980. I was sitting in a train compartment with
several young Germans, also university students on vacation.
As we traveled south through France and into Spain, we had
a stimulating discussion about German history, including the
Holocaust and its ramifications for our times. At that time I was a
fairly secular American Jew, so this discussion was eye-opening for
me, and I started to feel very Jewish for the first time throughout
the course of my trip which, by the time it was finished, covered
ten countries.

As time passed during my journey through southern Europe
and into Morocco through the desert, I met a small group of several
young Moroccans in the next compartment in our train car. They
were on their way home to Morocco after a year of study in a

Belgian university. They looked very westernized, wearing blue jeans, leather vests, and sneakers. They all had long hair, which in 1981 America was still very trendy. In short, there seemed to be a lot in common among us as we struck up a conversation. They were drinking beers and smoking cigarettes, a definite Moroccan no-no, especially during the month of Ramadan. After a while, a police officer came into their compartment, and they quickly handed me their beers and cigarettes so they wouldn't be arrested. There I was, with two beers in my hands and two cigarettes in my mouth! Anyhow, after the policeman left and we had a good laugh – the conversation continued, very light and very pleasant, until I suggested that I would like them to meet my young German friends who were still sitting in the adjacent compartment. Their smiles suddenly disappeared, and they all nodded in agreement as one of them named Rashid, declared, *We don't like them.* Appalled by his seemingly bigoted response, which apparently offended my New York liberal instincts, I answered, *How can you make a statement like that when you don't even know them? You haven't even met them!* To which he explained, *We don't like them because of Munich, because they caught our people!* I quickly realized that *they* was referring to the German police and *our people* to Palestinian terrorists. In the 1972 Munich Olympics, the German police had unsuccessfully attempted to rescue eleven Israeli athletes who had been kidnapped and eventually killed by Palestinian terrorists. Eight of the terrorists were killed in that abortive rescue attempt. Totally confused and outraged to hear that these westernized, college-educated Moroccans were actually identifying with terrorists, I demanded an explanation, which was quick in coming. Rashid stared me in the eyes, and shouted at me, with a wild, angry expression on his face and a clenched fist waving in the air, *Because Jerusalem is for all the Arabs!!!*

That was the last time I ever saw Rashid, but he forever changed my naive view of Islam – and ideologies in general. At that time I hardly knew anything about Islam, but he taught me my first lesson on that day. The dream of peace and love and universal spiritual harmony of the 1960s and 1970s America that I thought was realistic; the live-and-let-live liberalism that I believed in and that seemed to be a popular philosophical world-view in the Scandinavian countries where I spent part of my trip – all of this conflicted sharply with the Muslim mindset. It didn't matter that my Muslim *friends* had long hair and wore jeans and studied in European universities. It was irrelevant that they seemed *cool*, because once our discussion reached below superficial conversation, the incongruity of an authentic American, European or Israeli mentality with regard to the religion of Islam became blatantly evident. Peace, love and even tolerance of any non-Muslims were foreign concepts to these young men.

Despite their misleading Western appearance and their extensive European university education, they apparently still believed that terrorism, otherwise known as the religious obligation that they call *jihad*, is justified and proper against Jews and what they call infidels (Christians). These views they also hold against any non-Muslims or even Muslims who dare to convert to another religion, thereby defying the Muslim *thought police*. The fact was that these young men had a value system which had remained basically Islamic. The real danger is that the religious and cultural assimilation of Muslims into American and European society has been minimal. As a result of this, they are a dangerous fifth column within, and in many cases, actively working towards and waiting for the right moment to overthrow the oblivious, democratic societies in which they live.

> *Whoever changes his Islamic religion, kill him.*
> (Hadith Sahih al-Bukhari 9:57)

> *And those who are with him are severe against disbelievers, and merciful among themselves.*
> (Sura 48:29)

> *Allah's Apostle said, I have been ordered to fight with the people till they say, "None has the right to be worshipped but Allah..."*
>
> (Hadith 4:196 Narrated Abu Huraira)

Much attention has been paid by the media to the courageous Dutch parliamentarian and leader of the Dutch Freedom Party (PVV), Geert Wilders, who has sounded the warning to Holland and Europe that drastic action is needed to halt the raging Islamic tsunami in its tracks. Wilders produced the powerful film called, *Fitna*, in which he identifies Islam for the dangerous ideology that it is and exposes the lie that it is merely a peaceful religion. For this, he is now on trial in Holland, being charged for *hate speech*, even though he mainly used quotes from the Koran. Unlike some other right-wing European parties with similar views about the Islamic threat, his party is also strongly pro-Israel. This alliance can only help him, and perhaps will encourage many Christians to open their eyes about the pivotal role being played by the small Jewish state and about the task that Israel must soon undertake in the war on Islamic terrorism. As I always say, Israel is on the front lines of the war on Islamic terrorism, but the ultimate target is Western civilization as we know it today.

Brigitte Gabriel grew up in a Christian family in Lebanon. For some time, Lebanon was a cosmopolitan European island with a Christian majority in the heart of the Islamic-dominated Middle East. But all that changed when Muslims soon became the majority – to the extent that the Islamic terrorist organization Hezbollah has become a major player in the Lebanese government, which has not moderated the organization's genocidal Islamic views or goals against Israel and Western civilization. Gabriel continues to deliver a potent message to those in the West who are willing to listen – about how what happened in her formerly tolerant, Western-cultured, Christian-dominated nation on Israel's northern border can also happen in both Europe and America:

We were the majority, the Muslims were the minority, but as the years went by, the Muslims became the majority because of their birth rate, but also because of our open-border policy. We welcomed everyone into our country, Gabriel said, and people didn't realize that the minority, the Muslims in the society, were not tolerant and did not believe all people were equal. The result, Gabriel said, was that a radical terrorist organization tied to Islam, Hezbollah, now rules in Lebanon.[28]

What happened in Lebanon is a bitter lesson for Europe to learn, but at this late stage, awareness is not enough. It won't be easy to halt the looming Islamic takeover of the Old Continent without drastic action. Can the New World be far behind?

Chapter Six
A Light In The Land Of Zion

The Hebrews have done more to civilize men than any other nation ... (God) ordered the Jews to preserve and propagate to all mankind the doctrine of a supreme, intelligent, wise, almighty sovereign of the universe which I believe to be the great essential principle of morality, and consequently of all civilization.[1]

(President John Adams,
February 16, 1809
in a letter to Judge F.A. Van der Kemp)

For the truth is in the Koran, as verified by the words of the prophet Muhammad, that the decisive battle will be in Jerusalem and its environs: "The resurrection of the dead will not occur until you make war on the Jews..."[2]

(Sheikh Ibrahim Madhi, officially-appointed Imam
of the Palestinian Authority on official
Palestinian TV, August 11, 2000)

For many years, the American Administration and Congress have been hailing the historic bonds linking the United States and Israel. The ties between the two nations are often proclaimed to be due to Israel being *the one true democracy in the Middle East.* America's political leadership has consistently given lip service to the importance of the relationship. Some presidents have been more positive than others toward Israel, but it has always been clear that this was a unique relationship. When U.S. President Barack Hussein Obama was elected, it was apparent that the theme of his campaign, *change,* extended in part to America's relationship with Israel.

Although some American presidents have been friendlier than others, Obama was the first American president who has had close alliances with the avowedly anti-Israel, and anti-American, Arab-Americans. This included Rashid Khalidi, the Palestinian-American activist and former official spokesman for WAFA – the news agency for the P.L.O. terrorist organization. Khalidi currently holds the Edward Said Chair of the Middle East Studies program at Columbia University. This anonymously-funded position (rumored to be from an Islamic donor living in the Persian Gulf) is named for the late P.L.O./Yasser Arafat advisor and intellectual-hater of Israel, Edward Said, formerly of Columbia University. After years of using his carefully constructed image as an oppressed, poor Palestinian who was driven from his country, in order to bash Israel in high academic and political circles, the truth about Said was finally revealed after the publication of his autobiography. There were significant parts of the book that were fabricated – in particular that he grew up as an oppressed Palestinian Arab. In reality, Said was raised in very privileged Egyptian and American homes.[3]

The extent of Barack Obama's relationship with Said is still unclear, but there is little doubt of his long-time relationship with Rashid Khalidi. Obama served as a paid director on the board of the Woods Fund – a Chicago-based non-profit organization – along with an unrepentant ex-terrorist William Ayers. Ayers' Weather Underground terrorist group intended to overthrow the U.S. government and took responsibility for bombings at New York City Police headquarters in 1970, the U.S. Capitol building in 1971, and the Pentagon in 1972.[4]

I don't regret setting bombs. I feel we didn't do enough.[5]
(William Ayers, September 11, 2001)

In 2001-2002, the Obama-Ayers directed Woods Fund provided two grants which totaled $75,000 for the Arab American Action Network (AAAN). This virulently anti-Israel activist group was co-founded by Khalidi – his wife even serves as president. Khalidi also held an AAAN-sanctioned fundraising event for Obama's failed bid for a U.S. House of Representatives seat in 2000.

Asked several years later about Obama's role in funding the AAAN, Khalidi claimed he had *never heard of the Woods Fund until it popped up on a bunch of blogs....* He terminated the call when petitioned further about his links with Obama. Contacted by phone, Mona Khalidi refused to answer questions from WorldNetDaily (WND) about the AAAN's involvement with Obama. Obama's campaign headquarters did not reply to a list of questions that were sent via e-mail from the WND to the senator's press office.[6]

Three years later, an evening tribute event was held in honor of Khalidi, who was leaving Chicago for a job in New York. According to the *Los Angeles Times, a special tribute came from Khalidi's friend and frequent dinner companion, the young State Sen. Barack Obama. Speaking to the crowd, Obama reminisced about meals prepared by Khalidi's wife, Mona, and conversations that had challenged his thinking. His many talks with the Khalidis, Obama said, had been "consistent reminders to me of my own blind spots and my own biases. It's for that reason that I'm hoping that, for many years to come, we continue that conversation – a conversation that is necessary not just around Mona and Rashid's dinner table, but around 'this entire world.'"*[7]

A True Freedom Fighter: *Civil Rights leader Dr. Martin Luther King Jr. not only spoke out and sacrificed on behalf of freedom, but courageously criticized the hatred and the incitement to violence of the Black Muslims.*

These are not Obama's only questionable colleagues. They have also included associates of the racist and anti-Semitic leader of the Nation of Islam, Louis Farrakhan. Obama's long time membership in a church that awarded Farrakhan with its greatest honor was also particularly troublesome.

> *The other force is one of bitterness and hatred, and it comes perilously close to advocating violence. It is expressed in the various black nationalist groups that are springing up across the nation, the largest and best-known being Elijah Muhammad's Muslim movement.*[8]
>
> (Martin Luther King Jr.,
> Birmingham, Alabama, April 16, 1963)

This of course brings us to the infamous Jeremiah Wright, Obama's pastor and mentor for 20 years. This is a man with views that most Americans should find repulsive:

> *No, no, no. Not God bless America. God damn America. That's in the Bible. For killing innocent people. God damn America for treating citizens as less than human.*[9]
>
> (Pastor Jeremiah Wright,
> 2003 sermon at Trinity United Church of Christ)

At first, candidate Obama tried to downplay the numerous anti-American, anti-Semitic and racist statements made by his pastor, Rev Jeremiah Wright. Obama said that Rev. Wright *is like an old uncle who says things I don't always agree with.* He tried to further downplay the statements by telling a Jewish group that everyone has someone like Rev. Wright in their family.[10]

Once it became evident that this answer wasn't going to satisfy people who had read the shocking quotes, seen the videos, and realized that Obama considered Pastor Wright to be his *mentor*, the campaign shifted into damage control mode. Obama resigned from his church and repudiated the statements of the pastor who had married him, had baptized his daughters, and had been the inspiration for the title of Obama's book, *The Audacity of Hope*. The most troubling part of this whole affair is that despite the many problematic videos which surfaced during the campaign and Wright's reputation that was well-known in his community and beyond, Obama still insisted that in the 20 years that he had attended the church, he had never heard any of these controversial speeches.

> *Had I heard those statements in the church, I would have told Reverend Wright that I profoundly disagree with them, Obama said. He added, What I have been hearing and had been hearing in church was talk about Jesus and talk about faith and values and serving the poor.*[11]

During the 2008 election campaign, there were warning signs for all supporters of Israel and those who wanted a strong America, yet paradoxically, the liberal Jewish community proved that its ideology and knee-jerk rejection of Republicans was more enduring than its attachment to Israel. Obama managed to maintain the support of American Jews and eventually won 78% of their votes.[12] Nonetheless, in an unnecessary attempt to maintain and expand on his already strong Jewish support, Obama spoke positively about the relationship between the U.S. and Israel up until Election Day, even though his focus shifted considerably after taking office; hence his unyielding pressure on Israel to surrender its historic heartland and parts of its capital city to hostile Arabs – land it had won in a defensive war. The tone of the U.S.-Israel relationship soured further when the Obama Administration sought to send subtle – and not-so-subtle – signals of cooperation to the Muslim world. This included the White House-released photograph of President Obama speaking to Israeli Prime Minister Benjamin Netanyahu during Obama's first year in office. In the photograph, Obama has his legs on his desk with the soles of his shoes clearly facing the camera. In Arabic culture, this is a clear sign of insult and it is considered rude even to display the sole of one's shoe to a fellow human being.

It seems unlikely that Obama could have so easily forgotten about the infamous "shoe attack" on President George W. Bush

A Shoe For Israel, A Message for the Islamic World: *President Obama speaks to Prime Minister Netanyahu in this White House released photo, as heavy pressure is applied on Israel to halt all building in its heartland communities, including Jerusalem. Were the figurative shoe soles in the Israeli face an intentional message to the Muslim world?*

in December of 2008 when an Iraqi television journalist hurled two shoes at President Bush. The President was holding a joint news conference with Iraqi Prime Minister Nouri al Maliki to mark the signing of a U.S.-Iraq security agreement. The journalist responsible for the political statement, Muthathar al Zaidi, tossed his shoes at Bush and yelled, *This is a goodbye kiss, you dog.*

Furthermore, President George W. Bush's national security adviser and subsequent secretary of state, Condoleezza Rice was referred to by the particularly insulting first name Kundara – meaning shoe – in many Arab circles.[13]

Another example of how the Obama Administration has sent subtle messages to the Arab and Muslim world about Israel occurred with Secretary of State Hillary Clinton's publicized telephone berating of Netanyahu. The Jerusalem municipality had announced that the Israeli government had approved a building

In Your Face: *Showing the soles of a person's shoes to someone has long been a non-verbal sign of contempt or insult in Arab culture.*

project in a northern Jerusalem neighborhood. This announcement, which came during Vice-President Joseph Biden's visit to Israel, supposedly embarrassed the Vice President, and Netanyahu almost immediately apologized to Biden for the perceived insensitivity. The problem comes from the fact that Muslim nations object to all Jewish building in Jerusalem, which Jews have recognized as Israel's eternal capital since the time of King David, nearly 3,000 years ago. America's approach of bashing Israel as a way to pander to the Muslims raises some crucial questions, and not just about Obama's integrity. Must the American government automatically accept the Arab position on existential questions concerning Israel's very existence? Would the Obama Administration accept criticism from another nation in regard to a building project in the American capital, Washington, DC? Are the occasional platitudes about the positive bonds with Israel based solely on the desire to be seen as a nation that supports Israel but is merely used as a tool for electoral gain? Does the United States see the wealth from Arab oil and their extensive land mass as more valuable to the United States than its relationship with Israel? In fact, Israel has virtually no oil and has a geographical land mass smaller than New Jersey. It also is regularly condemned by the Islamic and Third World dominated United Nations. Recognizing these facts, what possible value can Israel have for the United States?

The Founding Fathers of the United States established their nation on biblical foundations and they understood that these foundations originated in the Israel of the Bible. The Land of Canaan spoken about in the Bible is the land where Abraham and Sarah walked, where Isaac and Rebecca slept, and where King David reigned. It is in that very same place where the mission of God's *chosen people* remains as vital today as it was in any other time in history. Many of the secular founders of the modern state of Israel tried to create *a nation like all the other nations* – that would be respected and take its rightful place in the family of nations. Israel's accomplishments, from re-establishing an ancient nation located on rocky desert hills and in malaria-infected swamps, was remarkable and is worthy of great praise. However, I have to adamantly disagree that the dream of returning after almost two thousand years of exile from our land was for the sole purpose of being a nation like all the other nations. I firmly contend that the Jewish state was recreated to fulfill Israel's historical and spiritual mission – to become *a kingdom of ministers and a holy nation*. Israel continues to be singled out for unreasonable criticism or hatred by the United Nations and by world leaders, but the simple truth is that the nation is judged by a different compass than the other nations because it is truly a unique nation.

> *Our society is illuminated by the spiritual insights of the Hebrew prophets. America and Israel have a common love of human freedom, and they have a common faith in a democratic way of life.*[14]
>
> (Lyndon B. Johnson)

> *Moses ascended to God, and the Lord called to him from the mountain, saying, "So shall you say to the House of Jacob and*

relate to the Children of Israel. You have seen what I did to Egypt, and that I have borne you on the wings of eagles and brought you to Me. And now, if you hearken well to Me and observe My covenant, you shall be to Me the most beloved treasure of all peoples, for Mine is the entire world. You shall be to Me a kingdom of ministers and a holy nation.

(Exodus 19:3-6)

Despite the majestic words in the Book of Exodus that describe perhaps the loftiest mission that people have ever been given, there has always been confusion about the vital role of the Jewish people in their quest to redeem the world as it is known today. The world is overwrought by war and terrorism, hunger and despair, and a destructive cynicism and self-indulgence. Step by step, this is tearing away the fragile social fabric of Western civilization. The Israeli people have a mission to improve the world; to fix a world that has lost its way; and, in effect, to create a world of light that is now incomplete from the world that God intentionally created.

There is a misconception garnered from these words that someone who believes in an omnipotent God cannot also believe that He created imperfection; but there is no inherent contradiction in His plan. God created a world filled with both good and evil; and he urges Jews to choose good. This is the meaning of *free choice* and is a fundamental concept in Judaism. Jews believe that they have the obligation of *Tikkun Olam* (repairing or fixing the world), by which they are commanded to be active players in fighting against evil and performing good deeds in order to improve the world. There is an expression in Hebrew, *Hakol L'Tovah*, which literally means *everything is for good*. The point is that everything happens for a good reason. It may be difficult to find the reason, but something good is supposed to come out of every seemingly negative event, and it is each person's responsibility to bring that to fruition.

Thus the heaven and the earth were finished and all their

hosts. And by the seventh day God completed His work which He had done, and he abstained on the seventh day from all His work which He had done. God blessed the seventh day and sanctified it because on it He abstained from all His work which God created to make.

(Genesis 2:1-3)

A basic premise of faith-based biblical scholarship is the idea that there are no redundant words or expressions in the Torah. If so, why does the last line in the above verse follow the words *which God created – with to make?* The answer to that question can be found in the words of Rabbi Joseph B. Soloveitchik, which analyze various commentaries about the elaborate Genesis story. Soloveitchik points out that biblical commentators have asked numerous questions regarding the reasons for the nature and style of the Creation story, including questions which delve into its chronology and/or its literal meaning. Soloveitchik makes it clear that, based on those discussions, one can derive many hidden lessons for humankind, which are intended to guide us as we seek an understanding of the deeper meaning of life. He explains that there are two kinds of creations: God can and often does create *yesh me'ayn* (ex nihilo – something from nothing), whereas man can only create *yesh me'yesh* (something from something). Nonetheless, that doesn't diminish its importance. The words *God created* are referring to God's initial creation. The words *to make* are referring to our task, of continuing and perfecting the imperfect world that God intentionally created that way.[15]

Furthermore, in the Midrash (Bereshit Rabah 3:9):

Rabbi Abbahu taught the principle of multiple creations: "And there was evening and there was morning, the first day" (Since the sun was not yet created how could there be morning?). Says Rabbi Abbahu: "This indicates a time arrangement prior to this (biblical) creation; that God built (previous) worlds and destroyed them, built worlds and destroyed them, until He said, 'This world pleases Me and the others did not please Me.'" Here we have God, not only creating, as in the biblical text, but also recreating, rebuilding after destructions.[16]

What does this come to teach us? Obviously, the omnipotent God doesn't need to experiment; he could have created a perfect world on the first try. But since we are created in His image and, therefore, we seek to emulate His example, He teaches us that despite our natural failings and mistakes, we need to persist in our efforts. We need to improve ourselves and to fix or better the world, not just once, but to rebuild again and again after destruction, which is often much more difficult to do after the first time. That is the challenge that God has issued to us – we are encouraged to persist in that challenge, despite the obstacles that are placed in our way or constructed through our uniquely human limitations and flaws.

The role of the Jewish people is to lead the process of *Creation Completion*, and that is where the Land of Israel enters into the equation. The homeless and often persecuted Jews living in other lands contributed greatly to those nations as individuals, but the reestablished nation in the Land of Israel has provided an appropriate vehicle for the prophetic vision of working towards a better world. That has always been Israel's mission, to be carried out from its deep-rooted base in the Land of Israel.

The aspiration for a Jewish homeland is rooted in a tragic history that cannot be denied. Around the world, the Jewish people were persecuted for centuries, and anti-Semitism in Europe culminated in an unprecedented Holocaust.[17]
(U.S. President Barack Obama
speaking in Cairo, Egypt on June 4, 2009)

While the centuries of persecution and the Holocaust were cruel and undeniable, President Obama missed the point. Whether this is intentional or unintentional is irrelevant – he over-emphasized the connection between the Holocaust and the rebirth of Israel as a sovereign nation and alienated a significant portion of his audience. The Muslim nations who were listening attentively to the speech, heard Obama heap abundant praise upon Islam and its supposed respect for *the principles of justice and progress; tolerance and the dignity of all human beings.* Undoubtedly, upon hearing the reference to the Holocaust, Muslims wondered why they should even agree to the existence of a Jewish state in the predominantly Muslim Middle East. Why should they bear the responsibility for what the Nazis did to the Jews?

If one were to ignore the thousands of years of Jewish history and disregard the events that have transpired over the past hundred years, such a question is reasonable and consistent with the Muslims' (and apparently President Obama's) line of reasoning. Obama implied that the nation of Israel was created as a response to the Holocaust and has no roots in the Land. For a Muslim to spread such falsehood is dishonest and ignorant, but understandable, given his primary role model and value system. However, Obama himself – despite reports to the contrary – insists that he has always been a Christian, not a Muslim. He also claims to be a student of history. Despite these self-assertions, Obama reveals a remarkable level of ignorance regarding the history of the evolution of his religion. Not once during his speech in Cairo did he mention the deep roots in the Land of the Bible that Israel possesses, that he wants to hand over to Muslim control. Let's examine what that means.

If President Obama had some basic knowledge of Christianity's roots, he would be well aware that Christianity would not – could not – exist if it weren't for the Torah and Judaism. The man known to the world as Jesus was a Jew who lived in the Land of Israel. While Christians and Jews are in sharp disagreement about whether he was the Messiah and what the significance of his presence in Israel was some 2,000 years ago, there is no doubt that any Christian recognizes that biblical history did not start with this particular man. Jesus was born in the Judean hills in the region otherwise known to much of the world as the Israeli-Occupied West Bank, which past presidents have proposed handing over to the so-called Palestinians with hopes to establish an independent state for them in the biblical heartland of Israel. Jesus the citizen of Bethlehem later moved to Nazareth in the Galilean hills. In modern politically correct semantics, he would today be stereotyped in the media as a child born to a religious settler family and his parents would no doubt be vehemently opposed to any proposal to force them to surrender their home in Bethlehem to a hostile Islamic terrorist entity.

Since 2008, there have been countless accusations that President Obama is actually a Muslim, an ideology which shows through many of his policies. He has rejected this allegation vehemently and continues to assert his Christian faith. So let's take him at his word and assume that during a 2008 television interview, when he referred to his Muslim faith, it was just a slip of the tongue and didn't reflect reality.[17a]

If so, how do we explain his acceptance of the Islamic narrative about Israel? Certainly, the Christian Obama should find his own anti-biblical policy which places Jesus and his family in what the Obama Administration has referred to as occupied territory incredibly offensive. The parameters of his policy disallows natural growth and severely restricts Jewish settlement. Has President Obama considered that under this anti-biblical policy, Jesus would not have been born in Bethlehem – perhaps not at all!

Another historical example of an ancient settler lies in the background of the great leader and Psalmist, King David. Although it was hundreds of years earlier, King David was also raised in Bethlehem and was appointed the King of Israel by Samuel the Prophet:

> *The Lord said to Samuel, "How long will you mourn over Saul, when I have rejected him from reigning over Israel? Fill your horn with oil and go forth – I will send you to Jesse the Bethlehemite, for I have seen a king for Myself from among his sons."*

> (1 Samuel 16:1)

The son of Jesse, who was referred to, was actually King David, who unified Israel by establishing Jerusalem and the future home of the Temple on Mount Moriah. Jerusalem remained the unified capital for 440 years.

Today, when we speak about Israel, we are not talking about an oppressed people born on the ashes of the Holocaust. We are not referencing a people with no prior roots in the Land who were given a new country to atone for the shame that the world felt because of the Holocaust. No, modern-day Israel is an indigenous people who are coming home to retake possession of their formerly sovereign and God-given Land, exactly as prophesied in the Bible:

> *I will sanctify my great name that is desecrated among the nations, that you have desecrated (by being) in the midst of them. Then the nations will know that I am the Lord, says the Lord God, when I will be sanctified through you before their eyes. I will take you from among the nations and will gather you from all the countries and will bring you into your own Land.*
>
> (Ezekiel 36:23-24)

> *The degradation of Israel is the desecration of the name of God.*
>
> (Biblical commentator Rashi on Ezekiel 39:7)

The degradation of the Jewish people – as a historically persecuted and scattered people without a land and without independence – was, in and of itself, a desecration of God's name. Therefore, the converse is also true: the homecoming of the Jewish people with full sovereignty constitutes a sanctification of God's name among the nations. After the nearly 2,000 years of forced conversions, ghettos, expulsion, beheadings, *Dhimmitude*, and death – culminating in the horrible Holocaust during World War II – the return of the Jewish people to their historic homeland is a sanctification of God's name, a confirmation of the ever-lasting covenant between God and His people Israel.

The declaration of the state of Israel in 1948 was the

culmination of a pre-ordained return to the Land of Israel. This was the return of the only nation that was ever indigenous and sovereign in the land, as had been promised several thousands of years ago to the Patriarchs of Israel, Abraham, Isaac, and Jacob. Yes, even impending persecution and slavery in Egypt was foretold to the Patriarch Abraham – the founder of Judaism – but the promise of the Land as Israel's Divine inheritance was implied even then:

> *And He said to Abram (Abraham), "Know with certainty that your offspring shall be aliens in a land not their own (Egypt) – and they will serve them (the Egyptians), and they (the Egyptians) will oppress them for four hundred years."*
>
> (Genesis 15:13)

Many generations later, after the escape from slavery and the Revelation on Mount Sinai, the promise which was given to Joshua and the Israelites upon entry into the Land of Israel was much more explicit:

> *Moses My servant has died. Now, arise, cross this Jordan (River), you and this entire people, to the land that I will give to them, to the Children of Israel. Every place upon which the sole of your foot will tread I have given to you, as I spoke to Moses. From the desert and this Lebanon until the great river, the Euphrates River, all the land of the Hittites until the Great Sea (the Mediterranean Sea) toward the setting of the sun shall be your boundary.*
>
> (Joshua 1:2-4)

Anyone with a basic knowledge of Middle East geography would know that the biblical boundaries defined above are far more substantial than any land that Israel has possessed during the past 63 years. Israel's return to the Land was always a basic religious principle, even if it wasn't always practical. Given the biblical foundations of the United States, it is not a surprise to learn that the return of Israel to its Land was supported by American presidents throughout history, long before it was close to becoming a reality:

> *...I could find it in my heart to wish that you had been at the head of a hundred thousand Israelites... and marching with them into Judea and making a conquest of that country and restoring your nation to the dominion of it. For I really wish the Jews (were) again in Judea an independent nation...*[18]
>
> (John Adams, Letter to Mordecai Manuel Noah, 1819)

> *(I believe in the) rebuilding of Judea as an independent nation.*[19]
>
> (John Quincy Adams,
> Letter to Major Mordecai Manuel Noah)

Judea is the southern part of what most of the world now calls the West Bank – in the heart of the ancient Land of Israel. Before the Temple was destroyed by the Romans and the Jews were expelled from the Land in the year 70, Judea was the final remnant of what had once been David's unified kingdom.

Not long after the Emancipation Proclamation, President Abraham Lincoln met a Canadian Christian Zionist, Henry Wentworth Monk, who expressed hope that Jews who were suffering oppression in Russia and Turkey be emancipated *by restoring them to their national home in Palestine.* Lincoln said this was a noble dream and one shared by many Americans. The President said his chiropodist was a Jew who *has so many times put me upon my feet that I would have no objection to giving his countrymen a leg up.*[20]

It is impossible for one who has studied at all the services of the Hebrew people to avoid the faith that they will

Honest Abe: *Long before it seemed realistic, President Lincoln expressed sympathy for the rebirth of Israel in its historic homeland.*

*one day be restored to their historic national home and there
enter on a new and yet greater phase of their contribution to the
advance of humanity.*[21]

(President Warren Harding)

*I had faith in Israel before it was established, I have faith in it
now. I believe it has a glorious future before it – not just another
sovereign nation, but as an embodiment of the great ideals of
our civilization.*[22]

(President Harry S. Truman, 1952)

President Truman was known for his toughness, as exemplified
by the famous slogan, *Give 'em hell, Harry!* His visibly emotional
moments were rare, but Israel was one topic that touched his
heart. Truman biographer David McCullough reported:

*I have about three instances where Truman cried in public.
They are very few and they are always real.*[23]

(Truman biographer Michael T. Benson
author of *Harry S. Truman and the Founding of Israel*)

When Chief Rabbi Yitzchak Isaac HaLevi Herzog of the
newly established state of Israel came to visit President Truman
in early 1949, the two had a very moving exchange, in which the
rabbi expressed his thanks to the president for his recognition of
Israel.

He then went on to say the following words to the
president:

*God put you in your mother's womb so that you could be
the instrument to bring about the rebirth of Israel after almost
two thousand years.*

Truman was visibly moved. Herzog then opened his Bible,
and with the President reading along in his own Bible, the Rabbi
read from the Book of Ezra (1:2), in which the Persian King Cyrus
spoke the following words:

The Lord, God of Heaven has given me all the kindness of

Appreciating Truman's Divine Mission: *The Chief Rabbi of Israel, Dr. Isaac Herzog, walks with his entourage on his way to visit one of several children's homes in Israel, carefully carrying a Torah scroll in his arms.*

the earth; and he has commanded me to build Him a house (Temple) at Jerusalem, which is in Judah.

On hearing these words, Truman rose from his chair and with great emotion, tears glistening in his eyes, he turned to the Chief Rabbi and asked him if his actions for the sake of the Jewish

Biblically-Connected: *President Truman receives a Menorah from Israeli Prime Minister David Ben-Gurion in 1951 as Ambassador Abba Eban (center) looks on.*

people were indeed to be interpreted thus and (that) the hand of the Almighty was in the matter. The Chief Rabbi reassured him that he had been given the task once fulfilled by the mighty King of Persia, and that he too, like Cyrus, would occupy a place of honor in the annals of the Jewish people.[24]

(Truman biographer Michael T. Benson)

In 1961, then-Prime Minister of Israel David Ben-Gurion, on his final trip to the U.S., visited former President Truman in a New York hotel suite to once again express his appreciation:

I told him that as a foreigner, I could not judge what would be his place in American history; but his helpfulness to us, his constant sympathy with our aims in Israel, his courageous decision to recognize our new State so quickly and his steadfast support since then had given him an immortal place in Jewish history. As I said this, tears suddenly sprang to his eyes. And his eyes were still wet when he bade me good-bye. I had rarely seen anyone so moved.

I tried to hold him for a few minutes until he had become more composed, for I recalled that the hotel corridors were full of waiting journalists and photographers. He left. A little while later, I too had to go out and a correspondent came up to me to ask, "Why was President Truman in tears when he left you?"[25]

Truman's emotional bonds with Israel seem to reflect a spiritual, biblical connection that transcends the usual ties of interest between nations. As the plentiful quotes from American presidents show, the dream of Israel's return to the Land after 2,000 years of exile was something that was always expected in the eyes of biblically-literate people, because the prophecies predicted it. Truman and so many of his predecessors were biblically bound to believe that the return to the Land was destined to happen. The only question was when, for the Land without its people was barren and depressed. Remember, this Land was promised to Abraham, Isaac, and Jacob, and their descendants by God. This was the land that Moses wanted to reach, but it was not meant to be. This was the Land where the Tabernacle – the precursor of the Temple – stood in Shiloh for 369 years in the times of Joshua, Hannah, and Samuel the Prophet. This was the Land where David and Solomon reigned in Jerusalem and where the first Temple on Mount Moriah in Jerusalem was built by Solomon, which was eventually destroyed by the Babylonian ruler, Nebuchadnezzar.

The Temple symbolized Israel's spiritual and physical sovereignty in the Land of Israel. After the destruction of the First Temple, the Northern portion of the Kingdom of Israel was exiled to Babylon – but Ezra and Nehemiah led the return of a small number of Israel's exiles to rebuild the Temple, once again on Mount Moriah in Jerusalem. Although there was religious autonomy during the succeeding few hundred years, the Land was under foreign political control, first by the Persians (including the benevolent Cyrus), then by the Greek Hellenists. Eventually, the Romans conquered, once again destroying the Temple and forcing the Jews into exile – this time for almost 2,000 years. When they sent the Jews away, they changed the name of the land to Palestina – after Israel's arch-enemy, the Philistines – as a seemingly effective semantic way of totally erasing Israel's history and presence from the Land. There was certainly no independent country known by that name. Nonetheless, from then on the Land was called Palestina, or Palestine, except by the Jews, who, throughout the succeeding centuries, continued to pray at least three times a day for the prophetic return to Zion – the Land of Israel.

> *Sound the great Shofar for our freedom. Raise the banner to gather our exiles and gather us together from the four corners of the Earth. Blessed are you O Lord, Who gathers in the dispersed of His people Israel.*
> (From the weekday Amidah prayer)

> *May our eyes behold Your return to Zion in compassion. Blessed are You O Lord, Who restores His Presence to Zion.*
> (From the weekday Amidah prayer)

The Land of Israel, known to most of the world as Palestine, was much like an orphaned young child; it remained alive, but just barely. The Land had many rulers during the approximately 1,900 years that Israel was away. The Byzantine Christians were in control from 313-636, then came the Arab Muslim conquest from 636-1099, during which time the Dome of the Rock mosque was built on Mount Moriah. The Dome was built exactly on top of the site where the two Temples had stood, in an apparent attempt to prevent it from being rebuilt again and to demonstrate Islamic conquest. The Muslim rule was disrupted by the Christian Crusaders who invaded the Holy Land, intending to evict the Muslims. The Christian Crusaders ruled from 1099-1291. After that, the Muslim presence returned, although in a different form, when the Mamluks took control from 1291-1516. The Ottoman Empire was the next Islamic conqueror, until the year 1918 and the conclusion of World War I. Following World War I, the victors ended Ottoman rule over the Land of Israel and the British were given what was called the Palestine Mandate by the League of Nations.[26]

> *It is manifestly right that the scattered Jews should have a national center and a national home and be reunited, and where else but in Palestine, with which for 3000 years they have been intimately and profoundly associated?*[27]
>
> (Winston Churchill, 1920)

The first two decades of the 20th century saw increasing Jewish immigration to the Land, with many agitating for an independent Jewish state in order to restore Jewish sovereignty to the Land once again. While the majority of activists were Jewish, one individual who will forever be recorded in Zionist history was the British Foreign Secretary Arthur James Balfour (later Lord Arthur Balfour). Balfour, while representing the British Government, wrote the statement of principle known as the Balfour Declaration, which expressed official British approval for *the establishment of a homeland for the Jewish people in Palestine.* At that time, this *homeland* referred to a broad geographic area, including what is now Israel and Jordan and extended eastward into what is now Iraq and northward toward Beirut, although the borders were very roughly defined. France was given the Mandate over the region of the Ottoman Empire which is now called Syria.[28]

The Balfour Declaration was a significant political recognition in the Zionist struggle to reestablish Jewish sovereignty over the ancient homeland. However, it was destined to be short-lived. As an article on PalestineFacts.org so aptly describes:

> *...the British underwent a change of heart about the establishment of the Palestine Mandate. The reasons were related to political developments that had taken place in the region between 1920 and 1922. The result was that Abdullah, a (Muslim) Arab from the Hejaz (now Saudi Arabia), was abruptly installed as the Emir of Transjordan (meaning on the other side of the Jordan River) by the British. In a British memorandum presented to the League of Nations on September 16, 1922, it was declared that the provisions of the Mandate*

document calling for the establishment of a Jewish national home were not applicable to the territory known as Transjordan (today called Jordan), thereby severing almost 80% of the Mandate land from any possible Jewish Homeland.[29]

Thus, after September of 1922, the proposed Jewish homeland had been reduced to just 23% of the British Mandate, in the area west of the Jordan River. The same PalestineFacts.org article details:

From the moment of its creation, Transjordan was closed to all Jewish migration and settlement, a clear betrayal of the British promise in the Balfour Declaration of 1917 and a patent contravention of its Mandatory obligations.[30]

The 1920s and 1930s also saw a sizeable rise in Islamic terrorism against Jews in the Land. Muslims made it clear that they would not accept Jews in their midst – certainly not as a free and sovereign nation – and they were prepared to do everything in their power to stop them. The sword of Islam commenced its attacks on the peaceful Jewish inhabitants of the Land. During the riots and massacres, hundreds of Jews were brutally murdered, wounded, and raped by Arab mobs in cities throughout the Land of Israel. There were no limits, it seemed. Elderly men, pregnant women, young children – none were shown mercy in the rampages that followed the calls from the mosques in the Land.[31]

My heart is full of sympathy for Zionism.[32]
(Winston Churchill,
visiting the not-yet-completed
Hebrew University of Jerusalem, 1921)

In 1945, after World War II, the League of Nations disbanded and the British mandate came to an end. The United Nations was established and the new body eventually gave its approval for an increasingly truncated Jewish state of Israel, and Jerusalem would be internationalized. Though its borders reflected only a small fraction of the historic Jewish homeland, it was a day of celebration – the sovereign nation of Israel officially returned to its Land after 1,900 years of dispersion and national homelessness.

Upon hearing this news, the Arabs rejected the vote and declared war on the nascent state. The new sovereign state of Israel declared its independence on May 15, 1948 and the Arabs surrounded Israel on all sides, heavily outnumbering its meager army both in weaponry and soldiers. The Arabs launched a coordinated war against Israel; a painful battle in terms of deaths and territory lost to Israel's newly reborn nation. A full one percent of the population of the reestablished state fell in the fighting, half of whom were civilians. The historically biblical, mountainous regions of Samaria, Judea and eastern Jerusalem had fallen into the hands of the newly independent Kingdom of Jordan, Gaza was taken by the Egyptians, and the Golan Heights captured by the newly independent Republic of Syria.[33]

Israel was left with a tiny state – a thin strip of coastal land in the west-central part of the country where most of its cities and population were concentrated. Therein existed a dangerous, almost indefensible situation that led Arab leaders to call for war:

> *We intend to open a general assault against Israel. This will be total war. Our basic aim will be to destroy Israel.*[34]
> (Egyptian President Gamal Abdel-Nasser,
> May 26, 1967)

> *The sole method we shall apply against Israel is total war, which will result in the extermination of Zionist existence.*[35]
> (Egyptian Radio, *Voice of the Arabs*, May 18, 1967)

> *I, as a military man, believe that the time has come to enter into a battle of annihilation.*[36]
> (Syrian Defense Minister
> Hafez al-Assad, May 20, 1967)

The existence of Israel is an error which must be rectified ...
Our goal is clear – to wipe Israel off the map.[37]

> (Iraqi President
> Abdur Rahman Aref, May 31, 1967)

The result of these verbal attacks and the military maneuvers that accompanied them was the Six-Day War in June of 1967. Once again attacked from all sides, Israel fought another valiant war armed with hopes of survival – the results were nothing short of miraculous. Israel recaptured Judea with the ancient cities of Hebron and Bethlehem (where the patriarchs and matriarchs of the nation are buried); Samaria, with Shiloh, Bet El, and Shechem; and eastern Jerusalem, including the Temple Mount (Mount Moriah) and its famous Western Wall, which had often been called the Wailing Wall because of the tears that had been shed by Jews over the destruction of Zion. Israel also recaptured the Golan Heights in the north and the Gaza region in the south. The dangerous, fragile borders of Israel from 1948-1967 have been known to many as *The Auschwitz Borders* which were penned as such by former Foreign Minister and U.N. Ambassador Abba Eban, serving as a bitter memory of the notorious Nazi death camp.

> *We have openly said that the map will never again be the same as on June 4, 1967. For us, this is a matter of security and of principles. The June map is for us equivalent to insecurity and danger. I do not exaggerate when I say that it has for us something of a memory of Auschwitz. We shudder when we think of what would have awaited us in the circumstances of June 1967, if we had been defeated; with Syrians on the mountain and we in the valley, with the Jordanian army in sight of the sea, with the Egyptians who hold our throat in their hands in Gaza. This is a situation which will never be repeated in history.*[38]

> (Abba Eban, Der Spiegel)

Meanwhile, in May of 1964, the Arab League, which was comprised of fourteen Arab countries, established a political body to deal directly with the problem of the Palestinian Arabs.

They called it the Palestine Liberation Organization (P.L.O.). The P.L.O.'s first leader was an Egyptian, Ahmed Shukairy. In 1969, the most notable leader of the P.L.O. – Fatah leader Yasser Arafat – was elected chairman of the organization. The P.L.O.'s stated goal was to eventually destroy the Jewish state. Its immediate goal? To create a Palestinian people and use it as a tool to destroy Israel. Up to that point, the term *Palestinian* referred more to Jews than to Arabs or Muslims.

My father-in-law, who was born in Jerusalem in 1939 – nine years before the state of Israel was established – has always said that, if there is such a thing, he is more of a Palestinian than Cairo-born Arafat ever was. Ten years later at the 1974 Rabat Summit of Arab nations, which included the P.L.O., the armed struggle against Israel was reaffirmed, and a unanimous resolution was passed. For the first time ever, the P.L.O. was declared *the sole*

Creating New History In Cairo: *P.L.O. Chairman and P.A. Founder Yasser Arafat, born in Cairo, Egypt, participated in the creation of the "oppressed" Palestinian people in 1964 to capture the Jewish people's underdog image. He was glowingly successful at the Islamic art of speaking out of both sides of his mouth, words of jihad in Arabic to the Muslims and words of peace in English to the "infidels."*

legitimate representative of the Palestinian people. The summit also declared that the Arab world would accept any parts of the Land of Israel that Israel would agree to surrender peacefully. Thus, began the policy of shooting at and bombing Israel with one hand, while simultaneously holding *peace* negotiations with the other.

> *Peace by persuasion has a pleasant sound, but I think we should not be able to work it. We should have to tame the human race first, and history seems to show that that cannot be done.*[39]
>
> (Mark Twain)

> *We plan to eliminate the State of Israel and establish a purely Palestinian state. We will make life unbearable for Jews by psychological warfare and population explosion... We Palestinians will take over everything, including all of Jerusalem.*[40]
>
> (Yasser Arafat, P.L.O. Chairman, speech in Stockholm, 1996)

When asked about his plans during an Egyptian television interview in 1998, Arafat explained that strategic pause was a venerable Islamic strategy, referring specifically to the *Khudaibiya agreement.* Through this agreement, the Prophet Mohammed made a ten-year treaty with the Arabian tribe of Kuraysh, but broke it after two years. During this time, his forces used the security of the pact to marshal their strength and then conquered the Kuraysh tribe.[41]

Since 1989, there has been a full-blown diplomatic process, often called *the peace process* or *the Oslo process,* named after the city where it originated. The focus of this process is to organize and initiate a movement spearheaded by the western nations to get Israel to withdraw from its biblical heartland of Judea and Samaria. The aim is then to have Israel hand Judea and Samaria over to the Palestinian Authority – the quasi-governmental structure that was created from the P.L.O. to further the establishment of a new Muslim state in the heart of Israel. The plan is to establish this state's capital in the ancient eastern part of Jerusalem – including the Temple Mount (Mount Moriah), where Solomon's Temple stood in the heart of Israel's capital. However, even though Israel recaptured the Mount in that miraculous war, the Temple Mount in recent years has been under Muslim control.

The sad truth is that Israel has been afraid to tempt the anger of the Islamic world by asserting its sovereignty over the place where God's presence (the *Shekhinah*, in Hebrew) dwelled. An unfortunate result of that lack of courage has been that all non-Muslims are forbidden from praying on the Temple Mount.

In addition to ancient Jerusalem, the new Islamic state would also encompass the city of Hebron, where the patriarchs

The Western Wall: *This retaining wall of the Temple Mount in Jerusalem, where the two Holy Temples of the Jewish People once stood, has become an enduring symbol of thousands of years of Jewish history in the Land of Israel.*

and matriarchs Abraham, Isaac, and Jacob, Sarah, Leah, and Rebecca are buried. It would include Shiloh, where Joshua set up the Tabernacle and the first capital of Israel, where Hannah prayed for a son, and where Samuel the Prophet grew up. Other key locations in this new state would be Bethlehem, Shechem, Beit El, and Elon Moreh, which are all deeply historic, biblical sites. I could go on and on, but the point is clear – these areas are all part of Israel's inheritance from the King of the Universe. This is a gift that Israel is obligated to protect and to treasure – certainly not to hand over to the hostile terrorist entity that openly seeks our destruction.

Before setting foot in the Land, the great leader Joshua was given some words of encouragement from the Almighty:

> *No man will stand up to you all the days of your life; as I was with Moses so will I be with you; I will not release you nor will I forsake you. Be strong and courageous for it is you who will cause this people to inherit the Land that I have sworn to their fathers to give to them.*
>
> (Joshua 1:5-6)

The exhortation continues with a reminder that God's commandments in the Torah need to be followed, and that a smooth conquest of the Land would depend upon that. The Philistines, the Hittites, the Canaanites, Amalek, and all of Israel's enemies were in an evil alliance against Israel. To stand against it required courage and faith in the rightness of the cause. It was not a time to set up a committee to examine the causes of anti-Semitism. It was not a time to examine various ways to ease the plight of the Philistines.

Today, the long arm of terrorism is still threatening our world and an evil alliance has again been formed. The alliance is made up of different players, but the goal is the same. Among these evil allies are the Palestinian Authority (PA), otherwise known as Fatah; the main terrorist group in the P.L.O., Hamas, the component of the Palestinian Authority which controls Gaza;

Hizbollah, which controls much of Lebanon; and al-Qaeda. All these terrorist groups are being heavily supported and funded by Iran, Syria, Saudi Arabia, and the other Islamic Gulf states. Some support it loudly and some discreetly, but they are all involved. They also have collaborators in the Knesset, Israel's parliament. For example, in an interview with the Kol El-Arab newspaper, Arab MK (Knesset member) Masoud Ranaim, a member of the Re'em-Ta'al political party and of the southern branch of the Islamic Movement, publicly called for the establishment of an Islamic Caliphate that would include Israel.[42]

To say that Israel is faced with challenges would be a tremendous understatement, but let there be no misunderstanding: while Israel may be on the front lines in the struggle against the Islamic terrorist organizations, terrorists are also targeting the United States, Europe, India, and anyone else who doesn't share their evil ideology. Yes, I know that political correctness and moral relativism keeps us from using terms such as *evil ideology* because ideologies, in general, contain a certain amount of relative truth. Well, I choose not to bend to the doctrine that wishes to silence contrary voices, so the *thought police* will have to forgive me. In a perfect world, they would at least consider my points as we continue to honestly examine the religious ideology that plants fear in the hearts of innocent people around the world.

The culture of death that is rooted in the teachings of Muhammad has been promoted ceaselessly by the Palestinian Authority, which both the European Union and the United States governments have backed and continue to heavily support, both financially and militarily. The stated reason for this support is because the leader of the Fatah terrorist group that controls Judea and Samaria is more moderate than the Hamas terrorist group that currently controls Gaza. However, it is the mainstream, moderate Palestinian Authority (PA) leadership that has actively promoted suicide bombing and terrorist attacks and becoming a *Shahid* (a martyr), by repeatedly describing – often on PA television in dramatic fashion – the eternal rewards that await the Muslim who dies while performing acts of terrorism. The most prominent reward that Palestinian male martyrs are repeatedly promised are 72 dark-eyed virgins in Paradise. Palestinian religious leaders tell their flock that this is authentic Islam, the purpose of which is to fill Muslims with desire for Paradise.

Let's read several texts from the official PA media (courtesy of Palestinian Media Watch):

He (Muhammad) said (in a Hadith, Islamic tradition): (There is) a palace of pearls in Paradise and in it seventy courts of ruby ... And in each court (there are) seventy houses of green emerald stone. In every house, seventy beds. On every bed, seventy mattresses of every color, and on every mattress a woman.

The writing of the Prophet (Muhammad in this Hadith) ... is intended to fill Muslims with desire for Paradise ... to be worthy of it, because only three dwell there: Prophets, Righteous and Shahids (Martyrs for Allah).

(Al-Hayat Al-Jadida, January 2, 2004)

The Al-Aqsa Martyrs' Brigades (Fatah) took responsibility for killing Israeli Rabbi Meir Avshalom Hai in a drive-by shooting. Israel killed three of the terrorists involved. The response of the PA has been unequivocal support and glorification of the killers as Palestinian heroes and Shahids (martyrs).

A Fatah poster honors the three terrorists and is signed with condolences from PA Chairman Mahmoud Abbas.

(The following is the text on the poster with pictures of the terrorists:)

With honor and admiration to those who are more honored than all of us.
The Palestine Liberation Organization, Fatah, accompanies to their wedding. (Reference to Islamic belief that Martyrs marry virgins in Paradise)

The Martyr, Commander, Hero: Rassan Abu Sharah
The Martyr, Commander, Hero: Ra'ed Al-Sakargi
The Martyr, Commander, Hero: Anan Sobh
The Director General of the Presidency expresses condolences to the Nablus Martyrs – in the name of the President (Abbas).

And what happens to a female terrorist after she is killed? Are there 72 male virgins waiting for her? No – she becomes one of the 72 dark-eyed virgins.

PA TV host:

Had you succeeded in (a suicide) mission, what would your reward have been?

Female terrorist:

The reward was from Allah, in Paradise. The female Martyrdom-seeker becomes one of the Dark-Eyed (Maidens), and she marries one of the Shahids (martyrs).
                (Interview with female terrorist arrested
                       before her suicide terrorist mission,
                          IBA News, October 1, 2004)[43]

Jerusalem and its environs are a trust of Allah. Saving it from the settlement monster and the danger of Judaization is a personal commandment incumbent upon all of us.[44]
         (Palestinian Authority President Mahmoud Abbas,
           speaking at an Arab League gathering, March, 2010.)

PA leaders such as Mahmoud Abbas are always welcomed and honored in Washington's corridors of power, but they are the prime sponsors and promoters of the glorification of the Shahid.

The sick mentality that is represented by the Islamic terrorists' culture of death seems to think that the people of Israel will be so frightened that they will surrender entirely. Muslims believe that they will be able to take control of the Land by virtue of the *scare factor*. In other words, they don't believe that Israel will have the level of commitment needed to withstand the pain of terrorism and war. They are hedging their bets on their belief that Israel will not be able to continue to fight. According to that theory, Israel will surrender its biblical heartland – Judea and Samaria and eastern Jerusalem – through the intimidation of terrorism and war combined with American and European pressure. From that point on, Israel would lose its *raison d'etre*, its reason for existence – namely, its historic biblical heartland.

Many Muslims believe that Barack Hussein Obama, a significant portion of the Democratic Party, and a smaller segment of oil-dependent Republicans are willing to apply what they see as the necessary pressure on Israel; and the Muslims may indeed be correct. Whether this means that Israel will cave in to such pressure is still uncertain. Despite the secular Left elite in Israel that endlessly preaches the virtues of establishing a Palestinian state in the biblical heartland of Israel, there is a growing faction of idealistic, dedicated Israelis that are well-versed in the history of their people and they are integrally bound to their land. They are not prepared, in any circumstance, to hand over their land to the sons of Ishmael.

> *May You shine a new light on Zion, and may we all speedily merit its light.*
>
> (From the Jewish prayer book)

The light in Zion is the presence of God's nation that has returned to its land after two thousand years of exile – never to be forced from their land again. Jews believe that the proverbial blossoms are on the trees and that their land is once again bearing its fruit. The prophecies foretold in the Bible are coming to life for all to see; and the heart and spirit of that national resurgence is in the hills of Judea and Samaria. These territories – often referred to as the West Bank – that the recent succession of presidents, and even the world, refuse to recognize as the property of Israel, are actually the cradle of Judeo-Christian civilization. Israel's resettlement of the land actually fulfills biblical prophecy.

I shall yet rebuild you and you shall be rebuilt, O Maiden of Israel; you will yet adorn yourself with drums and go forth in the dance of merrymakers. You will yet plant vineyards in the mountains of Samaria; the planters will plant and redeem.

(Jeremiah 31:3-4)

The return to the Land of Israel is an ongoing process that is central in the redemption of the entire world. Even if all Islamic terrorists united, they would be unable to stop this process. They may cause death and wounds and great destruction, but in the end they will fail. As I see it, the bigger question is where the rest of the free world will stand in this process – it, too, is threatened by the monster of Islamic terrorism. Will the world stand strong with Israel in its noble battle and stop the Koranic terrorists from taking over the free world?

For there will come a day when watchmen will call out on Mount Ephraim…

(Jeremiah 31:5)

Chapter Seven
The Sleeping Giant

...Their mouths speak with arrogance. As we step forth, they immediately surround us; they fix their gaze to spread over the land.

(Psalms 17:10-11)

While the threat to the future of Europe as we have known it seems imminent, the United States of America may not be far behind. As in the case of World War II, the United States is self-absorbed and doesn't seem to understand that the greatest threat isn't necessarily another massive terrorist attack, but that the longer term threat is the threat from within. The sleeping giant of Western civilization doesn't seem to have noticed the creeping demographic changes in American society that may soon threaten its existence.

I had heard about a raucous anti-Israeli demonstration in Fort Lauderdale, Florida on December 30, 2008, during Israel's war against the Hamas Palestinian terrorist army in Gaza. I was told that there were actually Americans in the streets of Florida shouting to send the Jews *back to the ovens*, referring to the death furnaces at Auschwitz death camp in Poland, established by the Nazis to mass slaughter hundreds of thousands of Jews. With the exception of the rare cases of Neo-Nazi youth, such vile expressions of hatred seemed incongruous in the USA that I knew so well, until I saw the actual video footage of violent Muslims rioting in Fort Lauderdale and shouting those very words.[1] It was shocking, but I immediately understood the reason why for years there had been violent, anti-Israel demonstrations in the streets of Europe.

The Islamic demographic numbers in the United States are smaller than in Europe, but the trends are the same, as are the reasons. The Muslim population is the fastest growing segment of the American population and that growth shows no immediate signs of abating. According to the 2000 U.S. Census, the annual Muslim growth rate was 6% versus 0.9% for the total U.S. population.[2] This is a product of a high birthrate and massive immigration, although illegal immigration was most likely not included in the census.

Apparently, the illegal immigration across the Mexican border doesn't just consist of poor, hungry Mexican natives looking for a better life, but includes substantial numbers of Arab Muslims, an influx that has been organized by al-Qaeda. Tens of millions of Muslims, mostly of Arabic descent, live in Latin America. It has been revealed that al-Qaeda, Hezbollah, and the Islamic Resistance Movement (Hamas) are all active along the various borders in Latin America, such as Colombia, Paraguay, Brazil, and Argentina in creating routes for illegal immigration, in drug and uranium smuggling, and in counterfeiting U.S. currency. FBI Director Robert Mueller has reported that many of the illegal aliens crossing into the United States are people with Middle Eastern names who have adopted Hispanic last names before entering the U.S.[3] Furthermore, it has recently been reported that Venezuela, under the leadership of its anti-American, anti-Israeli President Hugo Chavez, and in alliance with Iran, may be taking a leading role in coordinating these efforts, as a new cold war against the United States and the free world heats up along the southern border.[4] The Iranian-Hezbollah Islamic involvement was further verified by Navy Admiral James Stavridis, who oversees U.S. military interests in the South America region as head of U.S. Southern Command. He expressed concern about the Iranian-Hezbollah axis' involvement in "proselytizing and working with Islamic activities throughout the region."[5] All of these activities have contributed to the lawlessness on the United States-Mexico border.

Alongside the demographic struggle, there is a multi-faceted and intensive financial/cultural/propaganda war that is being carried out by the Islamic activists, supported by the wealthy Muslim states, using their oil wealth to win a battle for the hearts and minds of what they (perhaps accurately) see as the naive American public. This is not a Middle Eastern desert mirage and my vision is not being blurred by the Israeli desert sand. The Christian Arab-American scholar Dr. Anis Shorrosh has highlighted 20 practical steps that the Islamists have been taking in recent years to minimize the ability of the American public to resist the demographic onslaught that has already begun, toward their goal of accomplishing in the United States what is already happening in Europe:

1. Terminate America's freedom of speech by replacing it with hate crime bills state-wide and nation-wide.

2. Wage a war of words using black leaders like Louis Farrakhan, Rev. Jesse Jackson and other visible religious personalities to promote Islam as the original African-American's religion while Christianity is for the whites! Strangely enough, no one tells the African-Americans that it was Arab Muslims who captured them and sold them as slaves, or the fact that the Arabic word for *black* and *slave* is the same, *Abed.*

3. Engage the American public in dialogues, discussions, and debates in colleges, universities, public libraries, radio, TV, churches and mosques on the virtues of Islam. Proclaim how it is historically another religion like Judaism and Christianity with the same monotheistic faith.

4. Nominate Muslim sympathizers for political office to promote legislation that is favorable to Islam. Support potential sympathizers by utilizing a block voting system, in which candidates are ranked on the ballot from most to least preferred, making it easy to pinpoint the Muslim sympathizers and vote accordingly.

5. Take control of Hollywood, the media, TV, radio and the internet by purchasing certain corporations or a controlling stock.

6. Yield to the fear of imminent shut-off of the lifeblood of America – the black gold. America's economy depends on oil – over 1,000 products are derived from it – as does its personal and industrial transportation and manufacturing – 41% of America's/ of the world's oil comes from the Middle East.

7. Yell criticisms such as foul, out-of-context, personal interpretation, hate crime, Zionist, un-American, inaccurate interpretation of the Koran, etc. whenever Islam or the Koran are reproached or analyzed in the public arena.

8. Encourage Muslims to penetrate the White House, specifically with Islamists who can articulate a marvelous and peaceful picture of Islam. Acquire government positions, gain membership on local school boards. Train Muslims as medical doctors to dominate the medical field, research, and pharmaceutical companies. Take over the computer industry. Establish Middle Eastern restaurants throughout the U.S. to connect planners of Islamization in a discreet way. Ever wonder why there is a plethora of Muslim doctors in America while their own countries need them desperately?

9. Accelerate Islamic demographic growth via:

a. Massive immigration – there has been 100,000 annually since 1961.

b. No birth control whatsoever – every baby of Muslim parents is automatically a Muslim and cannot choose another religion later.

c. Muslim men must marry American women and Islamize them (10,000 annually) – then divorce them and remarry every five years – since one cannot have the Muslim legal permission to marry four at one time. This is a legal solution in America.

d. Convert angry, alienated black inmates and turn them into militants (so far 2000 released inmates have joined al-Qaeda world-wide). Only a few have been captured in Afghanistan and on American soil. (So far – sleeping cells!)

10. Reading, writing, arithmetic and research through the American educational system, mosques and student centers (now totaling 1500 in the U.S.) should be sprinkled with dislike of Jews, evangelical Christians and democracy. There are 300 exclusively Muslim schools with loyalty to the Koran, not the U.S. Constitution.

11. Provide very sizeable monetary Muslim grants to colleges and universities in America to establish "Centers for Islamic studies" with Muslim directors to promote Islam in higher education institutions.

12. Let the entire world know through propaganda, speeches, seminars, local and national media that terrorists have hijacked Islam. In actuality, this is not true; the truth is that Islam hijacked the terrorists. In January of 2002, Saudi Arabia's Embassy in Washington mailed 4,500 packets of the Koran and videos promoting Islam to America's high schools, which were received free of charge. They would never allow us to reciprocate – meaning that Saudi Arabia would never allow such distribution of the Bible and promotion of anything but Islam in their society.

13. Appeal to the historically compassionate and sensitive Americans for sympathy and tolerance toward the Muslims in America – these people are portrayed as immigrants from oppressed countries.

14. Nullify America's sense of security by manipulating the intelligence community with misinformation. Periodically terrorize Americans with impending attacks on bridges, tunnels, water supplies, airports, apartment buildings and malls. We have experienced this often since 9-11.

15. Form riots and demonstrations in the prison system and declare that the American justice system is not the way of life – Islamic *Sharia* is.

16. Open numerous charities throughout the U.S. but use the funds to support Islamic terrorism with American dollars.

17. Raise interest in Islam on America's campuses by insisting

that every freshman take at least one course on Islam. Be sure that the promoter is a bona fide American, Christian, scholarly and able to cover up the violence in the Koran and express the peaceful, spiritual and religious aspect only.

18. Unify the numerous Muslim lobbies in Washington, mosques, Islamic student centers, educational organizations, magazines and papers by Internet and an annual convention. These outlets will be used to coordinate plans, propagate the faith and engender news in the media.

19. Send intimidating messages and messengers to the outspoken individuals who are critical of Islam. Take whatever measures necessary to eliminate them.

20. Applaud Muslims as loyal citizens of the U.S. by spotlighting their voting record as the highest percentage of all minority and ethnic groups in America.[6]

The Islamic ideologues understand that all of these steps are needed to prevent resistance from an American society that still has maintained some of its biblically-based roots. This is in contrast to agnostic Europe, where political correctness took over many years ago, hence the relative passivity (i.e., a lack of action) regarding the Islamic threat. Does this mean that people in Europe are apathetic? I don't think so, but I do believe that they are intimidated that the unofficial *thought police* will accuse them of Islamophobia.

This shocking anti-democratic, anti-First Amendment silencing of those who dare to issue a warning about the Islamic threat is also happening in the U.S., where the Islamic big brother, aided by pagan leftists, is watching carefully. They accuse those who expose their facade and their misrepresentation of themselves as an oppressed minority, of being racist. One example of this occurred in the summer of 2010 in Tennessee, when a small newspaper, The Rutherford Reader, published a guest column that referred to Islam as *evil* and called for an end to Muslim immigration to the U.S. *until Muslims acquiesce to living within the legal structures of their host nations...* The newspaper was banned from a grocery store chain and a KFC outlet for allegedly publishing *hate speech*. The paper then threatened to sue, rightly asserting that its First Amendment rights had been violated.[7]

The reaction after the attack at Fort Hood by seemingly civilized, educated United States Army psychologist Nidal Malik Hassan is another prime example of how Americans have already been cowed into submission. After hearing about the attack, I was shocked by the fact that people seemed wary of stating that Hassan appeared to be an Islamic terrorist. It was immediately clear to me that this was not an isolated crazy individual, but a Muslim terrorist who, no matter how westernized and educated by American society (as was his imam), was committed to a fanatical ideology rooted in his belief in mainstream Islam. It is frightening that we do not know how many Hassans are in the on-deck circle, scheming, plotting and waiting for their moment of fame.

Then, of course, there was the new phenomenon of the American *Jihad Jane*, the blond-haired, blue-eyed, converted Muslim terrorist, quietly arrested in October 2009 by U.S. authorities. *Jihad Jane* was accused of planning to murder a Swedish artist who had depicted Muhammad in a cartoon, thereby enraging Muslims and setting off the usual death threats, attacks, and other forms of violence from the faithful devotees of the *religion of peace*. The indictment charged that from June 2008 to October 2009, Colleen LaRose, who called herself Fatima Rose, searched the Internet attempting to recruit male fighters for the cause, convincing women with Western passports to marry them and to raise money for *jihad* (the holy war).

Other related *Jihad Janes* were detained in Ireland in March 2010, including Jamie Paulin-Ramirez, a 31-year-old Colorado woman whose mother said she began talking about *jihad* with her Muslim stepfather and soon spent most of her time online, according to U.S. officials.

Paulin-Ramirez left Leadville, Colorado on September 11, 2009, with her 6-year-old son and told her family that she had married for a fourth time, to an Algerian whom she met online. Irish officials later said they had released the American woman, but she was subsequently arrested by U.S. authorities.[8]

There are millions of good Americans who practice the Muslim faith who love their country as much as I love the country, who salute the flag as strongly as I salute the flag.[9]
(President George W. Bush, September 19, 2001)

While one can understand President Bush's motivation for making such an unsubstantiated declaration just eight days after 9-11 (he hoped to lower the tensions in the aftermath of the attacks), it is not clear that his statement is true. It is also not known how many quiet Muslim supporters of terrorism there are in America. The United States needs to beware of the increasing number of terrorist threats made by the mild-mannered Hassans who are already in its midst. However, the greatest threat is the demographic time bomb of a population that bears, to a great extent, an allegiance, not to the U.S. flag or Constitution, but to the Koran, which represents an ideology that is contrary to the principles of the Constitution and the Bible on which it is based. The mosques in the Middle East, in Europe, and yes, even in America are not tranquil havens of peace, love and goodwill towards men and women, but rather are breeding grounds for hatred:

Do you realize what the mosque is? It is a prime factory educating men to fear and please Allah; (it is) the prime factory educating jihad fighters...[10]
(Al-Aqsa official on Hamas TV, April 24, 2009)

There are those who rush to the defense of Islam by pointing out the issue of fairness or discrimination. How can we impinge on religious freedom in the mosques? How can we complain about the growth of the Muslim population? Christians, Jews, or people of any other religion would never accept such an infringement upon their rights, so how can it be done to the Muslims? Perhaps those same fairness advocates would even recall the earlier historical chapter about the Egyptian enslavement of the Hebrews, pointing to what appears to similar complaints made by Pharaoh that the Hebrew population was growing too quickly. Their challenging question is obvious: Why are the Muslims in Europe or America any different than were the Hebrews in Egypt or the Jews in any other country? Don't the Muslims also have the right to peacefully have large families?

In opposition to the current State of Israel, where there is an ongoing debate concerning the extent to which Jewish historical jurisprudence should be the law of the land, it is clear – even plainly stated in Judaism – that a Jew is obligated to honor and respect the law of the country that he lives in, and not to attempt in any way to change it. This has always been the instruction given by rabbinical leaders through the centuries of dispersion amongst the nations. Jews have continuously internalized this tradition, honoring and respecting the laws and the norms of whatever country they have lived in.[11] This is fundamentally different than the message that Muslims hear from their religious leaders.

As we discussed earlier, before the Hebrews in Egypt were enslaved, they were characteristically loyal Egyptians. They rapidly abandoned their unique religious traditions in order to assimilate, with the intent to be better accepted into Egyptian society. The Hebrews had no interest in rebelling against the prevailing system in Egypt. The same was true regarding the Jews of Germany before World War II. Years earlier, many of the Jews in Germany began calling themselves *Germans of Mosaic Persuasion*. The Reform Movement in Judaism that had started in Germany many years prior, was conducted in an effort to more closely resemble the customs of the German Christian society in which they lived. The Reformists started using organs in their Sabbath services, stopped wearing head-coverings in synagogue worship and in some cases, even changed their Sabbath observance day to Sunday. All of this was done in an effort to fit in and be accepted by their Christian fellow citizens. Their primary loyalty was clearly to Germany and to their own personal self-interest as they perceived it – specifically to work hard and succeed as accepted individuals in German society – but changing Germany or its system of government, laws, and values or culture was never even considered nor desired, not by individual Jews and not by the Jewish leadership.[12]

> *The Hebrew is never a beggar; he has always kept the law – life by toil – often under severe and oppressive civil restrictions.*[13]
> (President Benjamin Harrison,
> in his Third State of the Union Address, December 9, 1891)

The contrast between Jews in the Diaspora (scattered around the world) and the European and/or American Muslims could not be greater, as the obvious Jewish desire to blend into American society has never been replicated by the Islamic-American communities. The insularity on one hand, and aggressiveness on the other, is only one aspect of the social ramifications of the Islamic desire to change America.

In a recent *Newsweek* article, the journalist Roqaya Ashmawey, deputy editor of a Muslim newspaper in Los Angeles, called on Arabs to write *Arab*, instead of *White*, in the census, the slogan of the campaign being, *Check It Right, You Ain't White*. The stated goal was to get more funding for Arab communities, but it seems somehow strange that they wouldn't be happy to be totally accepted into the majority ethnic category when given the opportunity.[14] It is instructive to read the following description of the serious nature of the problem as analyzed by socio-political commentator Daniel Pipes. This was taken from an article written shortly after the terrorist attacks on 9-11:

> *The Muslim population in this country (the United States) is not like any other group, for it includes within it a substantial body of people – many times more numerous than the agents of Osama bin Laden – who share with the suicide hijackers a hatred of the United States and the desire, ultimately, to transform it into a nation living under the strictures of militant Islam. Although not responsible for the atrocities in September, they harbor designs*

for this country that warrant urgent and serious attention.

In June 1991, Siraj Wahaj, a black convert to Islam and the recipient of some of the American Muslim community's highest honors, had the privilege of becoming the first Muslim to deliver the daily prayer in the U.S. House of Representatives. On that occasion he recited from the Koran and appealed to the Almighty to guide American leaders "and grant them righteousness and wisdom."

A little over a year later, addressing an audience of New Jersey Muslims, the same Wahaj articulated a rather different vision from his mild and moderate invocation in the House. If only Muslims were more clever politically, he told his New Jersey listeners, they could take over the United States and replace its constitutional government with a Caliphate (a government ruled by Sharia, Islamic Law). "If we were united and strong, we'd elect our own emir (leader) and give allegiance to him ... Take my word, if 6-8 million Muslims unite in America, the country will come to us." In 1995, Wahaj served as a character witness for Omar Abdel Rahman in the trial that found that blind sheikh guilty of conspiracy to overthrow the government of the United States. More alarming still, the U.S. attorney for New York listed Wahaj as one of the "unindicted persons who may be alleged as co-conspirators" in the sheikh's case.

The disparity between Wahaj's good citizenship in the House and his militant forecast of a Muslim takeover – not to mention his association with violent felons – is only one example of a larger pattern common to the American Muslim scene. Another example ... involves the American Muslims for Jerusalem, an organization whose official advocacy of "a Jerusalem that symbolizes religious tolerance and dialogue" contrasts markedly with the wild conspiracy-mongering and crude anti-Jewish rhetoric which its spokesmen indulge in at their closed events. At a minimum, then, anyone who would understand the real views of American Muslims must delve deeper than the surface of their public statements.[15]

Are these simply two isolated examples of the dual strategy of preaching peace and love to the American mainstream, while speaking of aggressive takeover to the Muslim masses? A Jewish chaplain in the New York area recently described to me a conversation that he had with his Muslim counterpart. They were discussing the nature of the *halal*, or the Islamic way of slaughtering animals. The imam told the rabbi that it is forbidden for a Muslim to put in his mouth any animal that was angry, so before slaughtering, the Muslims first attempt to calm the animal as much as possible. It appears to me that a frightening analogy can be made here with the present Islamic encounter in America. Islamic activists in the United States are doing everything in their power to calm the American public with soothing words in perfect English about the beauty of Islam, while simultaneously planning and working toward an aggressive takeover, preparing the animal for the slaughter. This is happening in the educational realm, where, in recent years, there has been a sharp increase in Islamic studies programs in American universities. There has also been an increase in religious programming. Both of these programs are heavily funded by the wealthy Persian Gulf nations. Do the heads of these college programs fit the Jewish-American model of assimilation and a passion for the land of the free and the home of the brave? Do these Islamic professors teach in the American university spirit of vigorous intellectual exchange of ideas? For the answer, let's go to the ivory tower of Yale University to hear from the intellectual elite of Muslim-American educators.

Zaid Shakir, formerly the Muslim chaplain at Yale University, has stated that Muslims cannot accept the legitimacy of the American secular system, which "is against the orders and ordainments of Allah." To the contrary, "The orientation of the Koran pushes us in the exact opposite direction."[16]

Whether and to what degree the community as a whole subscribes to the Islamist agenda are, of course, open questions. But what is not open to question is that, whatever the majority of Muslim Americans may believe, most of the *organized* Muslim community agrees with the Islamist goal – which is to gradually transform America. Sadly, the major Muslim organizations in this country are in the hands of extremists.

Not all these organizations and spokesmen are open about their aspirations. However, some are. For example, the International Institute of Islamic Thought in Herndon, Virginia, proclaims its academic purpose to be nothing less than *the Islamization of the humanities and the social sciences.* But the best-known organizations – those whose members are invited to offer prayers and invocations before Congress, to attend White House functions, or whose representatives accompanied the President on his September 17th visit to a mosque – tend to hide their true colors behind arch-respectable goals. The American Muslim Council claims to work *toward the political empowerment of Muslims in America,* the Council on American-Islamic Relations claims to be *putting faith into action,* and the Muslim Public Affairs Council seeks only to make American Muslims *an influential component in U.S. public affairs.*[17]

It behooves us to pay close attention, not to what is said in mainstream American public forums, in which Muslim leaders are careful about what they say and how they say it, but to what these Islamic organizational leaders generally reveal when they speak to their own people in Arabic, Farsi, or even occasionally in English. In fact, they are downright secretive and devious, for fear of being exposed for who they really are.

In a December 10, 2009 CNN interview, the generally well-respected Reverend Franklin Graham reiterated past statements that he had made calling Islam "an evil and wicked religion … True Islam cannot be practiced in this country," he told CNN's Campbell Brown. "You can't beat your wife. You cannot murder your children if you think they've committed adultery or something like that, which they do practice in these other countries."

Perhaps the most immediate and razor-sharp response came from The Council on American-Islamic Relations (CAIR). As previously alluded to, CAIR is a Washington-based

Victim of the Islamic Thought Police: Rev. Franklin Graham was blasted for voicing his opinion about the incompatibility of Islam with the values of America.

Islamic organization which presents itself as a moderate Islamic-American civil rights organization, but the reality is far less altruistic, to say the least.

In a letter sent to Rev. Graham, CAIR National Executive Director Nihad Awad called for an urgent meeting at which Graham would be offered accurate and balanced information about Islam. Awad wrote: "I believe your views on Islam are unworthy of a respected religious leader and are based on misinformation and misconceptions that could be cleared up in a face-to-face meeting with representatives of the American Muslim community..."[18]

On the surface, this sounds like a reasonable and respectable appeal for tolerance and dialogue in order to clear up what seemed to be Rev. Graham's misconceptions about Islam. The letter from CAIR Director Awad to Graham was well-publicized, but, in contrast, much less reported was the following quote from Omar Ahmed, Chairman of the Board of CAIR:

> Islam isn't in America to be equal to any other faith, but to become dominant. The Koran should be the highest authority in America, and Islam the only accepted religion on Earth.[19]

It seems that CAIR's Chairman of the Board inadvertently clarified the real agenda of the organization. Likewise, CAIR spokesman Ibrahim Hooper stated in a newspaper interview that he hopes to see an Islamic government over the U.S. some day, brought about not by violence but through *education*.[20] Had Rev. Graham accepted the invitation to meet with the leaders of CAIR, I highly doubt that he would have heard the words spoken by Ahmed or Hooper. However, when Ahmed, Hooper and others like them have a slip of the tongue, are speaking to their own Muslim people, or perhaps are not expecting to be in front of the general public, the message is almost always a message of *jihad*, dominance, and/or submission. The truth is only barely hidden. No, Rev. Graham didn't need a lesson in tolerance or an Islam 101 course. The Koran and his decades of experience as a Christian missionary in oppressive Islamic countries like the Sudan, taught Graham that Islam is intolerant, violent, and justifies the oppression of non-Muslims and women. For expressing those views, which were based on facts as well as on his perceptions, he was blasted as a bigot and an Islamophobe by the ostensible defenders of civil rights. The silencing process continued in May of 2010, when Rev. Graham, the honorary chairman of the 2010 National Day of Prayer Task Force, was disinvited from the event by the Defense Department. The Army, which oversees this National Day of Prayer event in Washington, DC and honors America's soldiers, reportedly feared that if Graham spoke, Islamic militants would publicize his comments. This would have supposedly fueled tensions in Muslim nations like Iraq and Afghanistan, where U.S. troops were currently deployed.[21]

Most proponents of *political correctness* see no problem with these attempts to silence those individuals who seek only to express their opinions about the danger of the Islamic ideology. As long as a Christian, Zionist or conservative activist is under attack, it's okay, since this is seen as an opportunity to bash and slander those with whom they disagree. In general, radical liberal and secular activists use the Islamic agenda freely in an effort to silence or hurt the people who they perceive to be their enemies. Nevertheless, I humbly suggest that they put aside those prejudices and take a careful look at the reality of the situation. I have no doubt that Islamists, once they achieve power, will demand *Dhimmi* status for them, as well. The Islamic *thought police*, now focused on intimidating and silencing Rev. Graham and many others, will eventually take aim at the secular leftists. Once *jihadists* no longer have any use for their former liberal allies, the Islamic tsunami will reach their doorsteps and will engulf them as well.

Chapter Eight

Education In The Land Of The Free

T he Islamists in North America use the democratic system to accomplish their undemocratic goals, not in lieu of the violence, terrorism, and intimidation, but as a supplement, along with a different, seemingly more peaceful form of intimidation. In a May 2010 interview with *FrontPage Magazine* reporter Jamie Glazov, Brooke M. Goldstein of the Legal Project at the Middle East Forum stated:

> One tenet of Sharia law is to punish those who criticize Islam, and to silence speech considered blasphemous against Islam, or its Prophet Muhammad. The Islamist movement has two wings – that which operates violently, propagating suicide-homicide bombing and other terrorist activities, and that which operates lawfully, conducting a "soft jihad," within our court systems, through Sharia banking, within our school systems and through organizations such as the Council on American-Islamic Relations and the Canadian Islamic Congress. Both the violent and the lawful arms of the Islamist movement can and do work apart, but often, their work re-enforces each other's.[1]

The university and legal systems are not the only ones being exploited to promote an anti-American agenda. The American public educational system is another frequent target, due to the fact that the cabal of Islamic ideologues, which is heavily funded by the Wahabi ideologues in Saudi Arabia, seeks to promote its oppressive, violent religion of submission to young and vulnerable children. It is presented as some sort of benign, harmonious source of spiritual bliss that can benefit all of humanity. Translations of the Koran into English often write God, instead of Allah, to imply that the Koran is speaking about the God of Abraham, Isaac, and Jacob, which the Bible speaks of. All of this is intended to make Islam comfortable and even familiar for the average American, as one of the *three great monotheistic religions.* Thus, they once again succeed in cynically taking advantage of America's famed tolerance and its openness to new ideas and pluralism – all religions and ideologies need to be considered equal, right? Not according to John Quincy Adams, the sixth President of the United States. Adams, while a firm defender of liberty, did not agree that truth and morality are relative:

*The precept of the Koran is, perpetual war against all who deny, that Mahomet (Muhammad) is the prophet of God. The vanquished may purchase their lives, by the payment of tribute; the victorious may be appeased by a false and delusive promise of peace; and the faithful follower of the prophet, may submit to the imperious necessities of defeat: but the command to propagate the Moslem creed by the sword is always obligatory, **when it can be made effective.** The commands of the prophet may be performed alike, **by fraud, or by force.** (Emphases mine.)*[2]

Before the Age of Political Correctness: *President John Quincy Adams didn't hesitate to voice his disdain for Islam and he was quite direct and unapologetic.*

(John Quincy Adams, 1829)

What exactly is the nature of the educational principles that the Saudis and other Gulf oil states are exporting to America?

After fifteen of the nineteen 9-11 terrorists were found to be born or raised in Saudi Arabia, the Saudi Arabian government shifted its propaganda machine into high gear, concerned about the public relations disaster that could ensue from the knowledge that most of the 9-11 terrorists were from their soil.

The Saudi leadership promised to purge its educational curriculum in order to remove all remnants of intolerance, later announcing through its embassy that this had been accomplished. Nina Shea, director of Freedom House's Center for Religious Freedom, investigated these claims and found them to be sorely lacking, to say the least. Here are some highlights of her report in the Washington Post:

> *A review of a sample of official Saudi textbooks for Islamic studies used during the current academic year reveals that, despite the Saudi government's statements to the contrary, an ideology of hatred toward Christians and Jews and Muslims who do not follow Wahabi doctrine remains in this area of the public school system. The texts teach a dualistic vision, dividing the world into true believers of Islam (the monotheists) and unbelievers (the polytheists and infidels).*
>
> *The Saudi public school system totals 25,000 schools, educating about 5 million students. In addition, Saudi Arabia runs academies in 19 world capitals, including one in Fairfax County, just outside of Washington DC. These academies utilize those official Saudi religious texts.*
>
> *Saudi Arabia also distributes its religion texts worldwide to numerous Islamic schools and madrassas that it does not directly operate. Undeterred by Wahabism's historically fringe status, Saudi Arabia is trying to assert itself as the world's authoritative voice on Islam – a sort of Vatican for Islam, as several Saudi officials have stated – and these textbooks are integral to this effort.*
>
> *As the report of the commission investigating the September 11 attacks observed, Even in affluent countries, Saudi-funded*

Wahabi schools are often the only Islamic schools available.

Here are but a few samples from the official K-12 curriculum: (Note that this English translation uses the word God instead of Allah, but you will see that the God spoken about here is very different from the God of the Bible.)

Sixth Grade

Just as Muslims were successful in the past when they came together in a sincere endeavor to evict the Christian crusaders from Palestine, so will the Arabs and Muslims emerge victorious, God willing, against the Jews and their allies if they stand together and fight a true jihad for God, for this is within God's power.

Eighth Grade

As cited in Ibn Abbas: The apes are Jews, the people of the Sabbath; while the swine are the Christians, the infidels of the communion of Jesus.

God told His Prophet, Muhammad, about the Jews, who learned from parts of God's book (the Torah and the Gospels) that God alone is worthy of worship. Despite this, they espouse falsehood through idol-worship, soothsaying, and sorcery. In doing so, they obey the devil. They prefer the people of falsehood to the people of the truth out of envy and hostility. This earns them condemnation and is a warning to us not to do as they did.

They are the Jews, whom God has cursed and with whom He is so angry that He will never again be satisfied (with them).

Some of the people of the Sabbath were punished by being turned into apes and swine. Some of them were made to worship the devil, and not God, through consecration, sacrifice, prayer, appeals for help, and other types of worship. Some of the Jews worship the devil. Likewise, some members of this nation worship the devil, and not God.

Twelfth Grade

Jihad (holy war) in the path of God – which consists of

battling against unbelief, oppression, injustice, and those who perpetrate it – is the summit of Islam. This religion arose through jihad and through jihad was its banner raised high. It is one of the noblest acts, which brings one closer to God, and one of the most magnificent acts of obedience to God.[3]

The Saudi Arabians have already made significant inroads into the American educational system – including publicly-funded education – but the Saudi royal family isn't the only extreme example of wealthy Islamic ideologues using their oil wealth for nefarious purposes. A secretive network of Islamic radicals known as the FGC (Fethullah Gülen Community) is named for a wealthy Turkish imam and Islamic ideologue who established a network of at least 85 publicly-supported Islamic charter schools throughout the nation. Gülen fled Turkey in 1998 to avoid prosecution, which charged that he was attempting to undermine Turkey's then-secular government and establish an Islamic government. He now lives in the United States. The recent rise of the Islamic AKP party – *Adalet ve Kalkinma Partisi*, a Turkish political party that advocates a liberal market economy and Turkish membership in the European Union – and its anti-American, anti-Israel alliance with the Iranian-Syrian axis prove that Gülen's efforts were eventually successful in Turkey. After Gülen's arrival in the United States, the Department of Homeland Security tried to deport him, but he successfully fought the effort in federal court due to a ruling which stated that he was an individual with *extraordinary ability in the field of education* – although he has no formal education training.

According to an article in the Jane's Islamic Affairs Analyst (February 2009), Gülen stated that *in order to reach the ideal Muslim society, every method and path is acceptable,* (including) *lying to people.* This public acknowledgement of *taqiyya* (employing deception to advance Islam) is highly pertinent to Gülen's activities in the United States and *indicative of the overall strategy employed by those planting the groundwork for the Islamic takeover of America.*[4]

> *And they (the disbelievers) schemed, and Allah schemed (against them): and Allah is the best of schemers.*
>
> (Sura 3:54)

The Arabic word used here for scheme (or plot) is *makara*, which literally means deceit. If Allah is deceitful toward unbelievers, then certainly Muslims in our times are allowed to do the same.

It is interesting to note that the Islamic concept of *taqiyya* jibes quite well with the philosophy of radical left-wing ideologue Saul Alinsky. Although he died in 1972, Alinsky, who called himself a "community organizer," was indirectly a mentor of none other than Barack Obama, who taught Alinsky's radical political philosophy for the ACORN political action organization in Chicago. As explained by political analyst David Horowitz:

> *Revolutionary warfare, which is not about compromise, must be conducted through deception. Thus the rules for the organizers of revolutions, laid down by Alinsky, are rules for deception.*[4a]

The concept of deception in radical Left philosophy and the Islamic concept of *taqiyya* both serve well their matching goals of destroying the American system. Despite their divergent concepts of radical Communist vs. Islamic rule, they cynically cooperate in their dishonest means to bring American liberty and justice to its knees.

Here are several glaring examples of Islamic abuse of the American free education system and its exploitation – which aim toward the ultimate purpose of eventually destroying the value system that it represents:

> *...Students at Friendswood Junior High in Houston were required to attend an Islamic Awareness presentation during class time allotted for physical education. The presentation involved two representatives from the Council on American-Islamic Relations, an organization with a record of Islamist statements and terrorism convictions. According to students, they were taught that there is one God, his name is Allah and*

that Adam, Noah, and Jesus are prophets. Students were also taught about the Five Pillars of Islam, how to pray five times a day and to wear Islamic religious garb. Parents were not notified about the presentation; it wasn't until a number of complaints were submitted that school officials responded with an apologetic e-mail.

...At Lake Brantley High School in Seminole County, Florida, speakers from the Academy for Learning Islam (ALI) gave a presentation to students about cultural diversity that extended to a detailed discussion of the Koran and Islam. The school neither screened the ALI speakers nor notified parents. After a number of complaints, local media coverage and a subsequent investigation, the school district apologized for the inappropriate presentation, admitting that it violated the law.

Amherst Middle School transformed the quaint colonial town of Amherst, NH, into a Saudi Arabian Bedouin tent community. Male and female students were segregated, with the girls hosting hijab and veil stations and handing out the oppressive head-to-toe black garment known as the abaya to female guests. Meanwhile, the boys hosted food and Arabic dancing stations because, as explained in the article, the traditions of Saudi Arabia at this time prevent women from participating in these public roles. An Islamic religion station offered up a prayer rug, verses from the Koran, prayer items and a compass that pointed towards Mecca. The fact that female subjugation was presented as a benign cultural practice and that Islamic religious rituals were promoted with public funds is cause for concern.[5]

Along with giving money for textbooks and curricula, the Saudis are also involved in funding and designing training for public school teachers. The Saudi-funded Prince Alwaleed Bin Talal Center for Muslim-Christian Understanding (ACMCU) at Georgetown University now offers professional development workshops for K-12 teachers. The workshops take place at the hosting institution and provide teachers with classroom material. They are free of charge and include lunch, which is paid for by

ACMCU.

But this show of generosity likely comes with a catch, for the center is known for producing scholars and material with a decidedly apologist slant, toward both the Saudi royal family and Islamic radicalism. It's no accident that ACMCU education consultant Susan Douglass, according to her bio, has been an affiliated scholar with the Council on Islamic Education for over a decade. Douglass also taught social studies at the Islamic Saudi Academy (ISA) in Fairfax, Virginia, where her husband still teaches. ISA has come under investigation for Saudi-provided textbooks and curriculum that allegedly promotes hatred and intolerance towards non-Muslims. That someone with Douglass' problematic associations would be in charge of training public school teachers hardly inspires confidence in the system.[6]

As you can see, the evidence is extensive, and we have only scratched the surface. Islamic efforts at exploiting American liberty to further its gradual undoing are ongoing and well-funded. In a sense, it's understandable that when a budget-pressed school system is offered a totally funded, comprehensive, multi-media curriculum for its students, with staff and meals provided, it fails to see through the facade of openness, multi-cultural education, and pluralism. Understandable, yes. But acceptable? The goal of Muslim propagandists is to end the very openness that they exploit in order to get these programs into the educational system, but the long-term goal is not freedom of religion or free speech for all.

On February 8, 2010, the Israeli Ambassador and history scholar Michael Oren spoke to a group of a few hundred college students at the University of California, Irvine. From the very beginning of his speech, Oren was heckled continuously by Muslim students who, possibly incited by the rhetoric of the college's Muslim Students Union, shouted slogans and insults throughout. Despite repeated requests by the frustrated professors who organized the event, and appeals from other members of the audience, the Ambassador was not allowed to speak. Such intolerance and refusal to accept the American university tradition of the intellectual free exchange of ideas was apparently shocking for the organizing professors, as well as the non-Muslim students. However, it was in the finest Islamic tradition of intolerance towards those who hold beliefs that differ from Islam:

> *O Prophet! Rouse the Believers to the fight. If there are twenty amongst you, patient and persevering, they will vanquish two hundred: if a hundred, they will vanquish a thousand of the Unbelievers: for these are a people without understanding.*
>
> (Sura 8:65)

> *If the freedom of speech is taken away then dumb and silent we may be led, like sheep to the slaughter.*[7]
>
> (George Washington,
> Speech to Officers, March 15, 1783)

Freedom of speech and freedom of belief may not be the Islamic way, but it is certainly the American way. Do Americans really want this fifth column to cynically – whether the nature is violent or peaceful – use American freedom to destroy these very liberties which have made America great? It's much easier in the short-term to ignore the impending challenge, in other words, to look within and concentrate only on work, family and one's own backyard. Americans have become passive, indeed almost helpless, in the face of this assault on their values, but that state of mind is far more dangerous than the danger itself.

> *The world is a dangerous place to live, not because of the people who are evil, but because of the people who don't do anything about it.*[8]
>
> (Albert Einstein)

> *Those who stand for nothing fall for anything.*[9]
>
> (Alexander Hamilton)

Until the relatively recent assault on its values by the forces of moral relativism, America has always stood for the values of its

Judeo-Christian civilization. It has also fought to protect its system of *liberty and justice for all*. Indeed, for all of its social shortcomings in its history, the American mind is typically open to change, improvement, and advancement in all spheres of life.

The women's suffrage and the civil rights movements were products of American humility – the willingness to engage in self-introspection and to draw from that a vision that is necessary for social advancement. This sense of vision has also been evident in realms of scientific research and development.

It is certainly no accident that the U.S. was the undisputed world leader in space exploration, at least until the mysterious reversal of policy under the Obama Administration. In a July 2010 interview, NASA Administrator Charles Bolden, in an extraordinary display of candor, revealed the bizarre mission that had recently been entrusted to him by the President of the United States. NASA – National Aeronautical Space Agency – is the governmental body which is responsible for exploring new frontiers in outer space, sending astronauts to the moon, building rockets, spaceships and space stations for scientific research, and planning flights to other planets to advance human knowledge. Now NASA has a new high priority mission, assigned to its chief administrator by President Obama:

> *When I became the NASA administrator – or before I became the NASA administrator – he charged me with three things. One was he wanted me to help re-inspire children to want to get into science and math, he wanted me to expand our international relationships, and third, and perhaps foremost, he wanted me to find a way to reach out to the Muslim world and engage much more with dominantly Muslim nations to help them feel good about their historic contribution to science ... and math and engineering.*[10]

Isn't that sweet? Pandering to Islam is NASA's new mission. Helping the Islamic nations present a facade to the world by saying that they are in the forefront of scientific and

The Saudi-Obama Connection Exposed: *Formerly Manhattan Borough President, Cable TV mogul, and past lawyer for Malcolm X, Percy Sutton had no apparent reason to expose Obama's Saudi connections, but in what seemed to be a slip of tongue in an interview, he revealed the Obama-Prince Alwaleed connection.*

space research – that is the new primary mission of NASA! This fits neatly into the Islamist agenda of presenting a deceptively open-minded, progressive image to the Western world – quite the opposite of the *Sharia*-based vision that is their true intention.

The tentacles of Islamic aggression reached their highest levels of American influence when it was revealed that Barack Obama's higher education was likely financed and guided by the anti-American, anti-Israel alliance of secular leftists and Islamist ideologues. In 2008, Percy Sutton, the former Manhattan Borough President and media mogul who had previously served as lawyer for Malcolm X, appeared in an interview on the *Inside City Hall* program on the NY1 cable television channel. Sutton revealed that radical American Muslim ideologue Khalid al-Mansour, (a.k.a. Donald Warden), a former mentor to Black Panthers founders Huey Newton and Bobby Seale, had called him over twenty years earlier with a specific request.[11] Al-Mansour, who Sutton described as *the principal advisor to one of the world's richest men*, asked him to write a letter to Harvard University on behalf of a young law school applicant named Barack Obama. Sutton went on to say that al-Mansour *was then raising money* for Obama, apparently for his education, although the reason why al-Mansour would be raising money for a virtually unknown young student was not divulged. The wealthy man for whom al-Mansour was

King Abdullah's Man In Washington: Prince Alwaleed bin Talal of Saudi Arabia was revealed to have financed, although perhaps indirectly, the young Barack Obama's college education. It's difficult not to wonder – What else has he financed for Obama and more importantly, why?

the principal advisor was none other than Prince Alwaleed bin Talal of Saudi Arabia, the nephew of Saudi Arabian King Abdullah.[12] Before Sutton's revelation, Alwaleed was already infamous for his back-handed offer in 2001 to donate $10 million to New York City after the World Trade Center attacks, while simultaneously lecturing the United States that it *must address some of the issues that led to such a criminal attack* and *re-examine its policies in the Middle East.* New York Mayor Rudolph Giuliani turned down the donation, sharply criticizing the Saudi prince for drawing *a moral equivalency between liberal democracies like the United States, like Israel, and terrorist states and those that condone terrorism.* In April 2009, Alwaleed donated $20 million to Harvard University.[13] It was also reported that radical leftist and Obama associate William Ayers was the one who originally solicited al-Mansour back in 1987 to raise money for Obama's Harvard Law School education.[14]

This strange, complex collusion of anti-American, anti-Israeli extreme leftists – such as the radical Ayers – with anti-American, anti-Israeli Muslims attempting to influence governments and universities on behalf of aggressive, repressive Islamic monarchies such as Saudi Arabia fits a dangerous pattern that demands our immediate attention. The *friendly* Saudi royal family has been exposed for directly and discreetly providing financial support to terrorist groups like al-Qaeda in Iraq, so it's clear that the veil of moderation covering Saudi faces is a deceitful desert mirage.[15] Nonetheless, the royal family's apparent *peaceful* involvement with homegrown radical American Muslims such as al-Mansour is even more pernicious. Could it be that Obama's infamous bow to King Abdullah of Saudi Arabia had something to do with his gratitude to them for financing his college education?

It is a well-known fact that Obama raised more money for his 2008 presidential campaign than any candidate in history. Could the Saudis have had something to do with that? Sadly, the media betrayed its objectivity by allowing the White House to bury the Percy Sutton and Khalid al-Mansour story. The use of al-Mansour by the Saudis to nurture and groom young dynamic leaders like Barack Obama to further their anti-American and anti-Israeli agenda seems to jibe with the 20 practical Islamic strategies that Dr. Anis Shorrosh elucidated so well in the previous chapter. These are the battle plans for the Islamic Revolution in the West; it would be foolish to ignore the wealth of evidence that is becoming more apparent with each passing day. However, the problem is far greater than any one personality. Despite our current focus on Barack Obama, it is essential that we avoid the over-emphasis on personalities that is so prevalent in the West. Let me make it very clear: Obama is not the core problem – he is a symptom of a cancerous growth that will only get bigger until it is confronted head on.

We have discussed the preliminary manifestations of those strategies in action, which the Islamists have used to minimize the ability of the American public to resist the Islamic demographic onslaught, but those manifestations could be at a more advanced stage than we care to recognize. What is their long-term goal? The eventual, but complete replacement of the once magnificent American legal and educational system with an oppressive system of *Sharia* and the imposition of *Dhimmitude*, would essentially destroy the long-standing claim that the United States is *the land of the free*. This is not an illusionary scenario that I've created, nor is it simply a polemic from a Jewish Israeli American Zionist. I care deeply about both Israel and the U.S., and I believe, as I am sure that the Islamic radicals believe, that both stand squarely in the way of the Islamic Revolution's path to dominance. I have placed the facts before you to carefully examine without fear, but with a sense of hard realism and openness to recognizing the severity of the situation.

Victory for Islam on the Ruins of 9-11: Imam Feisal Abdul Rauf, the architect of the Cordoba Initiative at Ground Zero.

There has been much discussion in the news about *The Cordoba Initiative*, an Islamic effort with masked funding to build a 15-story mosque and Islamic cultural center next to Ground Zero in Manhattan. The name of the project is not without significance. Cordoba was the city in southern Spain where the first great mosque in Spain was built at the onset of the Islamic conquest in the eighth century. It also serves as a symbol of this conquest. The great mosque in Cordoba had been built on the foundations of a Christian Cathedral that they had destroyed. Could the goal of The Cordoba Initiative be a similar symbol at Ground Zero? After much contentious debate and public comment, Manhattan Community Board One gave the neighborhood residents' approval on May 25, 2010. *It's a seed of peace*, board member Rob Townley said. *We believe that this is a significant step in the Muslim community to counteract the hate and fanaticism in the minority of the community.*[16]

Sounds great, doesn't it? There can be no doubt that the Islamic movers and shakers want to show that Islam is a religion of peace and love and the American way. If that were actually the

On the Ruins: *After the attacks on the World Trade Center in Manhattan, several rescue workers stare at the ruins of the Twin Towers.*

case, all freedom of speech advocates would certainly agree, but when one removes the rose-colored glasses, the picture is quite different and very disturbing.

The Cordoba Initiative – which the Islamic movers and shakers are now shrewdly calling by its nice, friendly Manhattan type-name, Park 51 in order to hide the significance of the name Cordoba – has been spearheaded by the Imam Feisal Abdul Rauf. In his 2004 book, *What's Right With Islam Is What's Right with America*, Rauf referred to his goal of implementing *Sharia* in America, boldly proclaiming that *The American political structure is Sharia-compliant.* Even more revealing is the title of the Arabic version of his book, which was published in 2007, *A Call to Prayer from the World Trade Center Rubble: Islamic Da'wah (Proselytizing) from the Heart of America Post-9/11.* The title clearly reveals that the building of the 15-story mosque next to Ground Zero is seen as a symbolic victory for the cause of *da'wah* and *jihad.* The imam makes it quite clear that his goal is not to prop up the virtually nonexistent moderates, but rather to achieve the gradual imposition of *Sharia* in America.[17] As America is what he calls *Sharia-compliant,* the 15-story mosque and Islamic Center at Ground Zero would be a valuable weapon to be used against an innocent and unsuspecting population, whose liberal instincts cause them to assume the best intentions in others, even at their own peril. Would that same community board in Manhattan have approved a 15-story Nazi Center shortly after the outbreak of World War II? What is the value of freedom without a concurrent instinct for self-preservation?

It's not an accident that on the Temple Mount in Jerusalem, on the very site where Solomon's Temple stood in the heart of the Kingdom of Israel 3,000 years ago, the Muslims built the Dome of the Rock. This huge mosque was built exactly on the ruins of the Temple, at the holiest site in Judaism. Although the Torah mentions Jerusalem well over 700 times, Jerusalem is never mentioned in the Koran. Mecca and Medina in Saudi Arabia are clearly considered by Islam to be their holy cities, and Muslims

If I Forget Thee, O Mecca: *Muslims in prayer on the Temple Mount in Jerusalem, facing Mecca, away from the Temple site in Jerusalem. Since the days of Solomon's kingdom in Jerusalem, Jews have always prayed in the direction of the Holy of Holies, on the Temple Mount, in Jerusalem, in the Land of Israel.*

on the Temple Mount in Jerusalem pray with their rear ends in the direction of the Holy of Holies.

> *Their backs were toward the Temple of the Lord and their faces were toward the east, bowing eastward to the sun.*
>
> (Ezekiel 8:16)

Therefore, there were no innocent spiritual reasons to build the Dome of the Rock on the Temple Mount. However, it was considered high priority for the Muslims to build a symbol of Islamic victory on top of the ruins of the Jewish Temple. That was clearly the only reason for building it specifically at that site.

We have seen similar scenarios play out at other sites in Israel where mosques were built on sacred ground, such as the Tomb of the Patriarchs and Matriarchs of Israel in Hebron and at the Tomb of Samuel the Prophet, just north of Jerusalem. The purpose has always been to proclaim Islamic victory, as exemplified in the Islamic war chant, *Allah is greater!* The 15-story mosque and Islamic Center at Ground Zero is no symbol of moderation or sympathy for the victims of Islamic terror; it is clearly intended as a very visible symbol of Islamic victory, on the road to full domination and the eventual submission of the sleeping American giant.

If the proponents of Islamic victory and domination are successful, another such symbol would be the very site of Ground Zero itself. FOX News legal analyst Peter Johnson Jr. revealed that the Port Authority of New York and New Jersey, the owner of the Ground Zero site, is seeking a private partner to partially own and fully operate the proposed 1 World Trade Center building. One of the finalists in the bidding process was a company called The Related Companies, which is substantially bankrolled with billions of dollars in investments and/or loans by the most powerful Arab corporate interests in the world. These include companies with close ties to the Saudi and Abu Dhabi governments and royal families. If this sounds familiar, it's no accident. A particularly popular photo simulation seen widely on the internet after the 9-11 attacks showed an imaginary New York City skyline of

We Will Never Forget: *One week after the attacks, the rescue workers turned the rubble-strewn World Financial Center at Ground Zero into a memorial site, with the vow never to forget. Is a 15-story Islamic Cultural Center and mosque the proper memorial at the site of the largest single Islamic terrorist attack in this century?*

mosques. It was considered by many to be amusing, but this is no joke. The attempts to acquire the valuable real estate at Ground Zero are not innocent investments made by financially astute Arab businessmen who just happen to be Muslims. Rather, these are attempts to force a *Sharia-compliant* nation to submit to Islam at the site of its greatest *victory*, all in the name of American freedom.[18]

Even Fox News, long considered to be the sole bastion of right-of-center analysis and commentary among the major television networks, has seemingly failed to elude the tentacles of the growing Islamic takeover. Fox is one of the media giants owned by Rupert Murdoch's News Corporation. Here, too, Prince Alwaleed bin Talal of Saudi Arabia, through his Kingdom Holding Company, is making his presence felt. He now owns 7% of News Corp.'s shares, making his Kingdom Holdings the single largest shareholder, aside from members of the Murdoch family. Has Fox become the next target for his thinly-veiled radical Islamic agenda? The process seems to have already begun.[19] In 2005, just months after Alwaleed acquired his first 5.4% stake in News Corp., Fox News covered riots in Paris under a banner saying "Muslim riots." Alwaleed allegedly called Murdoch and had him change the banner to say "Civil riots." In addition, investigative journalist Joseph Trento reported that a comment he made on a Fox Network morning news show, *Fox and Friends*, about Saudi Arabian money still financing al-Qaeda, was edited out of the show.[20]

Is this merely the wonderful spirit of American finance and investment, or is it an attempt to exploit the free American business climate to gradually turn the media into a mouthpiece for Islam? We are confronted with the now classic question of whether a nation built on liberty has the obligation to allow misuse of that very liberty and to self-destruct in the face of a hostile takeover. What will be our response to this fatal question, the very same question that has guided the ongoing Ground Zero Mosque debate?

A story has been told about Rabbi Elya Meir Bloch, who was in a Chicago train station waiting to board a train to New York, while a few feet away stood an express train to San Francisco. He asked his students who were accompanying him, *How far apart are these two trains?* They speculated that there was a distance of eight, perhaps ten feet between them. He firmly disagreed: *These two trains are 3,000 miles apart; one is headed to California and the other to New York.*[21]

The two trains that Rabbi Bloch described, on the surface, appear to be nearly identical when viewed side by side, but because of their sharply conflicting destinations, they are actually miles apart. The Muslims of America may attend the same schools, shop in the same stores, and vote in the same elections as other Americans, but because of the deviant goals of Islam, they are on a train with a very different destination. They are seeking to steer the historical American train in a shockingly dangerous direction. As a wise man once told me, the end does justify the means, generally speaking, but if the end is rotten to the core, no means can justify it.

The challenge issued by the Islamic Revolution to the United States, Israel, Europe, and to the remainder of the free world, is clear and much more immediate than we have been led to or have wanted to believe. The American propensity for *looking after one's own backyard* can lead to passivity, but must be transformed into a renewed commitment to protect the common good and future generations from the violent and aggressive non-violent threat to Western civilization. This will require maturity of vision, ability to see the full picture, and a willingness to speak the truth without fear of being attacked for those beliefs. The fear of Islam is not a phobia, an anxiety, or an irrational fear that needs to be treated. It is a very real fear of an ideology that all Americans should be concerned about and prepared to do battle against it with eyes wide open.

Chapter Nine

Those Who Bless Israel

If Israel goes down, we all go down. To defend Israel's right to exist in peace, within secure borders, requires a degree of moral and strategic clarity that too often seems to have disappeared in Europe. The United States shows worrying signs of heading in the same direction. [1]

(Former President of Spain José María Aznar, June 2010)

I will bless those who bless you, and him who curses you I will curse, and all of the families of the earth will be blessed through you.

(Genesis 12:1-3)

The global recession that originated in the United States shocked American society in its entirety, from the upper echelons of the wealthy, all the way to the hungry and the poor. Economists in the United States and around the world have spent countless hours analyzing the events that initiated skyrocketing unemployment at all levels, caused massive housing foreclosures, and increased the national debt of the world's largest economy by trillions of dollars. Much of the blame fell on former President George W. Bush for his alleged mishandling of the economy, which caused the collapse of the markets in 2008, and his successor, President Obama, has been heavily criticized for multiplying the national debt in his attempts to stimulate the economy through big spending on national projects. Was this done recklessly? I will leave that debate to the financial and political analysts. What is clear, however, is that the ramifications of the actions (or inaction) of these politicians will be felt for years to come.

What most concerns me is that the spiritual component in this modern economic downturn is being ignored. It is certainly not considered "politically correct" to quote biblical verses on mainstream media, and especially not in the context of discussing current events like the recession, terrorism, or war. The separation of religion and state has become so ingrained in American culture that even when the debate concerns social/moral issues like abortion or homosexual marriage, it has become unacceptable to use the *G-word* on the air in any substantive way. In this context, it depends on which *G-word* – Gay is ok, while *God* is not. Concerning those two social/moral issues, it has somehow become out of bounds, and even a target of ridicule, to mention God in public, as if He can't possibly have an opinion on some topical issues. This unspoken, unwritten ban on the relevance of Scripture has prevented American society from confronting the deeper issues that threaten its survival as a world power. A nation that has lost its moral compass will eventually lose its will to live.

> *I am sure that never was there a people, who had more reason to acknowledge a Divine interposition in their affairs, than those of the United States; and I should be pained to believe that they have forgotten that agency, which was so often manifested during our Revolution, or that they failed to consider the omnipotence of that God who is alone able to protect them.*[2]
> (George Washington, March 11, 1792)

If Washington were alive today, he would no doubt want to remind his fellow Americans to once again look to the relevance of the Almighty God and to seek guidance from Him. That, in and of itself, is a challenge – to change the mind-set of a man-centered society, but once that barrier of knee-jerk rejection has been surmounted, how can one learn from His teachings? Upon opening the Bible – the bestselling book of all time – there is no mistaking the central issue on God's spiritual priority list. When it comes to biblical imperatives, the front page news should discuss the issue of what the Muslim activists derisively call *The Zionist Enemy*, otherwise known as Israel. The word Israel is mentioned 2,293 times in the King James version of the Bible. While not everyone is pro-Israel, Israel is not a topic that can be easily ignored, unless one remains blind to both the Bible and the evening news. There is no issue that unites the Islamic world greater than hatred of Israel. Often, it is couched in the semantic game of anti-Zionism, implying that their hatred is not for Jews, just for Israel; a specious explanation at best.

> *When people criticize Zionists, they mean Jews. You are talking anti-Semitism.*[3]
>
> (Martin Luther King Jr.,
> responding to an anti-Zionist remark
> by a student at Harvard University, 1968)

> *If Algeria introduced a (UN) resolution declaring that the Earth was flat and that Israel had flattened it, it would pass by a vote of 164 to 13 with 26 abstentions."*[4]
>
> (Abba Eban, former Israeli Foreign Minister)

The intense intra-Muslim rivalry between Sunnis and Shiites (or between Iran and Iraq), often thought of as brutal and lethal, recedes to the bleachers as soon as the uppity Jewish state steps up to the plate. The average Muhammad in the street – or, at the least, his political or religious leader – seethes with hatred whenever Israel wins a battle or scores an increasingly rare diplomatic victory. From where does this unusual degree of hatred and anger stem? Is it concern for the cause of the so-called Palestinians? Is it an expression of rage due to what they call Israel's *occupation of Arab land?* Why do *the settlements* cause such extreme reactions, to the extent that the most recent American presidents have felt the need to reach out to and even pander to the Muslim world on this issue? The comments of Washington, Adams, Lincoln, Truman, et al., seem to have been forgotten.

> *I will talk about Israeli settlement expansion, about how that is, that can be, you know, an impediment to success.*[5]
>
> (President George W. Bush)

> *The United States does not accept the legitimacy of continued Israeli settlements.... It is time for these settlements to stop.*[6]
>
> (President Barack Obama's Cairo, Egypt Speech, June 4, 2009)

> *We want to see a stop to settlement construction, additions, natural growth – any kind of (Jewish) settlement activity. That is what the President has called for.*[7]
>
> (Secretary of State Hillary Clinton, Al-Jezeera, May 19, 2009)

It appears to me that the undeniable Islamic hatred and exploitation of their oil wealth, which compels world leaders to bow to the Muslim world as President Obama did with the Saudi king, is clearly an eco-political outcome of a religious/ideological struggle that is deeply rooted in Islam. It seems to be a continuation of the typically violent Islamic reaction to Israel's covenant with the Almighty, and subsequent rejection of Muhammad's false claims to prophecy. This violent reaction is imbued with the intense passion that such deep religious conflict inevitably leads to. As discussed earlier, Islamic activists have found unlikely allies in the secular extremists and the anti-American, anti-Israel Left, who attempt to deny that such a religious conflict exists. They create a false class struggle narrative, in which the *oppressed* Third World Muslims are simply trying to affirm their *legitimate rights*. Such a narrative ignores the reality that Islam is not a peaceful *live and let live* religion, but an intolerant, aggressive ideological force seeking to dominate and force *dhimmi* status on all who refuse to accept their doctrines. There are many less-observant Muslims who choose not to accept what some have dubbed the *Islamist* view or *radical Islam*, but it is the Islamists who have clearly become the dominant force in Islamic activism, and this radicalism didn't arise in a vacuum.

Now some would suggest that we take a strictly secular view of this, saying that all organized religion is the root of this conflict, suggesting that if we abandoned such rigid positions that are based on religion and simply tried to understand each other, all of the problems could be resolved. However, there are two fundamental problems with this position. First, it doesn't change or show respect for the deeply held beliefs of the antagonists, and therefore it doesn't resolve the conflict. Second, this position is based on the presumption of truth being relative, that we all have our own truths and that they are all okay, which is a highly subjective perception in and of itself.

> *Imagine there's no heaven*
>
> *It's easy if you try*
>
> *No hell below us, above us only sky*
>
> *Imagine all the people, living for today*
>
> (*Imagine* by John Lennon)

However well-intentioned, we can't just wish away objective truth, as hard as many of the secularists of Hollywood (or in this case Liverpool) may try. If all truth was subjective or relative, would they agree that Muhammad's passion for beheadings of *Jews and infidels* is okay because it's *his truth*? Is Muhammad's legitimization of the rape and abuse of young girls acceptable because it's his truth? There are objective truths that are good and other claims of truth that are bad, and once we accept that reality, we can begin to come to terms with the painful issues that need to be confronted. Without that understanding, we will never have the moral clarity needed to confront the difficult challenges facing us in these dangerous times.

> *For moral absolutes, we have substituted moral ambiguity. We now communicate with everyone and say absolutely nothing.... Our society finds Truth too strong a medicine to digest undiluted.*

What Moses brought down from Mount Sinai were not the Ten Suggestions, they are Commandments. Are, not were. The sheer brilliance of the Ten Commandments is that they codify, in a handful of words, acceptable human behavior. Not just for then or now, but for all time.[8]

(TV news personality Ted Koppel)

When Moses, the legendary Israelite leader, brought those tablets of the Ten Commandments down from Mount Sinai, the world was forever changed. Aside from the implications for the role of Israel in the world, seeds were also planted that would eventually lead to the birth of the United States. No greater gift could have been given to the society that was later established in North America.

We can speak about modern Israeli accomplishments in the realm of intelligence and security, both overt – such as the destruction of the Iraqi and Syrian nuclear reactors – and covert – such as the activities of the Israeli Mossad intelligence agency that contributed to the defeat of Communism. We can also speak of the robust Israeli democracy, but it is the commonality of a deep core of values within the United States which ensures stability in the United States-Israel alliance. The same cannot be said of Islamic countries like Egypt, which can turn on the United States as soon as the Muslim Brotherhood overthrows the next dictator. Witness the rise of Erdogan in Turkey. Long considered to be a democratic Islamic country in which the latent but always present Islamic values came to the fore within just a few years, it was easy for Erdogan's Islamist party and its IHH terror group to quickly move his country into the Iran-Syria-Hizbollah-Hamas-al-Qaeda axis, against the West and against Israel. *The stability of common values is not just a slogan, but a tangible influence on current affairs.* Yes, there are indeed tremendous high-tech, medical, and scientific achievements by Israelis and Jews that have advanced world knowledge. This includes a grossly disproportionate percentage of Nobel Prize-winning scientists, medical professionals, and even comedians. Despite all of these great contributions, the most essential way that Israel has blessed America was to introduce the teachings of the Torah to American society, and letting God's lessons go forth from Zion to the world.

> *And this is the Torah that Moses placed before the Children of Israel according to God's word, through Moses' hand.*
>
> (The words recited in synagogue
> when the Torah scroll is raised in the air.
> Deuteronomy 4:44 and Numbers 9:23)

> *The Hebrews have done more to civilize men than any other nation… (God) ordered the Jews to preserve and propagate to all mankind the doctrine of a supreme, intelligent, wise, almighty sovereign of the universe… (which is) to be the great essential principle of morality, and consequently all civilization.*[9]
>
> (John Adams, February 16, 1809
> in a letter to Judge F.A. Van der Kemp)

> *Israel is the Lord's hallowed portion, His first fruits.*
>
> (Jeremiah 2:3)

One who denies this basic truth is either creating his own subjective *truth* or is innocently denying the veracity of the Bible (what Christians call the Old Testament) from which Judaism and Christianity both emerged. In fact, the Bible is the ongoing story, both wonderful and tragic, of the relationship between Israel and the one and only God. The Almighty frequently refers to this *stiff-necked people* who are often rebellious and repeatedly fall short of properly accepting their God-given role as a *kingdom of ministers and a holy nation.* (Exodus 19:6). Yet the covenant between Israel and the Almighty has never been abrogated; not by Israel and not by the King of the Universe.

> *For you are a people consecrated to the Lord, your God. Of all the peoples of the earth, the Lord your God has chosen you to be His treasured people. It is not because you are the most numerous of peoples that God set His heart on you and chose you – indeed, you are the smallest of people; it was because God*

loved you and kept the oath He made to your ancestors, that the Lord freed you with a mighty hand and rescued you from the house of bondage, from the power of Pharaoh, king of Egypt.
(Deuteronomy 7:6-8)

The Lord said to Abram, "Go forth from your land, from your homeland, from your father's house, to the Land that I will show you. And I will make of you a great nation. I will bless you and make your name great, and you shall be a blessing. I will bless those who bless you, and him who curses you I will curse, and all of the families of the earth will be blessed through you."
(Genesis 12:1-3)

The message in those words is clear and highly relevant today, for on this basis, nations have been judged and, consequently, have risen or fallen. Now, of course, there are those who would ignore or even ridicule such verses, claiming that the Bible is merely a collection of interesting fairy tales about a people and peoples who

From the Bondage of Communism to the Light of Torah: *A Jewish refugee from the former Soviet Union reads from the Torah in Jerusalem, during his Bar Mitzvah celebration at the Western Wall.*

may or may not have existed. This includes many Israelis.

On my first visit to Israel almost thirty years ago (before permanently relocating to the Land), I met my native Israeli cousins, who quickly informed me that one doesn't need to be religious in Israel and that in their secular schools they learn the Bible as history. Somehow, they leave out God, which to this day seems to me the height of incongruity, the Bible without God.

Another interesting phenomenon is the Christian who believes in God, but asserts that God somehow changed His mind and replaced the Jewish people as His *chosen people*. As we discussed earlier, this strange misreading of history is called Replacement Theology, a theory which claims that God at some point decided He made a mistake and that the Church would now be His new Israel. This brazen disregard for the integrity of God's decision-making process is a betrayal of the roots of their religion, which, I'm willing to bet, Christianity's Jewish messiah from Bethlehem would have found quite strange. Last but not least, we have the mouthpieces of Islam and their secular apologists, who simply deny that the Covenant with Israel was ever established, thereby denying all the commandments of the Bible pertaining to the Land of Israel. Despite archaeological evidence to the contrary, those rewriters of history enthusiastically deny that Judea and Samaria were the heartland of ancient Israel, that the Temples of Israel ever stood on the Temple Mount in Jerusalem, or that the State of Israel was built from the eternal bond which connects the God of Israel with His People, Torah, and Land. In fact, in 2000, when Israel's political leadership was negotiating with then-Palestinian Authority Chairman Yasser Arafat at the Presidential Camp David retreat in Maryland, negotiations collapsed when Arafat absolutely refused to concede that there was any historical Jewish connection to the Temple Mount (Mount Moriah) in Jerusalem.[10]

Another prime modern example of this Islamic revisionism is the darling of the Left/Liberal media Mahmoud Abbas (often known as Abu Mazen), Yasser Arafat's successor as president of the Palestinian Authority. Abbas's book, based on his doctoral

Committed to the Cause: *Despite his Holocaust denial and adulation for the worst of the terrorists, Palestinian Authority chairman Mahmoud Abbas presents a moderate image when speaking English. Consequently, he has always been honored and welcomed in the corridors of power in Washington and around the world.*

dissertation entitled: *The Other Side: the Secret Relationship between Nazism and Zionism,* refers to the Holocaust as a *Zionist Fantasy.* Perhaps he hasn't seen the thousands of documents and photographs from the concentration camps? Perhaps he hasn't heard about the documented names of the six million Jews who were slaughtered? It is highly unlikely that someone with Abbas's extensive education would be unaware of the facts of history. Whether intentional or not, it is evident that his research was built on the outright falsehoods that seem to be endemic in the *Palestinian* narrative.

For all of his lies and distortions, the founder of Fatah, and of the P.L.O. and the undisputed Father of Modern Terrorism, Yasser Arafat, received a Nobel Peace Prize. In turn, his successor – the Holocaust-denying Abbas – continues to receive international acclaim as a moderate, reasonable leader and a peace partner. Such are the leaders and peacemakers in our times. It is easier for us to simply ignore reality and pretend that all is well and peaceful.

> *We may hope for peace, but there is no goodness; for a time of healing, but behold, there is terror.*
> (Jeremiah 8:15)

> *For they have healed the hurt of the daughter of my people slightly, saying, "Peace, peace – when there is no peace."*
> (Jeremiah 8:11)

Nonetheless, the modern-day Muslim heroes notice, with pleasure, the moral cowardice of the European, the American, and even the Israeli leaders. When they speak in Arabic, they mock the naivety of the Bill Clintons and the Jimmy Carters, who fawn over them as they beg for them (in English) to speak and come to an understanding. Sometimes the frustration of American leaders is obvious. I recall at least one American politician saying, *If they would only sit down with us, like good Christians, and work things out.* But they aren't Christians, nor are they Jews. They are Muslims and their guide is the Koran, not the Bible. Sitting down with the Jews and the *infidels* is not their way.

> *Believers, if you yield to the infidels they will drag you back to unbelief and you will return headlong to perdition. We will put terror in the hearts of the unbelievers… The fire shall be their home.*
> (Sura 3:149-151)

> *You make of us an object of strife unto our neighbors, and our enemies laugh amongst themselves.*
> (Psalms 80:7)

Much of the world is in the dark – in a state of confusion about what is happening in our times – as the Islamic activists laugh at our confusion. But as a Gentile friend of mine once said:

> *It's all about Israel. Those who want to be on the right side of*

history had better get on board with Israel and fast. If America wants to recover from the challenges we are facing in our times, we need to be standing with Israel against the terrorists before the terrorists get to us.

How does one make that happen? It is one thing to call for people to stand with Israel and work together, but practically, how does one go about it? I suggest the following ten concrete steps:

- Pray for Israel to be courageous and faithful to the King of the Universe and His Torah.
- Let your political representatives know that Israel's defense is important to you and that you support the pioneers settling Israel's biblical heartland of Judea, Samaria and Jerusalem.
- Send monetary support to those projects/organizations that are making important contributions to strengthening Israel's hold on the Land and building for the future in the Land.
- Write letters to the media to let them know that you support Israel and why.
- Don't hesitate to contradict the Islamic propaganda machine, whether in private or in public.
- Educate yourself by reading about the facts in the Middle East. The best counterpoint to hatred and ignorance is knowledge.
- Visit and/or volunteer in the Land of Israel.
- Recommend important books and/or articles about Israel to others.
- When confronted with Islamic offensives, stand firm in your belief and don't be intimidated.
- Remember that for Israel and the Middle East, the Bible is your best source of historical truth, but there are also many others. Seek them out and learn!

Standing Together: *The USA and Israel are the two biblical pillars standing in the way of the Islamic tsunami, and therefore, need to be marching in tandem in these difficult times.*

It seems that Islamic terrorists are aiming their sights on the entire world, but Israel is the desired preliminary prize. Sure, the forces of Islam are out to take over the entire world, but Israel is on the front lines of that struggle; Islam would like nothing more than to control the Land of Israel. As they see it, what greater religious symbol of Allah's sovereignty over the Jews and the infidels could there be? As the Muslim preachers often say, *First the Saturday people, then the Sunday people!* After taking control of Israel, it would be an easy downhill walk.

> *Why should the nations say, where is their God?*
>
> (Psalms 79:10)

It is either Muhammad or Israel, the God of the Bible or the fictional deity called Allah. The choice could not be clearer.

> *See – I have placed before you today life and good, death and evil… I have placed life and death before you, blessing and*

curse, and you shall choose life, so that you will live, you and your offspring, to love the Lord your God, to listen to His voice...
(Deuteronomy 30:15-20)

How long will you be lax, in coming to take possession of the Land that the Lord God of your fathers has given you?
(Joshua 18:3)

According to Scripture, it is clear that Israel is both God's *chosen people* and God's chosen land and all other nations will be judged in comparison to Israel. There appears to be a direct correlation between the gradual decline of the United States as the world's undisputed superpower, the decline of Judeo-Christian civilization, and the rise of Islam, which threatens the idea that the United States continues to be the beacon of freedom and opportunity.

The rise of Islam is a serious threat to world peace and is already creating havoc in the social fabric of more than a few European countries. Much of this can be attributed to the European, and more recently, the American, penchant for blasting Israel for its insistence on being an independent, proud nation and allowing its people to build homes and schools. Perhaps this is a misguided attempt to placate the Islamic oil sheikhs of the Persian Gulf states or an outgrowth of latent anti-Semitism based on Replacement Theology that is still taught in far too many churches. Maybe it is a combination of the two. Either way, if this pressure and anti-biblical interference doesn't soon reverse itself, it is bound to lead to the destruction of Western civilization as we know it.

For behold, in those days and at that time, when I will bring back the captivity of Judah and Jerusalem, I will gather all of the nations and bring them down to the Valley of Jehoshaphat and I will contend with them there concerning My people and My possession Israel, that they dispersed among the nations, and they divided up my land...
(Joel 4:1-2)

Yes, God's Torah makes it clear that, eventually, a day of reckoning will come for every nation and every individual. While some may arrogantly choose to deride such thinking as primitive or uneducated, the facts of history speak differently. Each of Israel's enemies and those who have attempted to divide its Land has faded into the dust of history; these nations now cease to exist. Throughout the Bible we read about adversaries such as Amalek and the Philistines, both of whom denied Israel the right to its Land several thousand years ago. Those two bitter enemies tormented Israel for decades – even centuries – but they are now reduced to history lessons in Bible classes around the world.

> *Remember what Amalek did to you on the way, when you were leaving Egypt, how he confronted you by the way, and he struck those of you who were hindmost, all of the weaklings at your rear, when you were faint and exhausted, and he did not fear God. It shall be that when the Lord your God gives you rest from all of your enemies all around, in the Land that the Lord your God gives you, as an inheritance to possess it, you shall wipe out the memory of Amalek from under the heaven, you shall not forget.*
> (Deuteronomy 25:17-19)

On the Sabbath before the holiday of Purim, we read those verses in the Synagogue and over and over again, in every possible accent. Through this, we learn the lessons of history and understand the mistakes made while battling our enemies. These lessons help us learn how to confront them, especially when their raison d'être is to destroy the people of Israel. However, these lessons need to be adapted to our time and our current foes. Amalek as an identifiable, cohesive nation no longer exists, nor do the Philistines, Canaanites, Romans, Nazis, or any of the countless other once-powerful enemies that have risen up through history to annihilate the Jewish people.

The Bible verse says that Amalek would attack those who were most vulnerable. That is exactly what the Islamic terrorists continue to do. The disproportion of attacks on children is obvious and painful, but the strategy is the same: aim for the civilians and Israel will be weakened. Yet, Israel still stands and is still the target, and indeed is the obsession of the United Nations, representing a world gone mad. Israel has continued to survive and even thrive despite its tiny size, consistently miniscule population, difficult geographic location, lack of national resources, and, until recently, lack of national sovereignty for over 1,900 years.

> *The Egyptian, the Babylonian, and the Persian rose, filled the planet with sound and splendor, then faded to dream-stuff and passed away; the Greek and the Roman followed, and made a vast noise, and they are gone; other peoples have sprung up and held their torch high for a time, but it burned out, and they sit in twilight now, or have vanished... All things are mortal but the Jew; all other forces pass, but he remains. What is the secret of his immortality?*[11]
>
> (Mark Twain)

So, too, European countries have risen and fallen based on the treatment of the Jews. Medieval Poland, which welcomed thousands of Jewish merchants, had a thriving business climate until the Jewish population fell victim to anti-Semitic attack. Further southwest, in Western Europe, Jews held important professional positions and contributed their skills for the good of the Spanish Empire, until the forced conversions to Catholicism forced many Jews into spiritual hiding. Up to that point, Spain had been a prosperous nation and a major world power. Queen Isabella's monarchy had the means to finance expeditions to the New World, and helped fund the voyages of Christopher Columbus. Eventually, the expulsion order was given to its Jews in 1492, which officially ended the Golden Age of Spain.

Spain illustrates for us the *blessing and curse principle* on a national scale. Within a hundred years of expelling the Jews, Spain was no longer a dominant world power. They never again rose to the prominence in world affairs that was held before their persecution of the Jews.

In his book, *As America Has Done To Israel*, John McTernan examined the histories of Russia and the United States and each country's respective relationships with Israel and the Jewish people. His basic premise is that the United States has thrived because of its treatment of the Jews, starting with the biblically-inspired warm words of George Washington:

> *May the children of Abraham who dwell in this land continue to merit and enjoy the good will of other inhabitants, while everyone shall sit in safety under his own vine and fig tree – and there shall be none to make him afraid.*
>
> (George Washington, 1790)

On the other hand, Russia has been notoriously anti-Semitic as the scenes of pogroms, severe discrimination, and strict limitations on freedom of movement against its Jewish populations have been evident throughout their history. In addition, its anti-Israel policies, exemplified by its support of anti-Israel resolutions in the United Nations, have continued to this day.

The United States and Russia have been similar in many ways – both are historically Christian nations, large countries, rich in natural resources – but the United States has, until recently, been a strong supporter of Israel. It has welcomed large numbers of Jewish immigrants to its shores and, aside from isolated individual cases of discrimination, allowed Jewish citizens to demonstrate their abilities and pursue their inalienable rights.

Due to the blessings that the United States has bestowed on the Jewish people and on Israel, it has become an unrivaled world power and a bastion of Jewish creativity. Only in the past few American administrations have policies started to shift, as unjustified pressure has been put upon Israel to surrender portions of its God-given land to the sons of Muhammad. McTernan illustrates striking correlations between the pressure applied to Israel and the numerous hurricanes, floods, and other natural disasters that have hit America in recent years.[12]

Likewise, the Jews of Germany had been successful in

professional, business, and creative fields, until the rise of the Nazi party. Indeed the Jews were a great blessing until Germany turned on its Jews, which led to Germany's defeat at the hands of the Allies, its division after World War II, and abrupt decline as a world military power.

There are those who would call this analysis *religious fanaticism*, saying that we have no way of knowing what God plans and does. I agree that we don't know exactly what God is doing or what His considerations are. However, He gave us basic principles in the Bible with which we can attempt to understand His world. While I can't promise that every word of my analysis of history is true, the principles, trends and the patterns are, and are there for us to learn from.

Currently, the United States is facing serious economic challenges, including high unemployment and a raging national debt, but the longer-term threat is the Islamic encroachment on the American way of life. If not confronted, this danger will only continue to grow, at times manifesting itself in terrorism, but often employing a quieter, more subtle attempt to change America from within. With this change will come increasing pressure on the United States to turn against Israel, a pattern that we are already seeing in Europe.

The blessings that have shined on the United States since its inception may soon be coming to an end, as its successive administrations apply increasing pressure to surrender Judea and Samaria, its biblical heartland, and Jerusalem, its capital. This process was started over thirty years ago by Jimmy Carter, but the pressure under the Obama Administration has reached unprecedented levels, and alliances have shifted toward the Islamic countries. That shift accelerated near the end of the Bush Administration, when the firmness and moral clarity that President Bush had expressed after the 9-11 attacks started to deteriorate. Israel's enemies, such as Saudi Arabia, are being sold increasing amounts of American weaponry, the Palestinian army is being trained and equipped by the American government, and the hostile Islamic world is entering the nuclear age in Iran and elsewhere. All this while the American giant sleeps.

The loyalty of the Wahabi Islamists of Saudi Arabia will not be with the United States in the long run; this presumed loyalty will surely be captured by the Caliphate goal of world domination for Islam. They will quietly continue to fund the furtherance of *Sharia* and the transformation of the United States, for which Sunni and Shiite Muslims will gladly work together to achieve this mutual goal. While simultaneously spending billions of dollars on advertising and public relations, this goal, and the goal of convincing Americans that the Saudis and other Islamic states are loyal friends of the United States, will be achieved.

> *He'll put both his arms around you*
> *You can feel that tender touch of the beast*
> *You know that sometimes Satan comes as a man of peace.*
> (*Man of Peace* by Bob Dylan, 1983)

The Obama Administration are not the only ones who want to change the American affinity for Israel and move towards a more pro-Muslim slant. Farouk Shami, political activist, multi-millionaire hair care magnate, and failed 2010 candidate for the Democratic nomination for Governor of Texas is an American Muslim. Shami, a Houston Democrat, not only refuses to specifically condemn the Hezbollah, Hamas, and Islamic *Jihad* terrorist groups, but he was also honored by the American Task Force on Palestine, a pan-terrorist group which claims that all of Israel is actually considered *Palestine*. Furthermore, through his Sheikh Mohammed Shami Foundation (named for his father), he funds an extremist school in the so-called West Bank. Shami appeared at a Martin Luther King Day rally, wearing a keffiyeh scarf proclaiming, *Palestine: Jerusalem is Ours.* His scarf showed a photo of *Masjid Qubbat As-Sakhrah* – the Dome of the Rock mosque – which is built on the ruins of the holiest part of the destroyed Jewish Temple on Temple Mount in Jerusalem. Not only did this reveal a staunchly anti-Israel slant, but poor taste as well, as Dr. Martin Luther King Jr. in whose name the rally was held, happened to be unabashedly pro-Israel.[13]

> *Peace for Israel means security, and we must stand with all our might to protect its right to exist, its territorial integrity. I see Israel as one of the great outposts of democracy in the world, and a marvelous example of what can be done, how desert land can be transformed into an oasis of brotherhood and democracy. Peace for Israel means security and that security must be a reality.*[14]
>
> (Martin Luther King Jr., March 25, 1968)

Shami didn't succeed in his 2010 campaign for Governor, but he is symptomatic of a trend of American Islamic activism that will become more evident as their wealth and population grows. The expansion of Islam within the black community has been enormous, as exemplified by the growth of what is known as the National Ummah. This Muslim movement, strives to transform American cities into sovereign Islamic states and has gained a significant foothold in metropolitan areas throughout the country. It is led by Jamil al-Amin – former Black Panther H. Rap Brown – from his cell in a maximum security prison on the outskirts of Florence, Colorado where he is serving a life sentence for killing two police officers. Al-Amin continues to stand by his 1960s threat, *If America don't come around, we're gonna burn it down.*[15]

Some Ummah mosques maintain armed militias, while others provide training in martial arts and guerilla warfare. Almost all of these mosque militias operate beneath the radar of local, state, and federal law enforcement officials. Many African-American led mosques in America's major cities are affiliated with and/or influenced by the Ummah movement.

Imam Luqman Abdullah of the Masjid al-Haqq in Detroit – a mosque that was part of the Ummah network – was one of the founders of the Muslim Alliance in North America (MANA). Another founder was Siraj Wahhaj, the un-indicted co-conspirator in the 1993 bombing of the World Trade Center and imam of

Masjid al-Taqwa in Brooklyn. MANA was formed to defend Jamil al-Amin and to advance the Islamic take-over of the United States by *cultural jihad* – pushing for black/Muslim privileges under the guise of equal opportunity and civil rights. Imam Abdullah, who called upon his followers to launch an *offensive jihad* against United States officials, was killed in October 2009, when the FBI raided a warehouse and two houses in Detroit, which resulted in the arrest of eleven Ummah members. The charges were mail fraud, illegal possession of firearms, trafficking in stolen goods, and altering vehicle identification numbers.[16]

> *The other force is one of bitterness and hatred, and it comes perilously close to advocating violence. It is expressed in the various black nationalist groups that are springing up across the nation, the largest and best-known being Elijah Muhammad's Muslim movement.*[17]
>
> (Martin Luther King Jr.,
> Birmingham, AL, April 16, 1963)

> *A decree of death has been passed on America. The judgment of God has been rendered and she must be destroyed...*[18]
>
> (American Muslim leader Louis Farrakhan,
> speaking in Harlem, 1997)

It is unclear to what extent these movements influenced Barack Hussein Obama as he grew up in Chicago, but the shift away from Israel in American policy – at least in the Executive branch – has been manifested through official financial support provided directly to the Palestinian Authority (PA) by American government aid. This assistance, which started during the Clinton and Bush Administrations, has continued to be paid despite American laws that forbid aiding or honoring terrorists. The case of Dalal Mughrabi is a particularly poignant example of how enforcement of this law has been ignored. The following excerpt from an article by Itamar Marcus and Barbara Crook of Palestinian Media Watch exposes this immoral financial assistance and the deceit that the followers of Muhammad are notorious for:

> The PA chose to name its latest computer center "after the martyr Dalal Mughrabi," who led the most deadly terror attack in the country's (Israel's) history. Her 1978 bus hijacking killed 37 civilians, 12 of them children… The new center is funded by (PA leader) Abbas's office, which is bolstered by Western aid money (Al-Ayyam, May 5, 2009).
>
> U.S. law prohibits the funding of Palestinian structures that use any portion of their budget to promote terror or honor terrorists. But $200 million of the U.S.'s proposed $900 million aid package is earmarked to go directly to the Abbas government, which regularly uses its budget to honor terrorists. In fact, this latest veneration of Mughrabi is not an isolated case, but part of a continuing pattern of honoring terrorists that targets children in particular.
>
> Last summer the PA sponsored "the Dalal Mughrabi football championship" for kids, and a "summer camp named for martyr Dalal Mughrabi… out of honor and admiration for the martyr." It also held a party to honor exemplary students, also named "for the martyr Dalal Mughrabi," … at which Abbas's representative reviewed the heroic life of the martyr (Mughrabi). (Al-Hayat al-Jadida, July 23, 24 and August 8, 2008)
>
> Thirty-one years to the day after the Mughrabi murders, PA TV broadcast a special program celebrating the terror attack, calling the killing of 37 civilians "one of the most important and most prominent special operations… carried out by a team of heroes and led by the heroic fighter Dalal Mughrabi" (PA TV March 11). And it's not just Mughrabi who is a Palestinian hero. Despite professions in English by Abbas and other PA leaders that they reject terror, the PA has a long and odious history in Arabic of celebrating terrorists as role models and heroes, often involving U.S. money.
>
> USAID spent $400,000 in 2004 to build the Salakh Khalaf soccer field. After Palestinian Media Watch reported that Khalaf

was the head of the Palestinian terror group that murdered 11 Israeli athletes at the Munich Olympics and two American diplomats in Sudan, USAID publicly apologized and said it would demand that the PA change the name. The name was never changed.[19]

The deceitful Palestinian Authority has a history of speaking out of both sides of its mouth to further its goals. The misguided American support for the PA, at least until the blatantly pro-Islamic shift of Obama, has seemingly stemmed from an ill-advised desire to please the oil sheikhs. The U.S. operated under the belief that this was necessary to protect U.S. interests in the Middle East. The next logical step in the pro-Muslim shift would be letting Israel be destroyed, which would not be accepted within the grassroots American opinion. However, mere lip service for the biblical imperative to bless Israel is not enough. The Almighty wants Israel to be restored to its ancient homeland in the fullest sense and to be *a light unto the nations* in the full land of Zion. Just as Israel blessed the world with the Book of books, which it received through Moses on Mount Sinai, Israel's role is to be a blessing to the nations of the world. Crocodile tears for the fictional *Palestinian people*, which is just a vehicle created by the Arabs to wipe out Israel, should not even enter into American geo-economic considerations. When the Bible speaks of the abundant blessings to be derived by standing with Israel, it is not only theoretical, but also practical in the fullest sense of the word. We often enjoy poetry in the Bible if it makes us feel good, but we still make decisions based only on non-biblical or even anti-biblical considerations.

The true test of faith is to stand with Israel, knowing that the Islamic kings of oil are threatening to cut off the taps. Remember that they need the sales at least as much as the buyers need the oil. Stand firm, stand with Israel, and trust in the Real King!

Woe unto those who go down to Egypt for help and who rely on horses; they trust in chariots because they are many and in

horsemen because they are very strong, but they do not look to
the Holy One of Israel, nor do they seek out God.

(Isaiah 31:1)

It's not too late to turn things around. The great United States – which has been losing its sense of security and proud feeling of confidence since the 9-11 declaration of war – can start by returning to its roots. The first step in that process is to understand that without strengthening the country's connection with the moral, biblical basis on which it was founded, it cannot survive as a free nation.

The fundamental basis of this Nation's law was given to Moses on the Mount (Sinai).[20]

(Harry S. Truman, February 15, 1950)

I hope that you have reread the Constitution of the United States… Like the Bible, it ought to be read again and again.[21]

(Franklin D. Roosevelt,
Fireside Chat, March 9, 1937)

The second step is to recognize that one cannot genuinely return to biblical roots without recognizing the most miraculous event in modern times: the return of the Jewish people to their God-given land after almost 2,000 years in exile, a process that is unrivaled throughout the course of human history. What nation wins a war in six days (June 1967) and rests on the seventh day, thereby recapturing the biblical heartland of historical Israel? Events of this magnitude do not occur by accident and do not occur in a vacuum. These events are part of a lengthy spiritual process that is central to the world's continued existence in its current form, but it is also much more than that. This process will lead to the full redemption of Israel and of the world, to a time when the God of Israel's enemies will be defeated and true peace will reign among peoples.

Those nations that stand together with Israel in these challenging times will surely merit the spiritual rewards that are promised in the Book of Genesis:

The Rebirth of Israel: *An Israeli girl celebrates Israel's Independence Day by praying at the Western Wall in Jerusalem, with the national flag in hand.*

I will bless those who bless you, and him who curses you, I will curse; and all the families of the Earth shall bless themselves through you.

(Genesis 12:3)

It is not too late to restore those blessings to America.

Chapter Ten

Facing The Challenge

All that is necessary for the triumph of evil is that good men do nothing.

(Edmund Burke)

Even when I walk in the valley of darkness, I will fear no evil for you are with me.

(Psalms 23:4)

Umar Farouk Abdulmutallab, the suspect in the failed 2009 Christmas Day airliner attack told federal investigators that the radical U.S.-born cleric Anwar al-Awlaki directed him to carry out his attempt at mass murder.[1]

Brother Mujahed Umar Farouk – may God relieve him – is one of my students, yes. We had kept in contact but I didn't issue a fatwa to Umar Farouk for this operation.

I support what Umar Farouk did after seeing my brothers in Palestine, Iraq, Afghanistan being killed, he was quoted as saying. If it was a military plane or a U.S. military target it would have been better... (but) the American people have participated in all the crimes of their government.[2]

Al-Awlaki, who was born in New Mexico but relocated to his ancestral hometown in Yemen in 2004, exchanged up to 20 e-mails with the alleged shooter of the 2009 Fort Hood terror attack. U.S. Maj. Nidal Malik Hassan had apparently initiated the contact, seeking religious advice in the months before the attack.

Al-Awlaki had become popular among Islamic militants and their sympathizers for his English-language Internet sermons. During these sermons, al-Awlaki explained the ideology of violent *jihad* and martyrdom against the West to his mostly young and enthusiastic Muslim followers.

Throughout this book I have emphasized that we are living in dangerous but exciting times, and for whatever reason, that we have been given an extremely difficult challenge. Both biblical and modern-day Israel has been a nation that prides itself on going it alone. But in these times, with the tsunami that threatens to destroy us all, we need to focus on forming alliances that can work. Nonetheless, the common heritage and the values shared by these two biblically-based nations will be all for naught if the two nations don't face up to the reality of the Islamic challenge. We are talking about a growing force that is seeking to take over and subjugate the people of the world under its rule.

Will the United States and Israel both have the courage to recognize and stand up to the challenge? Only if the leaders of those two nations begin to understand that the current struggle is not one over land, human rights, or economic justice. It is an Islamic religious war: a jihad against Judaism, against Christianity (which came from Judaism), and against what is often called the Judeo-Christian civilization in the West, which emerged from both.

How are we to meet the challenge? Islamic propagandists have obviously learned the American expression, *The best defense is a good offense.* They have run many miles from the starting line and formed potent alliances with the secular Left in both America and Europe.

As we have seen, terrorism is only one component of their strategy.

> *Experience teaches us that it is much easier to prevent an enemy from posting themselves than it is to dislodge them after they have got possession.*[3]

(George Washington)

Has our sense of tolerance toppled over the edge to the point at which we have become practitioners of tolerance without values? Tolerance in the United States has been a wonderful value that many Americans take for granted, and it has been one of the country's great strengths. This is partially defined in the Establishment and Free Exercise clause of the First Amendment to the U.S. Constitution:

> *Congress shall make no law respecting an establishment of religion, or prohibiting the free exercise thereof...*[4]

The lack of an official religion originally meant that the various Protestant denominations of Christianity would tolerate each other and none would seek to be the official religion of America. That tolerance has gradually evolved and expanded over the years as the U.S. population has grown and diversified, to the extent that the tolerance has reached a degree perhaps unparalleled in human history. While the idea was always good in theory, it has been expanded to such a degree that it may, paradoxically, be detrimental to the very societal cohesion that it once supported.

The historian William Federer has described the progression of American tolerance from the beginning:

> *Originally, each colony had its own preferred Protestant denomination (Anglican, Puritan, Dutch Reformed, Lutheran, Presbyterian, Congregational, Baptist, Quaker, etc.). After the Revolutionary War, tolerance gradually extended to Catholics. In the early 1800s, tolerance extended to liberal Christian denominations (such as Unitarians and Universalists). In the middle 1800s, persecuted Jews from Europe immigrated and were tolerated. In the late 1800s, anyone who believed in a monotheistic God was tolerated. In the early 1900s, tolerance began to extend to polytheists and many new religions. In the middle 1900s, tolerance extended to atheists. Finally, tolerance extended to radical anti-religious, radical homosexual groups, radical Muslim groups, etc., who teach intolerance toward*

*the Judeo-Christian beliefs that began the entire progression of
tolerance.*[5]

American tolerance has always been one of its great attractions,
but how does a society determine when it has gone too far? Must
a nation remain dogmatic when it comes to basic principles such
as tolerance, even when that tolerance will be used to destroy
the society from within? To this question, the answer has to be a
firm *No.* No society, however free and tolerant, has an obligation
to commit national suicide, to self-destruct because of those
freedoms. If a society grants liberties which a malignant source
is then allowed to abuse, that society's principles and values will
have been grossly misused. For this society to suffer because the
force seeks to destroy the value system on which it was founded
would be much more reckless.

> *Muslims want you to make way for Islam, but Islam does
> not make way for you. The Government insists that you respect
> Islam, but Islam has no respect for you. Islam wants to rule,
> submit, and seeks to destroy our Western civilization.*
>
> (Geert Wilders, leader of the
> Dutch Freedom Party, in his film *Fitna*)

In a remarkable resemblance of the childhood of Muhammad,
the founder of Islam, a young German named Adolf Hitler was
orphaned as a child; both of his parents were dead by the time
he turned eighteen.[18] As with Muhammad, we will leave the
psychological analysis about little Adolf for the psychologists,
but eventually, he became an angry young man. He developed
his ideology throughout his life, as described in his infamous
guidebook of the Nazi doctrine, *Mein Kampf,* in which he writes
about the superior race, the Aryans, who he thought should rule
over all others. Hitler chose to attack a *race,* which he declared,
was vehemently against all the good things that the Aryans stand
for. This *race* was, of course, the Jews.

Hitler went on to say that subjugated peoples actually benefit
from being conquered because they come into contact with and

learn from the superior Aryans. However, he adds, they benefit only as long as the Aryan remains the absolute master and doesn't mingle or inter-marry with the inferior conquered peoples.

But it was the Jews, Hitler stated, who were engaged in a conspiracy to keep this master race from assuming its rightful position as rulers of the world. The Jews tainted the racial and cultural purity of the Aryans and even invented forms of government in which the Aryan came to believe in equality and failed to recognize his racial superiority.

The mightiest counterpart to the Aryan is represented by the Jew.[6]

Hitler's political views about conquering non-Aryans firmly placed the Jews in a separate, subjugated category from all others. His beliefs had a striking resemblance to Muhammad's views. However, the similarity doesn't end there. At the Nuremberg Trials, Adolf Eichmann's deputy Dieter Wisliceny (subsequently executed as a war criminal) testified about the role of the Grand Mufti Haj Muhammed Amin al-Husseini of Jerusalem in encouraging the mass extermination of the Jews in the death camps during the Holocaust:

> *The Mufti was one of the initiators of the systematic extermination of European Jewry and had been a collaborator and adviser of Eichmann and Himmler in the execution of this plan... He was one of Eichmann's best friends and had constantly incited him to accelerate the extermination measures. I heard him say, accompanied by Eichmann, he had visited incognito the gas chamber of Auschwitz.*[7]

The genocide, unparalleled in history, that Adolf Eichmann engineered, was carried out methodically under Hitler's enthusiastic leadership. Hitler's direction resembled Muhammad's ease and delight in mass beheadings and massacres, even though the Islamist passion for killing Jews, Christians and any others who were seen as infidels, hasn't yet reached Hitlerian proportions.

> *I am with you, so keep firm those who have believed; will cast horror into the hearts of those who have disbelieved, so smite them above the neck and smite them of every fingertip.*
>
> (Sura 8:12)

Last but not least, Hitler proved to be quite skillful at cynically using the democratic system to attain power for his Nazi Party. This is precisely what the Islamic ideologues are attempting to do, and are gradually succeeding at – first in Europe and then in America. As described earlier, they are engaged in a step-by-step struggle using the media, their oil wealth, and by abusing the tolerant system that they hope to someday destroy, according to the dictates of *the Prophet Muhammad*, as written in the Koran.

One key difference between Nazism and Islam that makes it difficult for a free society to identify Islam as a danger is that it is identified as a religion. Therefore, it is somehow considered to be untouchable because religious freedom is almost sacred in America. The Nazis and Communists weren't claiming to worship a God. But what if they were? What if Hitler's ideology had included belief in an unnamed God of the Nazis who they would then claim authorized the Nazi ideology? Would it have then been a violation of freedom of religion to confront them in World War II?

> *And fight against them until there be no temptations and their obedience be wholly unto Allah.*
>
> (Sura 8:39)

In recent years, Islamic attempts to influence the American political system have been focused on supporting candidates who are supportive of Islam, mainly in the Democratic Party. Several individual politicians have been seeking to work their way through the system, exploiting democracy in order to advance the tyranny of Islam. One such individual is Democratic Congressman Keith Ellison, a convert to Islam, who was elected as the first Islamic Congressman from his home state of Minnesota. Ellison was sworn into his new position by House Speaker Nancy Pelosi. The

Washington Post reported (January 3, 2007) that Ellison would be sworn in, not on a Bible, but on a Koran, that had been owned once by Thomas Jefferson.

This departure from congressional norms raised many an eyebrow. Ellison claimed that Jefferson appreciated the diversity of America and that the Koran was part of that.

> It demonstrates that from the very beginning of our country, we had people who were visionary, who were religiously tolerant, who believed that knowledge and wisdom could be gleaned from any number of sources, including the Koran, Ellison said in a telephone interview several days before the swearing in.[8]

However, there was another, much more practical reason why Jefferson made the effort to purchase and read the Koran. The United States was getting ready to go to war in the early 1800s against a group of lawless, radical Muslims. These were the Barbary Pirates, from the Barbary Coast of North Africa, who were creating havoc for American and European ships on the high seas, using the ports of the current Algeria, Libya, Morocco, and Tunisia – all of which were part of the Ottoman Empire – for their attacks. Thousands of vessels had been captured and large numbers of Europeans and Americans had been sold into slavery. The newly-formed United States government had no CIA or other intelligence services to research the Barbary Pirates and the Ottoman Empire for them, so Jefferson decided to do the research himself. What better way to understand the terrorists than to read their *Bible?*

In its infancy, the U.S. fought this international group of terrorists who, much like today's Islamic terrorists, crossed the definitions of states and operated beyond national borders. In their eyes, all traders and travelers were fair game. This ancient form of terrorism tormented the first five presidents, from Washington to Madison. Without a standing navy, the new United States was at a distinct disadvantage and had no choice but to succumb to the terrorists' demands. All the states of North Africa and the

Ottoman Empire joined in with this display of state-sponsored terrorism that would have instilled pride in the hearts of Iran, Syria, and Hezbollah. The Turkish terror group IHH (The Foundation for Human Rights and Freedoms and Humanitarian Relief), which gained notoriety because of its part in the armed Gaza flotilla raid, may also have favored this terrorism. The Barbary Pirates enjoyed this newfound enterprise; it was lucrative both for the pirates and also for the Islamic states that gave them refuge.[9]

The damage that this piracy and terrorism was causing to the American economy was extensive; the newly-formed American government had to take action. However, because of its weak position at that time, military action simply wasn't a realistic option.

In 1785, John Adams and Thomas Jefferson were sent to Tripoli's Ambassador in London as messengers. The men visited Sidi Haji Abdul Rahman and asked him by what right he extorted money and took slaves in this way. As Jefferson later reported to Secretary of State John Jay, and to the Congress:

> *The ambassador answered us that (the right) was founded on the Laws of the Prophet, that it was written in their Koran, that all nations who should not have answered their authority were sinners, that it was their right and duty to make war upon them wherever they could be found, and to make slaves of all they could take as prisoners, and that every Mussulman (Muslim) who should be slain in battle was sure to go to Paradise...*[10]

The new American nation, recognizing the limitations of its military, had no desire to enter into another war so far from its shores. The U.S. agreed to pay an exorbitant amount of tribute, which today would be called *protection money*, to the Muslim pirates and their cohorts from the Ottoman Empire.

They also signed the *Treaty of Tripoli*, in which the Americans agreed to refute that the U.S. was a *Christian Nation* and that it had no religious issues with Islam.

And so it happened that agreements were reached between

the United States and rulers of the Barbary Coast. In exchange for cash payments, the rulers pledged to guarantee the safe passage of American ships and to put a stop to the practice of maritime kidnapping. As the 18th century came to a close, Americans were cautiously optimistic that they had solved the Barbary problem.

By 1801, however, it became clear that the policy of appeasement had failed. The Pasha of Tripoli, who five years earlier had been satisfied with a payment of $56,000, now demanded increasingly larger sums. When they were not forthcoming, piracy resumed. The same held true for the other Barbary states. The Algerians received payments from the U.S. totaling $990,000 plus another $585,000 in 1793 to cover the ransom of 11 American ships.... These were extraordinary sums for a nation with a budget of no more than $7 million, but the appetite of the Muslim states seemed to grow evermore insatiable.

As America soon learned, a policy of accommodation only encouraged the brigands of the Barbary Coast to seize more ships and to take more captives. Far from providing safe passage to American and other foreign vessels, the North African rulers remained active accomplices to the crime of piracy, taking protection money while at the same time permitting the banditry to continue.[11]

President Jefferson changed course and saved the nation while it was in its infancy. His knowledge of the Koran, which he had read specifically for this purpose, gave him essential background, which confirmed for him the nature of the beast. Jefferson truly employed wisdom through the premise of *know thine enemy*. The Muslim terrorists pocketed not only the millions of dollars in tribute but American concessions as well, and they demanded more. This scenario is actually very similar to what the Muslim terrorists of the Palestinian Authority, Hamas and Fatah, have been doing for years in their recent dealings with Israel and the United States. They repeatedly demand concessions and *good-will gestures*, then the Saudi oil sheikhs bully the

Know Thine Enemy: *Thomas Jefferson, the third president, learned the Koran, not to absorb the wisdom of Muhammad, but in order to understand the mentality of the terrorists of his time, the Barbary Pirates.*

American administration into pressuring Israel. America then obediently applies pressure on the Israelis, who obediently make more concessions. More demands are subsequently made by the insatiable Muslim, who – from the perspective of the taker – well understands the motto, *Give an inch and they'll take a mile.* One would think that we should have learned our lesson by now.

William Welty describes the dramatic sequence of events from the point at which Jefferson, finally recognizing the failure of appeasing terrorists, decided to take action:

> In response to a declaration of war on the nascent United States of America by the Barbary Coast caliphates, Thomas Jefferson sent the USS Constitution to the Mediterranean in 1803. The fighting during these days saw many acts of heroism that established the U.S. Navy as a force to be reckoned with.
>
> Then, in 1805, the Constitution supported the landing of Marines "on the shores of Tripoli" in an action that was subsequently immortalized in the Marine Corps Hymn...
>
> The first blue-water ocean-going war machine of the new United States Navy turned the Tripoli harbor from state-of-the-art fortifications (state-of-the-art for 18th century Muslims, that is) back to 7th century piles of rubble. The United States Navy literally freed the Mediterranean and the world from domination by militant Islam for nearly 200 years.
>
> The crew of the USS Constitution annihilated those international terrorists, which led to a peace treaty that lasted for almost two hundred years, that is, until September 11, 2001, when conservative, Wahabi-type, radical Islam took the lives of

nearly 3,000 Americans.

Thomas Jefferson searched for his resolve to fight by reading the Koran, which, through his eyes, was the best source available to learn about Muslims, their heritage and their culture.[12]

When Keith Ellison spoke of the American founders as visionaries, he was right. They had a vision of what they wanted the country to be like and were prepared to fight for it, especially against the Islamic terrorists, whose entire value system was diametrically opposed to the tolerance and goodwill of the newborn American nation. And that is the real issue here. An aggressive ideology seeking dominance over a very different value system cannot live in harmony. The American value system, which is based on the Bible and the American Constitution, is precisely the reason why a Congressman swearing his allegiance to the U.S. with his hand on the Koran is problematic. It is difficult to ignore this inherent contradiction; the Koran justifies sexual abuse of women, *jihad* against non-Muslims, and supports death to the Jews. Would Washington, Adams, Jefferson, and Lincoln have agreed to this?

Beware of false prophets, which come to you in sheep's clothing, but inwardly they are ravening wolves.
(The Jefferson Bible 3:50)

Tolerance is a two-way street. If the American heart with its good intentions continues to reach out to the Islamic world and welcome them in with kindness and tolerance, America will be repaid by a hostile takeover from within.

So what can be done about this? Is the creeping *Sharia* unstoppable? Are the demographic trends irreversible?

Thirty years ago, American-Israeli Rabbi Meir Kahane sounded alarm bells in Israel about an emerging demographic threat because of the hostile and growing Arab Muslim population. He said, *I don't want to lose my country to bullets, or to babies.* Kahane advocated a controversial policy to encourage the hostile Arab population to emigrate from Israel. To justify this proposal, he cited the extensive forced transfers of European populations that had been jointly arranged and engineered after World War II by Truman, Churchill and Stalin as a way to bring peace within their respective countries after the war. Always a controversial figure due to his style and his message, Kahane was fiercely attacked both within and outside of Israel for daring to let the demographic genie out of the bottle. He was eventually assassinated in Manhattan by El-Sayyid Nosair, an Egyptian member of an Arab terrorist cell operating in New York in 1990. Nosair was one of the followers of Sheikh Omar Abdel-Rahman, who was later convicted of the 1993 World Trade Center bombing with his co-conspirators; today, he is serving life in prison. The gun that was used to kill Rabbi Kahane was supplied to Nosair by Wadih El-Hage – a member of al-Qaeda and who was convicted of conspiracy to kill American citizens in the 1998 U.S. embassy bombings. Ties within the Muslim terror network were established many years ago and have continued to grow, bound together by a shared ideology of radical Islam.[13]

The demographic warnings of 30 years ago spoke of a threat that continues to plague Israel, but, in truth, the scenario hasn't played out quite as badly as Kahane had predicted. Apparently his role as catalyst heightened awareness of the problem; there is a noticeable reversal of trends, which explains that the demographic threat within Israel is not as imminent as it once was.

Israel has witnessed a gradually rising Jewish birthrate in recent years and a simultaneous drop in the Muslim birthrate – the trend has clearly turned around. This development has been spurred on by the growing family-oriented, religious Jewish population in Israel; these families often have five or more children. That fact and others, including the slow but steady Jewish immigration to Israel, an increasing number of traditional Jewish families arriving with young children, and a trend of Arab emigration from Israel has greatly improved the demographic situation in the State of Israel. However, the trends still need to be very carefully monitored.[14]

The price of freedom is eternal vigilance.[15]

(Thomas Jefferson)

The demographic struggle can be won, but it requires self-sacrifice on the part of parents, who have to take on the challenge of having larger families and raising more children – a noble task which, especially in our times, requires full paternal involvement. This is not an easy task, but, as most parents in large families will tell you, there are incomparable personal pleasures in raising many children that make the sacrifice well worth it.

Then there is the issue of violent or less violent irredentism. Of the Muslims in Israel who are hostile to the Jewish State and agitate against its very existence – should they be expelled? Is it acceptable for elected Muslim Knesset members to consort with Israel's enemies? Is there no concept of treason anymore? There is a basic survival principle here which we seem to have forgotten. No country should allow a fifth column of traitors to remain within its borders and work toward the destruction of the country they live in. There is nothing moral about suicide, whether individual or national.

So what are the lessons from the Holy Land for the United States? The Prophet Isaiah said that the Torah will go forth from Zion, thereby spreading its wisdom to the entire world. What can the U.S. learn from the ongoing struggles between Israel and Islam? What are the solutions? I cannot speak for all Israelis, but I would propose to American (and European) leaders the following urgent steps, to counter both the imminent and long-term threats:

- Concerted efforts to assimilate the Islamic population into the American mainstream in all spheres of social life and norms, which, based on historic precedent, would lead to a reduction in the Islamic birthrate.
- Encourage the use of birth control among the Islamic populations.
- Strictly forbid polygamy.
- Encourage Christians and other non-Muslims to have

more children and to overcome passivity in the face of peaceful Islamic aggression.

- Halt immigration, both legal and illegal, from Islamic countries and encourage legal immigration from predominantly Christian countries, such as those in South America and Eastern Europe. Non-Muslim immigration from countries such as relatively poor, but industrious and populous India would also benefit America with a pool of hard-working immigrants eager to blend in.

- Encourage immigration from the industrious Asian/Oriental countries (China, Japan, and South Korea). This population has always proven itself to be loyal to the American way of life.

- Require the emigration of actively hostile Muslims, whether involved in terrorism or in other less violent, but no less dangerous forms of anti-American subversion.

- Encourage traditional Judeo-Christian values unapologetically at all levels of the educational and legal system.

- Encourage American patriotism based on the American biblical tradition and the religious values promoted by the Founding Fathers.

- Require the recital of the Pledge of Allegiance and The Star Spangled Banner at the start of each school day in all public schools.

- Prevent *hate speech* legislation, which in practice will be used as a *big brother* technique to curtail the free speech of those who dare to speak out against Islamic ideology.

- Discourage outward expressions of Islam in dress, especially those that can be used for terrorist purposes.

- Encourage multimedia exposés about the dangers of Islam.

- Forbid Muslims from publicly proclaiming their ideology from the minarets of their mosques.

Loudspeaker announcements from the minarets in neighboring Muslim villages call the faithful to prayer each morning at 4:00 a.m. These announcements, which are spoken in Arabic, wake my children and lack any regard for Jews, Christians or other non-Muslim *infidels* who may prefer to sleep at that early hour. A new law, passed in Switzerland, bans all construction for new minarets – this is a good start. If waking up for prayer is their real concern, there are perfectly good digital alarm clocks that can serve that purpose. In a similar vein, banning the wearing of face-covering veils, as has recently been implemented by the Belgian Parliament, is also a small step in the right direction. While few women in Belgium wear a face-covering garment, tensions have been heightened after a prominent burka-wearer, Malika El-Aroud, was arrested with 13 others in 2008 in connection with an alleged suicide attack plot. The arrests came on the day of an EU summit, although the police did not confirm the suspected target.[16] This ban, and similar bans such as the law against face-covering veils in France, will send a critical message that the ideology of Islam will no longer be welcomed in Europe. However, although it is a necessary message, sadly, it is the classic case of *too little, too late*. It is already the eleventh hour in Europe; all the steps that I described above need to be implemented if there is to be a reversal of the Islamic tsunami.

Anyone who makes the analogy that such a law is similar to restricting religious ritual for Jews or Christians is completely off base. Once again, we are not talking about an innocent spiritual movement that doesn't threaten anyone, but an evil force that is working to take over the world. We must remember that they are seeking to return the Caliphate and *Sharia* to a world that has not experienced its oppressive nature since the fall of the Ottoman Empire. Just as the World War II allies didn't worry about impinging on the rights of the Nazis, so too, Americans need not feel the least bit guilty in this case. The first step is for the U.S. to understand the mentality of the Islamic world in order to identify a way to defeat it. The second step is to use that knowledge, as

Jefferson did in the case of the Barbary Pirates, and to be vigilant. In our times, that means to quickly organize and stand against the rising Islamic tsunami, preferably in quiet coordination with the non-Islamic remnants of Europe. Also, it means standing strong and working closely with Israel as the situation gets more intense, which is a certainty, as the emboldened sons of Muhammad seek to emulate their ruthless leader:

I shall terrorize the infidels. So wound their bodies and incapacitate them because they oppose Allah and His Apostle.
(Sura 8:12)

We could go on and on with these quotes from the Koran, but the words speak for themselves, in the spirit of *the prophet.* All the Koranic quotes and their real-life ramifications that were discussed in this book reflect Muhammad's life, achievements, legacy, and, if it were up to him and his followers, his dominance over all of us in the coming years. Islam is the problem, and it has had a profound effect on world history. It is estimated that, since its inception approximately 1,400 years ago, Islam has left 270 million people – mainly Africans, Hindus, Christians, Buddhists, and Jews – in the death bins of *jihad.* This astounding number of people is comprised solely of those who chose not to surrender to a life of *Dhimmitude* under Muslim rule.[17]

The spectre of what may lie in wait because of Islamic influence in the era of nuclear and chemical warfare is indeed frightening.

Not long ago I spoke in the South (U.S.) to a vibrant group of mostly young, born-again Christians in a unique men's Bible class. The lecture was held in the morning at a local pub and, quite aptly did not include liquor. After I shared my message, and most of the attendees had left, I was approached by one of the event's organizers. He warmly shook my hand with both of his, and as his eyes welled up with tears, asked me if I could do him a favor. Not sure what was coming, I said, "Sure, if I can," to which he responded, "I'd like you to accept Jesus in your life."

Looking directly into his eyes and grasping his hands as well, I told him gently, "I really appreciate you sharing that with me, but we Jews have a direct relationship with the Creator that goes back several thousand years, long before Jesus was born. For Christians, it's different perhaps, but we who are directly descended from the Revelation to Moses on Mount Sinai don't feel the need for an intermediary between us and the Almighty." We ended the exchange amicably and he requested that I speak to his group again the next time I visited the area. To this day, I trust that his re-invitation was sincere. What can we learn from this particular exchange of hearts and minds? First, it is important to resolve any differences of opinion by talking about them honestly, openly, and with love, and to remember that sometimes it's necessary to agree to peacefully disagree. Such a situation is possible only if there is mutual tolerance and respect, with stress on the word *mutual*. There can be no *mutual* respect with one whose religion or ideology calls for beheading any who disagree with him. As I've said before, I would not object to those enthusiastic born-again Christians should they choose to put their energy and investment into weaning Muslims from the sword of Islam. I think that venture could be an important contribution to world peace. Quite a few ex-Muslims have overcome the violent threats made by their families and left Islam, exposing it for the dangerous ideology that it is.

A recent news topic is Mosab Hassan Yousef – son of jailed Hamas terrorist leader Sheikh Hassan Yousef – who was exposed as an undercover spy, working for Israel's intelligence agency on a volunteer basis – for more than a decade. Yousef converted to Christianity in the U.S. in 2007. According to the Israeli newspaper *Haaretz*, the intelligence that Yousef provided led to the arrest of several high-ranking terrorists, including Ibrahim Hamid – a Hamas terror commander in Judea and Samaria, Fatah strongman Marwan Barghouti and Hamas bomb-maker Abdullah Barghouti. In an interview with *FOX News* in 2008, Yousef said that when he was 18 years old, he was arrested and placed in an Israeli jail.

Hamas had control of its members inside the jail and I saw their torture; (they were) torturing people in a very, very bad way... Hamas leaders that we see on TV now, and big leaders, responsible for torturing their own members. They didn't torture me, but that was a shock for me, to see them torturing people: putting needles under their nails, burning their bodies. And they killed lots of them... I was a witness for about a year for this torture. So that was a huge change in my life... The problem is not Hamas, the problem is not people. The root of the problem is Islam itself as an idea.

Yousef said he saw no chance for Israel and the PA to make peace.[18]

Typically, once ex-Muslims abandon the ideology of Islam, they become friends of Israel and the West, since the sword of Islam no longer binds them. I remember speaking at a pro-Israel conference in California several years ago. As I was describing the horrifying but miraculous story of a terror attack in which my three-year-old son and I were wounded, I noticed an Arab man sitting in the audience with a pained look on his face, obviously moved by my story. After I finished my presentation, the man approached me and introduced himself as Walid Shoebat, a former Muslim terrorist who left Islam and is now a strong spokesman for ex-Muslims who live in America and support the Israeli-American alliance. As a result of their past experiences, these ex-Muslims usually become vocal opponents of Islam, using their insiders' knowledge of Islam to expose it for what it is. On a personal level, Walid informed me that it is not easy for them to leave, because their lives are often threatened by former co-religionists, including family members and friends, who act on the Koranic imperative to kill those who have left Islam. The following passage from the Hadith illustrates that violent, hateful doctrine:

Eight men of the tribe of Ukil came to the Prophet and then they found the climate of Medina unsuitable for them. So, they said, "O Allah's Apostle! Provide us with some milk." Allah's

241

Apostle said, "I recommend that you should join the herd of camels." So they went and drank the urine and the milk of the camels (as a medicine) till they became healthy and fat. Then they killed the shepherd and drove away the camels, and they became unbelievers after they were Muslims. When the Prophet (Muhammad) was informed by a shouter for help, he sent some men in their pursuit, and before the sun rose high, they were brought, and he had their hands and feet cut off. Then he ordered for nails, which were heated and passed over their eyes, and they were left in the Harra (i.e. rocky land in Medina). They asked for water, and nobody provided them with water till they died.
(Hadith: Sahih Bukhari, 4:52:261)

To resist such officially-sanctioned barbarity should be morally imperative, and therefore, helping Muslims leave Islam should be an organized goal and a high-priority project. Once again, it is not just *radical Islam*, but Islam itself that is the problem. By helping Muslims escape from this oppressive and evil ideology, we are helping to bring peace to the world.

I've spoken quite a bit in this book about the Barack Hussein Obama phenomenon as it relates to Israel and Islam, but it is important to avoid the tendency to overemphasize his personal aspects. Obama is not the main issue; the Islamic challenge to the world will not end once he is out of office. I wish to emphasize that Obama is just a distressing symptom of a much deeper, contagious illness – an illness that will likely spread if it isn't given the intensive care that I've outlined above. On a positive note, the rise of Obama – which is a product of the secular left-Islamic alliance – has provided ample clarification of the issues at hand. Hopefully, the damage that he is causing to the America-Israel relationship will be repaired once he is no longer in office. But the threat of the sons of Muhammad to the rest of the world will not go away until the above steps are taken.

Let us conclude with four quotes that encapsulate the problem and sum up the awesome challenge before us. The first quote is from Genesis, the first book of the Bible. It speaks about

Ishmael, the founder of the Arab nation, and the havoc that he and his descendants were predicted to create. This prophecy is still evident for all to see in our present-day encounter with Islamic terrorism.

> *And he (Ishmael) shall be a wild-ass of a man; his hand will be against everyone and (therefore) everyone's hand against him; and over all his brothers shall he dwell.*
>
> (Genesis 16:12)

This second quote is taken from a former President's essay about Ishmael's most prominent descendant – the founder of Islam – and the religion that he created as an extreme reaction to the rejection that he felt throughout his life.

> *In the seventh century of the Christian era, a wandering Arab of the lineage of Hagar, the Egyptian, combining the powers of transcendent genius, with the preternatural energy of a fanatic, and the fraudulent spirit of an impostor, proclaimed himself as a messenger from Heaven, and spread desolation and delusion over an extensive portion of the earth. Adopting from the sublime conception of the Mosaic Law, the doctrine of one omnipotent God; he connected indissolubly with it, the audacious falsehood, that he was himself his prophet and apostle... He poisoned the sources of human felicity at the fountain, by degrading the condition of the female sex and the allowance of polygamy; and he declared undistinguishing and exterminating war, as a part of his religion, against all the rest of mankind. THE ESSENCE OF HIS DOCTRINE WAS VIOLENCE AND LUST: TO EXALT THE BRUTAL OVER THE SPIRITUAL PART OF HUMAN NATURE.*[19] *(Capitals Emphasis by Adams)*
>
> (John Quincy Adams, 1829)

The third quote, composed by a noted American philosopher, is about the perilous danger of complacency and passivity. These hazards are derived from small-minded, selfish, or near-sighted thinking, with no regard for the greater society.

War is an ugly thing, but not the ugliest of things. The decayed and degraded state of moral and patriotic feeling which thinks that nothing is worth war is much worse. The person who has nothing for which he is willing to fight, nothing which is more important than his own personal safety, is a miserable creature and has no chance of being free unless made and kept so by the exertions of better men than himself.[20]

(John Stuart Mill – Economist and Philosopher)

This final quote is by another former President. It takes the proposed action to the next step, speaking of the potential for greatness that we all have within us.

You and I have a rendezvous with destiny. We will preserve for our children this, the last best hope of man on earth, or we will sentence them to take the first step into a thousand years of darkness. If we fail, at least let our children and our children's children say of us that we justified our brief moment here; we did all that could be done.[21]

(Ronald Reagan)

May we all be worthy of this lofty challenge and have the courage and ability to pursue it fully, for the sake of our nations and for our world. May the Almighty God of Israel bless our efforts!

Acknowledgments

Thanks:

To Julie and Paul: for the initial sources and encouragement.

To Joe and Haim: for sending several key sources and ideas my way.

To my hard-working, cross-ocean, cyberspace editing team: Jen and Kristen for the ideas, thoroughness, and perseverance; Chaim for being incredibly organized with editing and layout, for your calmness under pressure, and for patiently racing with me to the finish line.

To Yossi: for being the prototype of reliability and dedication to Am Yisrael.

To my children: for the unconditional love and the occasional quiet outside my office.

To Lisa: for sharing the passion for life, for the love, for the support, and for understanding.

To the Almighty G-d of Israel: for the true inspiration, the faith, and for bringing me to this day.

Photographic Credits

Front Cover Composite Image - ©Jens Carsten Rosemann
    and others from istockphoto.com
P. 43 - Flash 90
P. 133 - © Pete Souza/White House/Handout/CNP/Corbis
P. 155 - David Rubin
Getty Images Israel:
Back Cover Photo; P. 92; P. 108; P. 113; P. 134; P. 145;
P. 146; P. 175; P. 187; P. 188; P. 191; P. 192; P. 193;
P. 195; P. 205; P. 207; P. 210; P. 222

Endnotes

Chapter One

1. D'Souza, Dinesh. "What's So Great About America." Regnery Publishing, 2002.

2. http://www.jewishvirtuallibrary.org/jsource/US-Israel/roots_of_US-Israel.html

3. Sivan, Gabriel. "The Bible And Civilization." Jerusalem, Keter Publishing House, 1973: 236.
http://www.christianity-revealed.com/cr/files/
puritansweremorejewishthanprotestants.html

4. http://xroads.virginia.edu/~cap/liberty/lazarus.html
http://www.libertystatepark.com/emma.htm

5. Santayana, George. "The Life Of Reason." Vol. 1, 1905.

6. Winthrop, Robert Charles. May 28, 1849 Either by the Bible or the Bayonet address. "Addresses and Speeches on Various Occasions." (Boston: Little, Brown & Company, 1852): 172.
http://www.speakliberty.com/LibertyAndFreedom.pdf

7. Burke, Edmund. "A Letter to a Member of the National Assembly." 1791. Quoted in: Federer, William J. "Three Secular Reasons Why America Should Be Under God." Amerisearch, Inc. 2008: 45.
http://www.ourcivilisation.com/smartboard/shop/burkee/tonatass/index.htm

8. http://www.aproundtable.org/tps30info/beliefs.html
http://www.revolutionary-war-and-beyond.com/john-adams-quotations-2.html

9. Federer, William J. "America's God and Country: Encyclopedia of Quotations." St. Louis, Amerisearch, 2000: 392.

10. http://www.abrahamlincolnsclassroom.org/Library/newsletter.asp?ID=111&CRLI=159

11. Federer, William J. "America's God and Country: Encyclopedia of Quotations." St. Louis, Amerisearch, 2000: 10-11

12. http://www.inspirationalstories.com/1/106.html
http://george.loper.org/archives/2000/Feb/39.html

13. http://gwpapers.virginia.edu/documents/thanksgiving/transcript.html

14. http://etext.virginia.edu/jefferson/quotations/jeff0100.htm
http://www.monticello.org/reports/quotes/memorial.html

15. Rubin, David. "God, Israel, and Shiloh: Returning to the Land." Jerusalem, Mazo Publishers, 2007.

16. http://vftonline.org/EndTheWall/Mann.htm

17. Federer, William J. "Treasury of Presidential Quotations." St. Louis, Amerisearch, Inc, 2004: 245. http://www.calvin-coolidge.org/html/dedication_of_the_jewish_commu.html

18. http://en.wikipedia.org/wiki/Haym_Solomon

19. http://unitedisrael.org/blog/2008/01/04/george-washington-an-american-joshua/

20. http://www.beitbresheet.com/Heritage/Heritage.htm

21. http://www.resistnet.com/profiles/blogs/rebellion-to-tyrants

22. http://www.leaderu.com/orgs/cdf/onug/franklin.html

23. Katsh, Abraham. "The Biblical Heritage of American Democracy." (New York, 1977): 97.

24. http://thestateofamerica.wordpress.com/2008/01/29/jewish-roots-of-the-american-constitution

25. http://biblesearchers.typepad.com/destination-yisrael/2010/07/the-jewish-torah-roots-of-the-american-constitution-by-prof-paul-eidelberg.html

26. http://www.jewishvirtuallibrary.org/jsource/US-Israel/roots_of_US-Israel.html

Chapter Two

1. http://georgewbush-whitehouse.archives.gov/infocus/nationalsecurity/faq-what.html
http://www.submission.org/George_W_Bush/islam.html

2. http://waronjihad.org/muslims190505.html

3. http://www.topix.com/forum/religion/islam/TQBFHTDDGV8CBQ6F9
http://www.danielpipes.org/comments/32812

4. Ibid.
http://www.danielpipes.org/comments/32812

5. Santayana, George. "The Life of Reason." Volume One, 1905.

6. http://www.msnbc.msn.com/id/27940231/
http://www.bloomberg.com/apps/news?pid=newsarchive&sid=aZJ5vLosD3qM

7. http://www.etaiwannews.com/etn/print.php) (From AP News

Wire)

8. http://www.thaindian.com/newsportal/world-news/obama-fully-backs-bush-help-to-india-after-mumbai-attacks_100124990.html
http://www.usatoday.com/news/washington/2008-11-28-fbi-mumbai_N.htm

9. http://www.israelnationalnews.com/news/news.aspx/136165

10. AP and JPost.com staff. "Ahmadinejad Craves Zionist-Free ME", The Jerusalem Post, Feb. 25, 2010.
http://www.jpost.com/MiddleEast/Article.aspx?ID=169632

11. http://www.c-span.org/Transcripts/SOTU-2001-0920.aspx
http://archives.cnn.com/2001/US/09/20/gen.bush.transcript/

12. http://newsessentials.blogspot.com/2010_03_04_archive.html

13. Newsweek, Apr. 12, 2008
http://www.newsweek.com/2008/04/11/obama-s-world.html

14. The Christian Post, Dec. 13, 2009.

15. http://www.washingtonpost.com/wp-dyn/content/article/2010/02/28/AR2010022801912.html
http://www.brookings.edu/papers/2008/08_counterterrorism_hussain.aspx

16. http://teachingamericanhistory.org/library/index.asp?document=961
http://www.nationalcenter.org/ReaganEvilEmpire1983.html

Chapter Three

1. http://en.wikipedia.org/wiki/Idolatry

2. See Book of Genesis, Chapters 41-50.

3. Midrash Tanchuma: Exodus 5.

4. Midrash Sotah 12b-13a.

5. See Book of Isaiah.

6. http://www.jewishvirtuallibrary.org/jsource/Judaism/expulsion.html

7. Greenberg, Louis. "The Jews In Russia: The Struggle For Emancipation." Yale University Press: 1944.

8. "Encyclopaedia Judaica" Volume 13. Keter Publishing House, 1972.

9. http://www.brainyquote.com/quotes/quotes/d/davidbeng387794.html

10. "Am Sigula." Jerusalem, D'var Yerushalayim, later 19th century: 120-21.

11. Soloveitchik, Rabbi Joseph B. "Reflections Of The Rav." Besdin, Abraham ed. Jerusalem, Publishing Department of the Jewish Agency: 36.

12. Israel National News, Mar. 1, 2010.

Chapter Four

1. http://www.whitehouse.gov/the_press_office/remarks-by-the-president-at-cairo-university-6-04-09/

2. http://www.memri.org/report/en/0/0/0/0/0/0/1693.htm

3. http://thinkexist.com/quotation/mankind_must_put_an_end_to_war-or_war_will_put_an/13849.html

4. http://www.historyplace.com/speeches/churchill.htm

5. http://www.mtholyoke.edu/acad/intrel/WorldWar2/arsenal.htm

6. http://abcnews.go.com/Blotter/hasan-multiple-mail-accounts-officials/story?id=9065692

7. Anwar al Awlaki.com, Nov. 9, 2009.

8. Interview – Reported by Paula Newton, CNN, Jan. 10, 2010.

9. http://en.wikipedia.org/wiki/Muhammad

10. http://prophetofdoom.net/article.aspx?g=402&i=4222046
http://www.icbwayland.org/outreach/Muhammad.html
http://www.islaam.ca/downloads/Muhammad.pdf

11. Federer, William. J. "What Every American Needs to Know About the Qur'an – A History of Islam & the United States." St. Louis: AmeriSearch Inc., Jan. 2007.

12. Ibid.

13. Interview with Ali Sina, Jerusalem Post Magazine, June 20, 2008.

14. http://www.usatoday.com/news/world/iraq/2005-05-04-pleasure-marriage_x.htm

15. http://www.somalilandtimes.net/sl/2010/417/32.shtml

16. http://edition.cnn.com/2009/WORLD/asiapcf/10/26/ctw.afghanistan.sex.trade/index.html

17. Wright, Robin. "Islam's New Face Visible In a Changing Indonesia." Los Angeles Times, Dec. 27, 2009.

18. Associated Press – reported on Fox News – Mar. 9, 2009.

19. Guillaume, A. "The Life of Muhammad." Oxford University Press, 1955: 464.

20. http://www.historyplace.com/worldhistory/genocide/armenians.htm

21. http://www.agiasofia.com/armenia/armenia1.html

22. FoxNews.com, Mar. 15, 2007.

23. http://www.allaboutmuhammad.com/quotes-on-islam.html

24. http://www.palwatch.org/main.aspx?fi=157&doc_id=798
(Al-Moheet Arab News Network, May 10, 2009, Al-Hakika al-Dawliya, May 9, 2009.)

Chapter Five

1. http://www.telegraph.co.uk/news/newstopics/religion/6194354/ Mohammed-is-most-popular-name-for-baby-boys-in-London.html
2. Ibid.
3. http://www.telegraph.co.uk/news/worldnews/europe/5994047/ Muslim-Europe-the-demographic-time-bomb-transforming-our-continent.html
4. New York Times, Dec. 17, 2007. DPA. Earth Times. Nov. 22, 2007. Harrigan, Steve. Fox News, Nov. 26, 2004. (http://islamineurope.blogspot.com/2007/11/muslim-population-in-european-cities.html
5. New York Sun, Sept. 6, 2006.
6. Al Jezeera, Apr. 10, 2006.
7. www.memri.org/report/en/0/0/0/0/0/0/1286.htm
8. www.elaph.com – reported on Apr. 30, 2005.
9. http://waronjihad.org/muslims190505.html
10. Al Jezeera, July 27, 2006.
11. http://en.wikipedia.org/wiki/Battle_of_Khaybar
12. Federer, William. J. "What Every American Needs to Know About the Qur'an – A History of Islam & the United States." St. Louis: AmeriSearch Inc., Jan. 2007: 78-79.
13. http://en.wikipedia.org/wiki/Arab_slave_trade
14. Glick, Caroline. "Keeping Zionism's Promise." Jerusalem Post, Jan. 29, 2010.
15. Interview with Tom and Agneta in New York, Mar. 5, 2010.
16. http://www.historylearningsite.co.uk/Nazi_Germany_dictatorship.htm
17. http://www.jihadwatch.org/2008/07/fjordman-the-organization-of-the-islamic-conference-and-eurabia.html
18. http://www.coe.int/t/dg4/intercultural/ whitepaper_interculturaldialogue_2_EN.asp
19. http://www.jihadwatch.org/2008/07/fjordman-the-organization-of-the-islamic-conference-and-eurabia.html
20. "Never Give In: The Best of Winston Churchill's Speeches." Vol. 2003, Part 2.
21. http://thesop.org/usa/2009/03/29/would-america-be-better-off-under-sharia-law
22. www.wnd.com, July 9, 2007.
23. www.elaph.com

24. Michaels, Adrian, "By 2050 A Fifth Of The European Union Will Be Muslim." The Sunday Telegraph (London), Aug. 8, 2009.
25. Cherwell News, Oxford University, Feb. 9, 2010.
26. "Hardtalk." BBC television, Nov. 2, 2004.
27. Churchill, Winston. "The River War." 1st edition, Vol. II, London, Longmans Green and Co., 1899: 248-50.
28. www.wnd.com, Oct. 3, 2008.

Chapter Six

1. http://brothersjudd.com/index.cfm/fuseaction/reviews.detail/book_id/537/Gifts%20of%20the.htm
2. http://www.pmw.org.il/specrep-37.html
3. Weiner, Justus Reid. "My Beautiful Old House and Other Fabrications by Edward Said." Commentary Magazine, Sept. 1999.
4. http://www.mattkapko.com/indepth/wunderground.doc; www.wnd.com, Feb. 24, 2008.
5. Smith, Dinitia. "No Regrets for a Love of Explosives; In a Memoir of Sorts, a War Protester Talks of Life With the Weathermen." New York Times, Sept. 11, 2001.
6. www.wnd.com, Feb. 24, 2008.
7. Wallstein, Peter. "Allies of Palestinians see a friend in Obama." Los Angeles Times, Apr. 10, 2008.
8. http://mlkkpp01.stanford.edu/index.php/resources/article/annotated_letter_from_birmingham/
9. http://abcnews.go.com/Blotter/DemocraticDebate/story?id=4443788&page=1
10. Ibid.
11. www.cnn.com, Mar. 15, 2008.
12. http://www.ynet.co.il/english/articles/0,7340,L-3618408,00.html
13. http://news.bbc.co.uk/2/hi/7783325.stm
14. http://www.100000quotes.com/quote/Lyndon-B-Johnson-Our-society-is-illuminated-by-the-spiritual-insigh
15. Soloveitchik, Rabbi Joseph B. "Reflections of the Rav." Besdin, Abraham ed. Jerusalem, Publishing Department of the Jewish Agency, Chapt. 2.
16. Ibid.
17. http://www.whitehouse.gov/the_press_office/remarks-by-the-president-at-cairo-university-6-04-09/

17a. "This Week with George Stephanopoulos", ABC, Sept. 7, 2008.

18. http://www.jewishvirtuallibrary.org/jsource/US-Israel/adams.html

19. http://www.biblicalzionist.com/Quotes.htm

20. http://www.jewishvirtuallibrary.org/jsource/US-Israel/roots_of_US-Israel.html

21. http://www.jewishvirtuallibrary.org/jsource/US-Israel/presquote.html

22. http://www.icelebz.com/quotes/harry_s_truman/

23. Benson, Michael T. "Harry S. Truman and the Founding of Israel." Praeger Publishers, 1997: 191.

24. Ibid., 190.

25. Ibid., 191.

26. http://www.mfa.gov.il/MFA/Facts+About+Israel/History/HISTORY-+Foreign+Domination.htm

27. http://www.biblicalzionist.com/Quotes.htm

28. http://history1900s.about.com/cs/holocaust/p/balfourdeclare.htm

29. http://www.palestinefacts.org/pf_ww1_british_mandate_jordan.php

30. Ibid.

31. Kahane, Meir. "They Must Go." Grosset & Dunlap, 1981.

32. Makovsky, Michael. "Winston Churchill's Complex Zionist Evolution." Jerusalem Post, Oct. 31, 2007.

33. http://www.theisraelproject.org/site/apps/nl/content2.asp?c=hsJPK0PIJpH&b=883997&ct=4687261

34. http://www.mythsandfacts.com/conflict/10/resolution-242.pdf

35. Ibid.

36. Ibid.

37. Ibid.

38. Der Spiegel, Nov. 5, 1969.

39. http://www.quotatio.com/topics/humanity.html

40. http://www.cbsnews.com/stories/2004/11/12/opinion/main655409.shtml

41. Ibid.

42. Israel National News, May 10, 2010.

43. Sources from www.pmw.org.il

44. Jerusalem Post, May 12, 2010.

Chapter Seven

1. http://www.youtube.com/watch?v=j3Xl68kP4wo

2. http://www.allied-media.com/AM/index.html

3. "Islam on march south of border: Mexico agrees to monitor foreign groups as Muslim recruitment rate skyrockets." WorldNetDaily, June 7, 2005. "Osama's exploits south of border: al-Qaeda in league with Mexican radicals in plot to penetrate U.S., says M16 report." May 10, 2006.

4. http://myrick.house.gov/index.cfm?sectionid=22&sectiontree= 21,22&itemid=558

5. "US Military Commander Warns of Iran-Hezbollah Influence in Latin America." www.voiceofamerica.com, Mar. 17, 2009.

6. Shorrosh, Anis. "Islam Revealed: A Christian Arab's View of Islam." Thomas Nelson, Inc., 2001.

7. Macedo, Diane. "Newspaper, Businesses Feud in Tennessee Over Claims of 'Hate Rhetoric.'" Fox News, June 30, 2010.

8. http://www.csmonitor.com/USA/2010/0407/Jihad-Jamie-and-the-black-widows-Why-women-turn-to-terrorism

9. http://www.intervarsity.org/ism/news/39

10. http://www.reutrcohen.com/2009/05/hamas-says-mosques-are-for-educating.html

11. Talmud, Ned. 28a, *Git.* 10b, *BK* 113a, *BB* 54b-55a.

12. See Wertheimer, "Unwelcome Strangers: East European Jews in Imperial Germany."

13. A Compilation of the Messages and the Papers of the Presidents 1789-1897 Vol. IX, 198.

14. "Counting Arabs in California." Newsweek, Mar. 8, 2010: 8.

15. danielpipes.org/77/the-danger-within-militant-islam-in-america

16. Ibid.

17. Ibid.

18. prnewswire/.../cair-franklin-graham-repeats-attack-on-islam-79097332.html

19. San Ramon Valley Herald report of a speech to California Muslims in July 1998; quoted in Daniel Pipes' NY Post article, CAIR: Moderate Friends of Terror, Apr. 22, 2002.

20. Moore, Art. "DC Imam declares Muslim takeover plan." WorldNetDaily, May 10, 2010.

21. http://edition.cnn.com/2010/US/04/23/graham.islam.controversy/index.html

Chapter Eight

1. Glazov, Jamie. FrontPage Magazine, May 12, 2008.

2. http://www.apologeticspress.org/articles/240151

3. Shea, Nina. "This is a Saudi textbook (After the intolerance was removed)." Washington Post, May 21, 2006.

4. www.actforamerica.org/index.php/learn/email-archives/1069-fethulla-gulen-infiltrating-us-through-our-charter-schools/

4a. Horowitz, David. "Barack Obama's Rules For Revolution: The Alinsky Model." David Horowitz Freedom Center. Sherman Oaks, CA, 2009.

5. Stillwell. "Islam in America's Public Schools: Education or Indoctrination?" www.SFGate.com, June 11, 2008.

6. Ibid.

7. http://www.georgewashingtonsociety.org/Mission.html

8. http://www.tentmaker.org/Quotes/courage_quotes3.htm

9. Ibid.

10. http: //www.foxnews.com/politics/2010/07/05/nasa-chief-frontier-better-relations-muslims/

11. http://www.youtube.com/watch?v=4EcC0QAd0Ug

12. www.wnd.com July 21, 2009

13. http://en.wikipedia.org/wiki/Al-Waleed_bin_Talal

14. http://www.pr-inside.com/william-ayers-and-barack-obama-finally-r797225.htm ; http://www.wnd.com/index.php?pageId=74231

15. http://www.huffingtonpost.com/2009/06/23/new-evidence-links-saudi-_n_219877.html

16. "NYC board OK's ground zero mosque." AP, May 26, 2010.

17. "Hannity." Fox News, May 21, 2010.

18. http://video.foxnews.com/v/4238242/wtc-investor-controversy

19. http://en.wikipedia.org/wiki/News_Corporation

20. http://www.prwatch.org/node/8906

21. "Majesty of Man." Mesorah Publications, 1992: 282.

Chapter Nine

1. Aznar, Jose Maria. "If Israel goes down, we all go down." The Times (London), June 17, 2010.

2. http://www.revolutionary-war-and-beyond.com/george-washington-quote-4.html

3. http://www.boston.com/bostonglobe/editorial_opinion/oped/

articles/2009/01/07/yes_its_anti_semitism/

4. http://www.newworldencyclopedia.org/entry/Abba_Eban

5. http://www.reuters.com/article/idUSWAT00861920080103

6. http://www.whitehouse.gov/the_press_office/remarks-by-the-president-at-cairo-university-6-04-09/

7. http://www.haaretz.com/print-edition/news/clinton-calls-on-israel-to-halt-any-kind-of-settlement-activity-1.276415

8. Koppel, Ted. Commencement Address at Duke University, May 10, 1987.

9. Federer, William J. "America's God and Country: Encyclopedia of Quotations." St. Louis, Amerisearch, 2000: 12.

10. Morris, Benny. "Camp David and After: An Exchange." June 13, 2002.

11. Twain, Mark. "Concerning the Jews." Harper's Magazine article, Sept. 1899.

12. McTernan, John P. "As America Has Done To Israel." Liverpool, PA, Whitaker House, 2006.

13. http://www.debbieschlussel.com/15808/farouk-shami-pan-terrorist-muslim-texas-candidate-wears-anti-israel-keffiyeh-mlk-fest-father-led-pogroms-against-jews/

14. Lewis, John. "I Have a Dream for Peace in the Middle East: King's Special Bond with Israel." San Francisco Chronicle, Jan. 21, 2002.

15. http://en.wikipedia.org/wiki/H._Rap_Brown

16. http://thelastcrusade.org/2010/05/03/radical-islamic-movement-spreads-throughout-america/

17. http://mlk-kpp01.stanford.edu/index.php/resources/article/annotated_letter_from_birmingham/

18. http://www.allaboutmuhammad.com/quotes-on-islam.html

19. Crook, Barbara and Marcus, Itamar. Jerusalem Post, May 25, 2009.

20. http://www.amerisearch.net/index.php?date=2004-01-21

21. http://www.scribd.com/doc/22828866/What-Every-American-Needs-to-Know-About-the-Qur-an

Chapter 10

1. www.foxnews.com, Feb. 5, 2010.

2. http://abcnews.go.com/International/wireStory?id=9744188

3. http://www.leadership-skills-for-life.com/leadership-quotes-washington.html

4. http://www.usconstitution.net/xconst_Am1.html

5. Federer, William. J. "What Every American Needs to Know About the Qur'an – A History of Islam & the United States." St. Louis: AmeriSearch Inc., Jan. 2007: 274.

6. Hitler, Adolf. "Mein Kampf." 1925.

7. http://www.newsmax.com/PamelaGeller/Geller-mufti-holocaust-hitler/2010/02/09/id/349387

8. http://wcco.com/topstories/Keith.Ellison.Muslim.2.364092.html

9. Fishbein. National Interest Magazine, Winter 2001-2002.

10. Hitchens, Christopher. City Journal, Spring 2007.

11. Fishbein, op. cit.

12. Welty, William."Jefferson's Koran." Koinonia House, 2007.

13. "Inside 9/11." National Geographic TV, Aug. 2005.

14. http://www.israelnationalnews.com/News/News.aspx/125762

15. http://www.quotedb.com/quotes/2283

16. http://www.timesonline.co.uk/tol/news/world/europe/article7083103.ece

17. "The Infidel Revolution." www.FrontPageMagazine.com, Feb. 21, 2007.

18. Israel National News, Feb. 24, 2010.

19. http://www.apologeticspress.org/articles/240151

20. http://yankeefaninnc.blogspot.com/2010/06/united-nations-takes-action-against.html

21. U.S. Office of the Federal Register, Ronald Reagan, Vol. 1: 46.

Reference Notes:

1. The website http://www.quranexplorer.com/Quran/Default.aspx was consulted to verify accurate English translations of the Koran. Some translations were modified slightly for easier reading (i.e., you instead of ye).

2. In certain instances, very slight modifications to Old English text were made to enhance readability for the modern English reader.

3. In supplementing my own knowledge of biblical Hebrew to formulate the English translations of the biblical sources used in this book, I referred to *The Stone Edition Tanach of the Art Scroll Series* (Mesorah), *The Jerusalem Bible* (Koren), and *Judaica Books of the Prophets* (Judaica Press).